PACKAGED JAPANESENESS

Weddings, Business and Brides

D1368439

ConsumAsiaN Book Series

edited by

Brian Moeran and Lise Skov

and

Published by

The Curzon Press and The University of Hawai'i Press

Women, Media and Consumption in Japan
Edited by Lise Skov and Brian Moeran
Published 1995

A Japanese Advertising Agency
An Anthropology of Media and Markets
Brian Moeran
Published 1996

Contemporary Japan and Popular Culture
Edited by John Whittier Treat
Published 1996

Packaged Japaneseness
Weddings, Business and Brides
Ofra Goldstein-Gidoni
Published 1997

Australia and Asia
Cultural Transactions
Edited by Maryanne Dever
Published 1997

Asian Department Stores
Edited by Kerrie MacPherson
Published 1997

PACKAGED JAPANESENESS

Weddings, Business and Brides

Ofra Goldstein-Gidoni

UNIVERSITY OF HAWAI'I PRESS
HONOLULU

Published in North America by
University of Hawai'i Press
2840 Kolowalu Street
Honolulu, Hawai'i 96822

First Published in the United Kingdom by
Curzon Press
St. John's Studios, Church Road
Richmond, Surrey TW9 2QA
England

Printed in Great Britain

Library of Congress Cataloguing-in-Publication Data
Goldstein-Gidoni, Ofra.
Packaged Japaneseness: weddings, business, and brides /
by Ofra Goldstein-Gidoni.
p. cm. – (ConsumAsiaN book series)
Includes bibliographical references and index.
ISBN 0–8248–1954–3 (cloth : alk. paper), –
ISBN 0–8248–1955–1 (pbk : alk. paper)
1. Marriage customs and rites – Japan – Kōbe-shi.   2. Wedding supplies and
services industry – Japan – Kōbe-shi.   3. Weddings – Japan – Kōbe-shi –
Planning.   4. Wedding etiquette – Japan – Kōbe-shi.   5. Kōbe-shi (Japan)
– Social life and customs.   I. Title.   II. Series.
GT2784.K6G65   1997
395.2′2′09521874–dc21   96-49251
CIP

How Many Stories in a Wedding Dress? Not Only the Bride's
Carol Ann Duffy, poet

. . . Orient and Occident cannot be taken here as "realities" to be compared and contrasted historically, philosophically culturally, politically.

Roland Barthes, *The Empire of Signs*

CONTENTS

LIST OF TABLES AND FIGURES

Tables

Figures

LIST OF ILLUSTRATIONS

Plates

ACKNOWLEDGEMENTS

My first debt of gratitude is to the many people in Japan who helped me to carry out this research. In particular, I would like to thank the personnel of the wedding parlour where I gathered much of the information for this study. Mainly I would like to thank the beauty shop owner and her daughter-in-law and the beauty shop employees with whom I worked closely for two and a half years. Words of gratitude should be repaid with open thanks, yet confidentiality requires anonymity. Moreover, it would be impossible to mention all the many people who helped me: the wedding parlour manager and other personnel of Shōchikuden as well as other wedding entrepreneurs.

This research is based mainly on fieldwork conducted in Japan while I was a research student in the department of Anthropology of Osaka University. I appreciate the kindness and guidance I received from Professor Aoki Takamotsu and Professor Kajiwara. A special word of thanks goes to my colleague and friend in Japan, Patricia De Witte-Kuyl.

This book is based on a doctoral thesis that was written in the Anthropology Department in the School of Oriental and African Studies of the University of London. It is impossible to express adequately the debt I owe to Professor Brian Moeran who was my PhD supervisor. I thank him not only for his encouragement, advice and trenchant criticism, but also for his great support in the writing of this book. I would also like to thank Lise Skov for her valuable suggestions.

Thanks too are due to the department members for their support and especially, Nancy Lindisfarne for her thoughtful advice and criticism. Other members of the department helped me sharpen my study's focus. In particular, I would like to express my gratitude to Lola Martinez, Stuart Thompson, Lisa Croll and Chris Pinney. Special thanks are in order to Joy Hendry who acted as my external examiner at the PhD Viva.

Others have read this manuscript in one or another of its various forms and have given me criticism and advice. I would like to thank Haim Hazan for his most insightful suggestions, Eyal Ben-Ari who has always been enthusiastic and supportive about my work, and the two 'anonymous' readers of this manuscript, Grant Evans and William Kelly for their most valuable criticism and suggestions which shaped the final version.

I would also like to thank Norma Schneider for her editorial suggestions, Judy Fadlon for her help in the final stages of editing and Yael Kostrinsky who was my research assistant at the Department of Sociology and Anthropology at Tel Aviv University while writing this book.

I gratefully acknowledge the following support that made the fieldwork and writing possible: a Japanese government scholarship generously supported me for three years in Japan; a Japan Foundation endowment committee grant and a Sanwa Foundation research award provided additional support while I was completing my dissertation after returning from Japan. Grants from the Harry S. Truman Research Institute and the Israeli Council for Higher Education assisted in the process of writing. A grant from the Faculty of Humanities and the Faculty of Social Sciences at Tel Aviv University given through the help of the Deans of the two faculties, Professor Anita Shapiro and Professor Arie Nadler enabled the editing of the book.

EXPLANATORY NOTE

All Japanese terms are romanized in the Hepburn system. Macrons indicate long vowels.

Japanese words always appear in *italics*, except in cases of words which have already become part of the English language, such as kimono and obi. Names of cities always appear in their English version.

I follow the Japanese convention for personal names throughout, giving the surname first and given name last. In some cases I have adopted the convention of referring to people by their surnames. The use of given names is limited to such a use by the informants themselves.

I have created pseudonyms for Shōchikuden, Cobella, the Princess Palace, and the names of all other companies and persons in the wedding parlour to protect the confidentiality and anonymity of the people concerned.

British pounds equivalents in the text have been calculated at £1 = ¥250, which was the approximate rate of exchange during my fieldwork.

INTRODUCTION

I visited Japan for the first time in 1984. Of all the memories and impressions from that trip, the most vivid one was seeing two Japanese women clad in kimono and *tabi*, standing in front of the traditional *Bunraku* puppet theatre in Osaka, drinking Coca-Cola they had just removed from the slot of a vending machine. This image symbolized Japan for me: a country where tradition lives peacefully with modernity; where the 'Western' does not obliterate the 'Oriental'. When I returned to Japan in 1988 to conduct research on how this was possible, I found my initial impression challenged. How disappointing!

The Japanese bride, who is one of the main actors (or rather objects) of this study, begins the day of her wedding by being dressed in a many-layered traditional Japanese outfit, with a heavy wig in the traditional-Japanese style and the white, mask-like make-up customary for brides. As the day progresses, she is gradually transformed into a Western bride, with the requisite white bridal gown and sometimes another extravagant ball gown as well. While this process initially seemed to symbolize and express the modernization and Westernization of Japan, I gradually came to realize that what allegedly takes the guise of Japanese tradition is not always that old, and what wears the mask of the Western is not always really Western in origin. This becomes increasingly clear in the present study of the modern Japanese wedding industry, in which I have undertaken a critical examination of the terms 'traditional', 'Oriental' and 'Western' as they relate to the weddings produced by this industry.

In the late 1980s and early 1990s, when the fieldwork for this study was carried out, more than 80 per cent of urban Japanese chose to hold their weddings in commercial institutions: 30 per cent in wedding parlours, 40 per cent in hotels, which are considered more prestigious, and the remaining 10 per cent in other commercial facilities.

1

The Kobe Princess Palace – where I carried out my fieldwork as a part-time employee – is a modern wedding parlour located in the centre of a large city in central Japan. The parlour caters for about a thousand couples a year, although, like other wedding parlours, it has seen a decline in business since the mid-1980s, after a decade in which wedding parlours were immensely popular.

Most couples who get married at the Princess Palace are residents of the city, although some live in the surrounding area or in Osaka, a larger neighbouring city. Although it is difficult to draw an exact profile of those who choose to marry at the Princess Palace, they generally belong to Japan's large middle class, as do those who now prefer to have a comparable ceremony and reception in a hotel.

One of the reasons for the switch of venue from the wedding parlour to the hotel is that commercial weddings have always served as an opportunity for conspicuous display, and the more expensive hotel weddings provide the affluent middle class with a better opportunity to show their wealth than does the parlour. In addition, precisely because wedding parlours have become so popular, young Japanese and their parents – especially those in managerial positions – decided that they could not invite their colleagues to anything as 'common' as a wedding parlour. But it should be emphasized that the weddings offered by hotels are modelled on the pattern devised by the parlours.

The first organizations to offer lavish weddings outside the home were the *gojokai*, or 'mutual benefit' associations, which also provided services for other 'ceremonial occasions' such as funerals. Established in post-World War II Japan, the *gojokai* still control a large portion of Japan's wedding and funeral business and the company which owns the Kobe Princess Palace is one of the largest *gojokai* organizations.

I chose to work in the Kobe Princess Palace's Cinderella Beauty Shop because the beauty shop is the heart of the new style comprehensive wedding parlour which supplies every service and product related to weddings. The beauty shop is not only responsible for making-up and dressing the bride and groom and female participants in the wedding, but also manages the department which provides clothing worn on a rental basis. My work as an assistant dresser gave me an excellent vantage point from which to observe the laborious work that goes into producing the modern commercial wedding.

Another significant consideration in choosing to work at the beauty shop was that it is the main creator of the different 'appearances' – or 'Japanese' and 'Western' guises – which the bride is dressed and made

2

up for during the course of the wedding ceremony and reception. Participating in this work therefore provided me with a perfect spot for my investigations into the relationship between the 'traditional-Japanese' and the 'Western'.

While the present work is concerned with the Japanese commercial wedding, it differs from most studies of the subject in several ways. First, unlike most other wedding studies it puts more emphasis on the 'producers' of weddings than on those usually considered the main actors. In this respect, too, my work with the producers allowed me a better insight into their method of operation and their motivations. Second, I do not study marriage in general in Japan, but concentrate on the Japanese wedding and the confined space in which it is produced. Thus, most of the material presented herein is about the people who 'belong' to this space, whether as customers/clients or workers.

Edwards (1989) also studies Japanese wedding-parlour weddings. However, whereas he focuses on the formal ceremony, it is my intention to give a more comprehensive view of the production of a Japanese wedding by discussing and analysing the wedding from the point of view of its producers, that is by looking behind the overt ceremony, which is usually of interest to scholars or the general public.

Taking the point of view of the producers is the source of another crucial difference between this study of weddings and those by others, e.g. Charsley (1991) and Edwards, who analyse the wedding as a ritual of society. Instead, I view the Japanese wedding as a 'cultural product'. There have been some attempts to treat weddings in this light, or at least, in separation from their role as rituals as perceived by their principals. Nicholas Harney (1992) uses 'the communal event of the wedding as a "cultural artifact" through which to observe the many businesses and interests that benefit from the perpetuation of this event' (1992:275). However, his account is of weddings of an ethnic minority – Italians living in Canada. A much clearer connection between events such as weddings and concepts of national or cultural identity is drawn by Laurel Kendall (1994) in her study of Korean weddings where 'in the eyes of the state and in popular opinion, such rituals are, in and of themselves, vehicles of morality and of personal and national identity (1994:166)'.

In this study I look at the commercial Japanese wedding as a 'cultural product' whose 'traditional-Japanese' and 'modern-Western' images have been and continue to be invented in order to further the business interests of the purveyors of this product. Even more importantly, looking at the wedding as one cultural product among

3

many in the same 'market' allows us to see the wedding business, including the media which surround and promote it, as a purveyor of a sense of cultural identity.

My emphasis on the production of weddings is partly related to my intended stance of taking the point of view of the wedding producers rather than that of those usually considered its principals. However, looking at the wedding event as a 'cultural product' is primarily a theoretical stance, related to a wider discussion about the construction and consumption of Japanese cultural identity. This discourse has taken two major directions. A great concern has been given to the revived interest in things Japanese and in *dentō* (tradition) as part of a general nostalgia boom that has overtaken Japan since the 1970s (cf. Moeran 1984a; Kelly 1986, 1990; Ivy 1988; Robertson 1987, 1991; Bestor 1989). While these studies are concerned with the problematic and contingent nature of 'tradition' in Japan, another absorbing discussion has evolved concerning the 'West' in Japan (see Tobin 1992) and regarding the co-existence of the Japanese and the Western (see Creighton 1992; Ivy 1995).

Thus, the wedding as a cultural product is indeed not a sole actor in the process of the construction of a sense of cultural identity. This sense of identity, or of Japaneseness, is constructed in an ongoing process which implies also the dynamic, negotiable and contested nature of culture itself (Jackson 1995). Moreover, like Jackson (1995:19) who questions the validity of the clear-cut distinction between '"culture" and "indianess"', I challenge the distinction between 'culture' (and the production thereof) and 'Japaneseness'.

I use the term 'production' deliberately because it lends itself to my view of the customers of wedding services (mainly brides) as 'objects' that are processed by an assembly line. However, while I am aware that viewing human beings as objects has its pitfalls, I would like to point out that I do so on the methodological but not on the theoretical level. In so doing, I actually reverse Appadurai's (1986:5) approach, for although he, too, distinguishes between the theoretical and the methodological, he humanizes objects, and I objectify human beings. In both cases, however, the social analysis cannot 'avoid a minimum level of what might be called methodological fetishism' (Appadurai 1986:5)

Another important way in which this study differs from other wedding studies is that most of them are interested in continuity and thus survey traditional practices (e.g., Hendry 1981). In the Japanese case, this leads to viewing modern Japanese wedding practices as products of the emulation of customs of the warrior class (e.g., Yanagida 1957:167; Kamishima 1969:82; Edwards 1989:40). Although I by no means disregard past wedding customs, the manner in which past traditions have been brought into the modern age interest me less than the way in which they have been manipulated and re-invented by wedding producers to create something that never existed.

In this regard, Raymond Williams (1977) contends that tradition 'is always more than an inert historicized segment' (p.115); it is an 'intentionally selective version of shaping past and preshaped present', which offers an 'historical and cultural ratification of contemporary order' (p.117). In his study of a Tokyo neighbourhood, Bestor (1989) too distinguishes between tradition as an aspect of historical continuity and 'traditionalism' which he views as 'the manipulation, invention, and recombination of cultural patterns, symbols and motifs so as to legitimate contemporary social realities by imbuing them with a patina of venerable historicity' (p.2). In the present study, we shall see how the producers of weddings treat 'tradition' as something to be manipulated, reconstructed and even invented. Indeed, as Handler and Linnekin (1984:280) have put it: 'the invention of tradition is *selective*: only certain items . . . are chosen to represent traditional national culture, and other aspects of the past are ignored or forgotten' (my emphasis).

The idea of the 'invention of traditions' is usually related to Hobsbawm and Ranger (1983). In this respect, Hobsbawm's (1983a:307) distinction between 'spontaneous generation' and 'invention' is relevant to the present study in that instead of describing the process of creating current wedding customs as one of continuity or 'spontaneous generation', I prefer to show how the ceremonial occasions industry has involved itself in an ongoing process of 'invention'.

Ever since Hobsbawm and Ranger (1983) coined the phrase 'invention of tradition' it has been used to show how 'tradition' can be manipulated. Hobsbawm (1983b) – like others in the same volume – claim that '"traditions" which appear or claim to be old are often quite recent in origin and sometimes invented' (p.1). While this 'invention of tradition' is found in several spheres of life, the one they consider most relevant is the 'comparatively recent historical innovation, the "nation", with its associated phenomena: nationalism, the nation-state, national symbols, histories and the rest' (p.13). Hobsbawm (1983a) concludes that the creation of traditions may be a product of either political or social powers (pp. 263, 307), both of which are strongly connected with the modern state.

Several authors compare Hobsbawm's invention of the nation with Benedict Anderson's 'imagined communities' (see, e.g., Smith 1991; Tanaka 1993:264; Yoshino 1992:78). I would venture to suggest an even broader application of 'invention of tradition': that, in cases such as that of the Japanese wedding industry, traditions have been and still are being invented to satisfy financial considerations.

The term 'invention of traditions' implies a distinction between 'invented' and 'genuine' traditions. However, if we take Williams' (1977) (and Handler and Linnekin's (1984)) view that tradition is a 'selective version' of the past, this distinction seems artificial if not inaccurate. For, as Giddens (1994:93) puts it 'all traditions, one could say, are invented traditions'. What gives tradition its 'genuineness' for Giddens is not that it may have been established for generations, or that it may accurately encapsulate past events, but that 'tradition is the very *medium* of the "reality" of the past' (p.94).

Moreover, while Hobsbawm's distinction between 'genuine' and 'invented' traditions implies that invented traditions are immanently 'false', Anderson's (1991) view that what distinguishes communities is not their falsity or genuineness, but the style in which they are imagined, is also relevant to 'traditions'.

Hobsbawm contends that traditions are invented 'more frequently when a rapid transformation of society weakens or destroys the social patterns for which old traditions had been designed' (1983b:4), which may apply to the progression from tradition to modernity in the Western concept of history. But, in his *Archaeology of Knowledge*, Foucault (1972:209–210) asks an imaginary opponent 'What is the fear that makes you see beyond all boundaries, ruptures, shifts and divisions, the great historico-transcendental destiny of the West?' He then answers: 'It seems to me that the only reply to this question is a political one'.

One must therefore be wary of discussing the 'invention of tradition' uncritically in the Japanese context, to avoid running the risk of using Said's (1991) 'Orientalism' in connection with Japan. As Tanaka (1993:3) has put it, given the history of relations between Japan and the West, it is not surprising that (even) major Japanese historians have 'accepted the possibility of truth, objectivity, and progress . . . in Western enlightenment and Romantic historiography'.

Although Western historians of Japan like Carol Gluck (1985) use the term 'modern myths' instead of that of invented traditions, Gluck (and others) employ the same framework of analysis on Japan as Hobsbawm and Ranger and the others in their volume (1983) utilize for the British monarchy. Thus, instead of Western 'nationalism', Gluck speaks in terms of the 'ideology of the emperor' (*tennosei ideorogy*). According to her, 'The past was an obstacle for the future. The bureaucrats created a state of orthodoxy around the figure of the emperor and then imposed it on the people' (Gluck 1985:5). In other words, like Hobsbawm, she views ideology (which is another word for Hobsbawm's 'invented traditions') as being *imposed* on the people at times of rapid change. The new 'traditions', meant to veil the changes, then become ritualized themselves.

Gluck (1985:8–9) does not identify a single group of official myth makers. The cultural nationalism of interest to us (see Hutchinson 1987: ch.1) is fostered by journalists, intellectuals and public figures. Although in his study of cultural nationalism in Japan, Yoshino (1992) concentrates on 'intellectuals' and the 'intelligentsia' (who respond to the ideas and ideals of the nation's cultural identity) as prime developers, he also goes into great detail on how business elites are involved in systematizing and diffusing ideas of Japanese distinctiveness.

Yoshino's concentration on 'social groups with higher and further education' (1992:1) – similar to the view of Hobsbawm and others which emphasizes the hegemonic imposition of ideology – leads to a rigid and limited view of the process. This perspective, while neglecting the ongoing quality of such processes, also limits invention to specific historical periods. Thus, for Hobsbawm (1983a) the period of mass production of traditions in Europe was 1870–1914. Gluck (1985) describes the late Meiji (1890–1912) and the early post-World War II periods as times when Japan's modern myths were heavily articulated.

While the late Meiji period was a time of rapid transformation of society, and one in which 'unprecedented ceremonies' (Gluck 1985) like the Shinto wedding ceremony were introduced, the invention and manipulation of tradition is not, in fact, necessarily restricted to specific historical periods. For although historians like Gluck and Hobsbawm emphasize the question of timing, I suggest that we can broaden our understanding of the process through which traditions are invented by shifting from 'when' questions to questions of 'Who?', 'How?' and 'For what purposes?'.

As this study of the Japanese ceremonial occasions industry will show, the 'invention of traditions' – or, more generally, the construction of a cultural identity – is an ongoing process. Or, as Handler and Linnekin (1984:276) have clearly phrased it: 'the ongoing reconstruction of tradition is a facet of all social life, which is not natural but symbolically constituted'. In the case of the Japanese wedding, we shall see how 'Japanese' and 'Western' traditions are adapted, adopted, invented, and then tried on and either kept or discarded.

This aspect of 'invented traditions' may well be connected to my point about the possibility of financial motivations for the invention of tradition. My research on the modern Japanese wedding (and other ceremonial occasions) industry shows that, far from capitalizing on the inventions of others, these businesses are at the very heart of the process. This less 'hegemonic' approach to the process, which allows for reciprocity in the relationship between wedding producers and their customers, has been crucial to the evolution of my notion that so-called 'traditions' are no different from any other products or novelties in a consumerist society.

It is precisely because they are inventions and by-products of manipulation that the seemingly conflicting 'traditional-Japanese' and 'Western' elements included in the wedding packages provided by the commercial wedding parlour seem to co-exist without clashing. That is to say, just as the 'traditional-Japanese' aspects of the wedding are not products of historical continuity, the 'Western' elements should not be viewed as part of the 'Westernization' which Japan has allegedly undergone.

The relationship between 'Japanese' and 'Western' has always been of great concern to scholars of Japan. Analysing the modern Japanese approach to history, Tanaka (1993:18) contends that 'Japanese were using the West and Asia as other(s) to construct their own sense of Japanese nation as modern and Oriental'. The tension between the 'Oriental', which is often associated with the 'old' or the 'inferior' (Rosenberger 1993), and the 'Western', which has been seen as the 'modern' from the time of Commodore Perry, has resulted in the West becoming the Significant Other in modern Japanese society. As Roy Miller puts it: 'Any facet of Japanese life or culture is thrown into sharp relief when it is brought into direct confrontation with a similar or parallel foreign phenomenon'(1977:77).

In this connection, Befu (1984:62) argues that instead of being based on any objective classification, the 'Japanese' and the 'Western' are 'cultural concepts with a high degree of popular consensus'. The tendency to differentiate between 'Japanese' (*washiki*) style and 'Western' (*yōshiki*) style is obvious in the wedding producers' attitude towards the wedding they construct from artifacts like the Shinto ceremony and the kimono, which are considered 'traditionally Japanese', as well as from such 'Western' elements as the white wedding dress and the (inedible wax) wedding cake. The same division applies to the work of the beauty shop, where beauticians and dressers are characterized (and valued) by whether they work on the 'Western' or 'traditional-Japanese' appearances of the bride.[1]

Befu contends that being a cultural classification, the Japanese/ Western dichotomy is, 'while clear and evident to Japanese . . . not always comprehensible to non-Japanese'. I would venture to suggest that the Japanese concept of what is Western is a Japanese invention, and that a term like *Westanese* (Western-Japanese) might describe it more adequately. However, the ceremonial occasions industry manipulates both the Western and the traditional-Japanese – or shall we call it *traditionese*?

The pastiche-like co-existence of the Japanese and the Western in the modern commercial wedding is interesting not only in and of itself, but even more so as it represents some sense of cultural identity. In his recent book, Tobin (1992:8) says that in 'changing Japan, what people consume may be as important as what they produce in shaping a sense of self'. From this same consumerist perspective, the Western and the traditional-Japanese both contribute to the sense of Japaneseness.

The intriguing relationship between the Western and the Japanese and its role in constructing a sense of cultural identity, is a major concern of this study. Although this aspect is scrutinized on many levels, it is fascinating to observe, mainly through the role of the Japanese bride, the position of Japanese women in this ongoing discourse.

Indeed, most studies of weddings include analyses of marriage and kinship which bring up questions related to gender. Thus, Edwards' (1989) study of commercial Japanese weddings with its interest in 'gender, person and society' in Japan is not an exception. Moore (1988:1) suggests that 'women have always been present in ethnographic accounts, primarily because of the traditional anthropological concern with kinship and marriage' (see also Ortner and Whitehead 1981:10). This has resulted in feminist anthropology viewing kinship and marriage organization 'as the obvious place to start looking for important insights into the ways in which cultures construe gender' (Ortner and Whitehead 1981:11). Faithful to my concentration on the producers of the wedding rather than on the bride and groom and their families, I suggest additional points of entry for the study of gender in Japanese society.

There is no doubt that my choice of the wedding parlour beauty shop as the focus of my fieldwork has given this study a more 'feminine' approach. For the beauty shop employees and employers who appear throughout this book are all women, most of them middle-aged, who treat their work more as a feminine hobby than as a substantial job. Moreover, as becomes obvious from the title of this work, I concentrate my analysis of the wedding production on the bride and her packaging. This reflects not only my stated bias of a 'feminine' approach, but – even more so – the central role assigned to brides and bridal accoutrements by all those involved in the wedding industry, including the wedding parlour and its subcontractors as well as the media. Although the image purveyed by the industry is meant to convey the idea that 'weddings are made for brides', it turns out that brides are the objects as well as the customers of the wedding industry.

The argument that brides are more easily objectified and packaged than grooms is not new. Rubin (1975:175–176) suggests that we seek the locus of women's oppression in the way in which men ('the sexual subject') have treated them as 'semi-objects' for most of human history. From this point of view, 'many customs, clichés and personality traits – among them the curious custom by which a father gives away the bride – seem to make a great deal of sense. However, while Rubin and others speak about 'the traffic of women' in relation to the process a new bride undergoes when she enters her husband's household, I am more interested in the objectification of the bride. This is done, on the first level, through the wedding ceremony itself, which, as a ritual, produces symbols, including those of grooms and brides. And on the second level, by the wedding industry which cleverly uses this process of symbolization to its own, mainly financial, aims. This intriguing relationship between 'culture' and the 'market' is one of the concerns of this account.

In the following chapters I intend to provide a comprehensive account of the process of producing brides as well as traditions. Chapter One opens with a description of a day at the Kobe Princess Palace wedding parlour. Chapter Two delineates the history of the ceremonial occasions industry, as well as of the specific company under study. Chapters Three and Four are concerned with the production of weddings as well as with the people who produce these weddings. Thus, Chapter Three describes the wedding parlour's organization and work and elaborates the relationship between producers and customers, while Chapter Four discusses the structure and work of the Cinderella Beauty Shop and introduces the discussion of Japanese women, which is continued in Chapter Five. This chapter goes into more detail on the 'packaging' of the bride in both clothing and images. In Chapter Six I

10

show how the process of cultural production with which the wedding industry is so extensively involved can be explicated in terms of a dynamic approach to what is usually referred to as the 'invention of traditions'. In the concluding chapter I offer a more general look at manipulation of tradition and the construction of a Japanese cultural identity, which I locate in the Japanese consumer market.

1

A DAY AT THE KOBE PRINCESS PALACE WEDDING PARLOUR

It is only a twenty-minute walk from the bustling Kobe Motomachi station, and less than a two-minute walk from Kobe Business Centre, to what the Kobe Princess Palace describes as its 'gorgeous' building. Like many other wedding parlours in Japan, the building stands out noticeably from those surrounding it. It is not uncommon for these buildings – especially those of Shōchikuden, the company which owns this parlour and which is known as the most showy (*hade*) of all wedding-parlour companies – to have facades that resemble European castles or Walt Disney-style palaces.

The Kobe Princess Palace facade does not reveal that the building comprises three floors. Its long white columns and the large green windows which encircle it from the bottom to the top of the building, give viewers a mixed impression of something between the stereotypical church and mosque. The broad staircase through which one enters the main lobby reminds one of the one designed in Hollywood for Scarlet O'Hara's Tara. It is sometimes used for 'romantic' poses of the bride in her Western wedding dress. It is its columns, double staircase and the extensive grounds which surround the building that inspired one of the workers to suggest that it looks like the White House in Washington, DC. As one enters the grounds of the wedding parlour, either on foot or by car, one encounters a large board listing details of every event that will take place on that day. On exceptionally busy Sundays the board lists as many as seventeen family names of couples to be married on that day.

How can any one service provide for seventeen weddings to be performed in a single day? In fact, how does the 'Comprehensive Wedding Parlour' produce these weddings? In beginning to answer these questions, and in the following description of a wedding as it takes place at the Kobe Princess Palace, it is important to note that the weddings which take place there are similar to those conducted at all wedding parlours throughout Japan.

The wedding parlour

The Kobe Princess Palace is advertised as 'A Comprehensive Wedding Parlour', that is, one which provides everything involved in producing a wedding. In addition to the wedding ceremony itself, including clothing and beauty shop services, a bride and groom can and usually do choose their engagement and wedding rings, arrange their honeymoon abroad, purchase furniture for their new home and arrange for its delivery, all under a single roof. A glance at Figures 1.1 and 1.2 will indicate the extent of the services available at the Kobe Princess Palace and their arrangement in the parlour.

Most clients and visitors enter the palace's main floor by ascending the broad double staircase at the front of the building. After entering through the main door, they find themselves facing a small information desk, where one of the parlour's employees or sales women will refer them to the appropriate area on the ground floor where most of the services are located. Also on the main floor are a Shinto shrine and a small Buddhist temple. Although most couples choose a Shinto wedding service, the parlour also offers the choice of a Buddhist ceremony. In either case a priest is called in by the wedding parlour to perform the ceremony.[1]

The photography studio, which is used throughout the wedding for all photographs of the bride, groom and their families, is also located on the main floor. One room is set aside within the photo studio for the bride to change her attire and make-up during the wedding festivities. This floor also contains a large lobby, which is crowded with wedding guests on busy days, as well as two video screens for transmitting the Shinto ceremony while it is in process for the sake of friends and work associates who are invited only to the reception. In addition, the main floor has a small coffee shop for clients and wedding parlour workers. This shop, located at the front of the building, is the only room in the wedding parlour with windows open to the outside. Next to the large staircase leading to the first floor are two waiting rooms for the principals' families.

The first floor houses six banquet halls of various sizes and decor, as well as the kitchen which caters to all the ballrooms.

While the main and first floors are usually busy on wedding days, which are mainly Sundays, Saturdays and holidays, the ground floor is

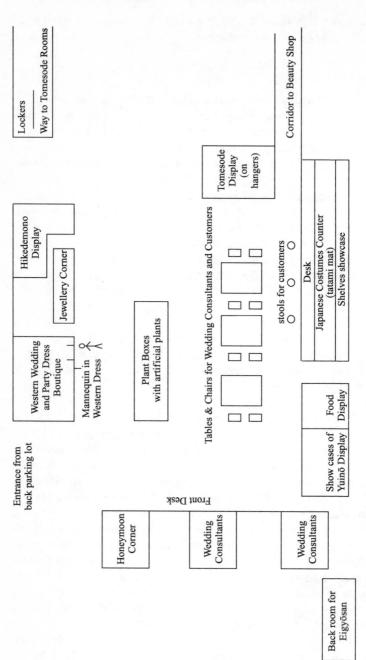

Figure 1.1 Kobe Princess Palace, ground floor main hall

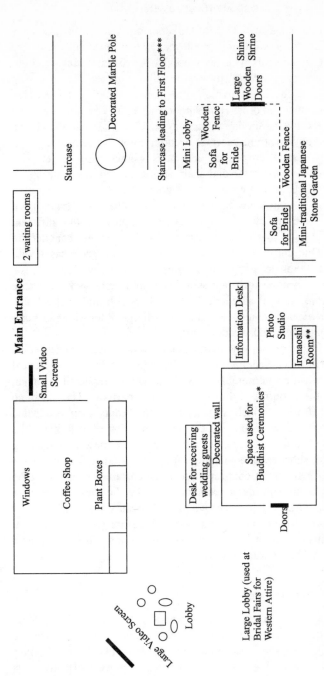

Main Entrance

Small Video Screen

2 waiting rooms

Staircase

Decorated Marble Pole

Staircase leading to First Floor***

Mini Lobby

Wooden Fence

Sofa for Bride

Large Wooden Doors

Shinto Shrine

Windows

Coffee Shop

Plant Boxes

Information Desk

Photo Studio

Ironaoshi Room**

Desk for receiving wedding guests

Decorated wall

Space used for Buddhist Ceremonies*

Sofa for Bride

Wooden Fence

Mini-traditional Japanese Stone Garden

Doors

Large Lobby (used at Bridal Fairs for Western Attire)

Large Video Screen

Lobby

*   This space is used for changing at Bridal Fairs.

**   This small room belongs to the beauty shop although it is located in the photo studio for convenience.

*** The first floor houses 6 banquet halls and the kitchen.

Figure 1.2 Kobe Princess Palace, main floor

almost always in use since most of the preparatory activities take place here. This floor, on which all employees are in uniform, houses the department which deals with reservations for weddings and wedding-related services. Next to the reservation counter is a smaller Honeymoon Counter at which the young couple can receive information about and order Honeymoon Packages. The most attractive sites for these five-to-six day excursions have been Hawaii and Guam, with Saipan and Australia recently becoming popular as well.

Wedding parlour employees and sales women also confer with clients at one of the table-and-chair arrangements which occupy a considerable area at the centre of the floor. Next to these consulting counters are a long show-case in which betrothal gifts (*yuinō*) are displayed,[2] and another in which wax samples of the different selections of food that may be ordered for the wedding banquet are displayed. One corner of the floor contains several show-cases with samples of items to be given as presents to the wedding guests (*hikidemono*). Among them are such household items as kitchenware and tableware, as well as edible food, such as fish and exotic fruits. Near the *hikidemono* display is a small jewellery corner which displays mainly engagement and wedding rings.

The bride and groom who marry at the Kobe Princess Palace – like those at most other wedding facilities throughout Japan – wear rented outfits. A considerable number of wedding guests, especially women, also rent their outfits from the wedding parlour. The costume department (*ishōbu*), which is managed by the beauty shop, is situated on the ground floor where it occupies two sides of that floor, the boutique for Western wedding and party dresses on one side, and a long counter with show-cases containing Japanese costumes on the other.

Dressing in the traditional-Japanese bridal costume and applying the special make-up considered essential for the Japanese bride is a complicated task which is carried out by beauty shop (*biyōshitsu*) professionals also on the ground floor. There are several additional rooms on this floor set aside for beauty shop workers to dress the groom and other wedding guests in their Japanese costumes.

The production of a wedding

The wedding parlour's work cycle is generally divided into two distinct parts, the quiet week days, when mainly preparatory work is being carried out, and the busy weekends (and holidays), when most weddings are held. The difference between the levels of activity on the quiet week days and the bustle of weekends is quite striking. On Sundays especially, the parlour is packed with clients and part-time workers preparing for as many as seventeen weddings. The first ceremony of the day is usually scheduled for 10 am to allow enough time for the bride to be dressed and made-up, as well as for other preparations, and the last ceremony is usually set at about 5 or 6 pm. This means that weddings are being prepared for and are taking place throughout the day and that the workers are constantly dealing with different stages at various weddings.

One of the first things that strikes an observer of the weddings taking place at the Princess Palace is their similarity. This is not to say that every wedding in which I participated as a worker and observed, or those similar wedding described by Edwards (1989), were identical. For every ceremony did, of course, have some distinct, personal aspects. The fact is, however, that at least from the mid-seventies on in Japan, when weddings began to be held almost exclusively in commercial institutions, they have tended to hold a fixed pattern. I shall discuss the reasons for this in Chapter Two. Here, I shall concentrate on describing the pattern of the weddings as I observed them in the Kobe Princess Palace. It is important to bear in mind that, although I describe a single wedding, there are several other weddings in different stages of preparation and performance at the same time. This is why it is so important to maintain a rigid time-table and maximum efficiency during the course of each wedding's production.

I do not use the term 'production' unintentionally. Not only does it refer to the 'performative' aspect (see Edwards 1989) of a wedding at the Princess Palace, in the same way that a film or a play is a 'production', but it also suggests the process of being produced or manufactured, especially in large quantities. The 'producers' of the entire event are the different departments of the wedding parlour, each of which is responsible for a particular aspect of the production, and all of whom together are accountable for the smooth manufacturing of the product known as a 'Japanese Wedding'.

Although the production of a wedding begins at least several months and usually up to almost a year before the wedding day itself, I will begin my description of the production as it takes place on the day of the wedding. Since I am interested in both the product, and its process of production, my description will pay as much attention to the work that takes place before and during the wedding in the area that might be regarded as 'behind the scenes' as to the formal aspect of the ceremony itself.

17

A wedding(s) day at the Princess Palace

The formal part of a wedding at the parlour takes four hours, including the gathering of all wedding guests, the Shinto ceremony, photographic sessions and the reception (*hirōen*), as well as short intervals of 'waiting time', when a wedding party must wait for the previous party to vacate its destined location before it can proceed to the next stage. However, especially for the bride, the duration of the wedding day is much longer. She must arrive at the parlour two and half hours before the ceremony to be made-up and dressed by the beauty shop professionals. Grooms are advised to arrive one hour before the ceremony, the same time when the wedding guests (*okyakusan*)[3] are supposed to arrive.

Dressing and gathering

The preparation of the bride for her first appearance in elaborate kimono, heavy make-up, wig and head covering is extremely complicated and time-consuming (see Edwards 1989:14–15; see also Chapter Five). Although the groom and many female guests don their clothing at the wedding parlour, their outfits are much less elaborate and usually require much less time than that of the bride. This is not the case for some female participants, especially those who play leading roles in the ceremony, who often have their hair set at the beauty shop so that it will suit the formal Japanese style that goes hand-in-hand with wearing kimono.

After being dressed on the ground floor, the bride is led to the main floor. From this time, she (and to a lesser extent, the groom) will be led by one or another of the wedding producers, who literally take her by the hand as her Japanese costume is confining and uncomfortable to walk in. On the main floor, the bride is led to one of the waiting rooms to meet her relatives, while the groom joins his family in an adjacent room. Most of those gathered in these two rooms – numbering around thirty – are close relatives. These are the people who will appear in the family photograph and who will participate in the religious ceremony to follow.

Included among them is a married couple who play the role of the *nakōdo*, or go-between. Though translated as a go-between or a matchmaker, this couple has not usually had anything to do with matchmaking as such (Edwards 1989:15). In fact, it seems that the roles of the actual go-between and the couple who takes this 'ceremonial'

18

role in the wedding are becoming increasingly separated. While the actual matchmaking is accomplished by either a man or a woman, the wedding ceremony requires a married couple, even though the term *nakōdo* normally refers only to the husband. This couple is supposed to provide an example of a stable married life. While in the past (and to some extent today in rural areas; see Hendry 1981:141, Bernstein 1983:45), the *nakōdo* was a respected family member (Omachi 1962:255) or a neighbour, in today's urban weddings he may be the groom's company superior (see Rohlen 1974:241–2; Kondo 1990:180). When I asked one bride how she and her fiancé chose their *nakōdo*, she replied that they chose the highest-ranking manager in the groom's company who agreed to accept the role. The symbolic importance of the *nakōdo* – as opposed to the person who actually introduced the couple – is evinced in the honourable seats (next to the bride and groom) which they occupy during the wedding ceremony and reception, as well as in the wedding portrait.

The short time spent by relatives in the waiting rooms is utilized for a briefing by a parlour employee as to what wedding participants are supposed to do, especially during the religious ceremony.[4] The Princess Palace employs two or three middle-aged women on a part-time basis to act as attendants (*kaizoe*). While on duty these women are dressed in plain kimono. Their explanations are considered necessary by the wedding producers, who tend to think that 'people nowadays do not know much about ceremony'.

Photographs

Upon receiving a signal from the photo studio that it is ready for the next wedding party, the attendant leads the bride and groom there. In a little while, the rest of the wedding party will be invited to join them for a 'group photograph'.

The photo studio occupies a relatively large space on the main floor. This space is divided into three areas, each one for a different type of a photograph. One area is for the bride and groom in their Japanese costumes. Next to it is an area large enough for group pictures. The third area, for bride and groom in Western dress (to be taken later, after the wedding ceremony) is at the other side of the studio. This allows studio workers[5] to handle the different stages of more than one wedding at the same time. This is extremely important in later stages of busy wedding days when brides and grooms leave the reception to change into Western dress and cannot be expected to wait in line while the more time-consuming photographs of other wedding parties are being taken.

Taking professional photographs of the bride in her different costumes, of the bride and groom together, and of their families, is considered as an essential part of the wedding parlour wedding as the Shinto ceremony or the reception which follows it. In fact, even couples who choose not to have any wedding service at the parlour make certain that they are photographed in traditional wedding clothing.[6]

The importance accorded the wedding portraits can be seen clearly in the manner in which the photographers treat the 'objects' of their professional services. Greatest attention is paid to the picture of the bride, who is the only participant in the wedding to be photographed on her own. This solo portrait is of the bride in her first costume, which is considered to be the most 'traditional-Japanese' costume of those that she is about to wear during the day.

Posing the bride for the photograph can take at least twenty minutes as every fold in her kimono is arranged by the studio workers. The pose itself, however – like that of the groom when he joins her for the second photograph – is fixed. In both these portraits, photographers immortalize their clients in positions which suit their Japanese outfits. Thus the bride always stands in profile, with her head facing the camera. This allows the camera to capture the full beauty of her elaborate kimono and its decorated long sleeves, as well as her traditional-Japanese make-up and hairdo. When the groom is 'added' to the portrait of the bride, he stands to her right, facing straight ahead, his feet placed in a stance which is wider than usual. His traditional dress includes a fan, held in his right hand and his left hand drawn into a lightly clenched fist. In this pose and costume – which he wears probably for the first and last time in his life – he is meant to resemble the Samurai.[7]

By the time the bride's and couple's portraits have been posed and photographed, the bride has been standing in a somewhat frozen position for quite a long time. This, together with the confining kimono and heavy wig, sometimes cause brides to feel faint – especially those who are pregnant. (Indeed, pregnant brides are not uncommon in the parlour. A rough estimation of about 20 per cent pregnant brides would not be an exaggeration.) The bride does occasionally complain, but not until she has obviously experienced great discomfort. It is interesting to note in this connection that I have witnessed many cases in which a bride has suddenly gone completely white without this being noticed by those around her, including the members of her family. Sometimes, when the bride is so uncomfortable and/or unwell that she cannot take it any more, she will convey her 'afflicting feeling' (*kurushii*) to her dresser, who may then try to ease the kimono binding. But the general attitude is that the bride must 'endure' (*gaman*), which her mother repeats to her several times during the course of the wedding day. The photographers, too, consider the slightest disturbance in the photo studio as an undesired flaw in the production process, and are impatient to continue their task: producing the perfect representation of the perfect bride.

After bride and groom have been photographed, the close family is invited to come to the studio by the same female announcer who summons them to other stages of the wedding on the parlour's loud speaker.[8] The relatives are generally familiar with posing for group photographs, either from other weddings in which they have participated or from photographs that they have seen.[9] They take their usual positions as follows: the *nakōdo* and his wife sit on either side of the bride and groom in the front row, he next to the groom and she next to the bride. The groom's father is seated next to the *nakōdo*, with his wife beside him, and the bride's parents are similarly seated next to the *nakōdo*'s wife. Next to the mothers of the couple, at each end of the front row, is seated another close family member usually a brother, sister or grandparent. The remaining relatives stand in the rows behind, attempting to place themselves on the bride's or groom's side of the photo with the rest of their kin. In rare cases a deceased family member may 'participate' in the wedding portrait. In a case like this which I witnessed, a framed picture of a deceased grandfather – the 'formal' type used for funerals (see Smith 1978:157–158) – was held by his widow, a further indication of the importance of representation and 'framing' that we shall see more of later on, as well as of formality.

As with bride and groom, posing those in the group photograph is a serious business, especially in the case of the *nakōdo* and close relatives in the front row. Their positions, in particular those of women wearing kimono, are arranged by the female assistant who positions their arms and legs, and makes certain that every fold of the kimono is in place – in short, does whatever necessary to create the 'perfect' portrait. This assistant may also be the one to make one final check of the bride in the group portrait, although this is usually done by a dresser. In fact, two or three experienced dressers are at hand throughout the picture-taking to powder the bride's nose or adjust her head cover while the studio assistant is responsible for spreading her over-garment (*uchikake*) on the floor.[10] After everything has been arranged to perfection and the photographer has done everything possible to engage the attention of the young children in the photo – including clapping his hand and pressing on a plastic duck to make it quack – the portrait is finally ready to be shot. At this point all smiles, if there were any to begin with, are erased; in Japan, formality requires seriousness.

The glossy hard-backed portraits that are the result of this exercise are considered an essential part of any wedding, and will be displayed throughout the years to come. But these professional portraits are by no means the only records made of a wedding. Most wedding guests bring their own cameras, and take photographs throughout the day, especially during the periods between different stages of the formalities. Some of these snapshots have already become part of the family wedding album, which always includes a picture of the bride and groom in front of the board bearing their family names that is taken on the way from their individual waiting rooms to the photo studio. Other snapshots are taken by wedding guests during the reception, especially of memorable moments such as the cutting of the wedding cake. Indeed, 'memorial moment' snapshots are encouraged by the wedding producers, who pose those concerned for the picture to create the frozen moments (or 'frames') which will become part of the permanent wedding memorabilia.

'Packing' the bride and preparing for the Shinto ceremony

After the group portrait, the relatives depart for the lobby, leaving the bride and groom, and sometimes the *nakōdo* and his wife, in the photo studio. For the next stage of the wedding agenda – the Shinto ceremony – the bride's flowing overgarment, which is untied for the photographs, must be re-tied. This binding, or 'packing' (*karage*), usually accomplished by two dressers, is necessary so the bride can walk. However, packing is also significant in regard to the whole process of 'packaging' the bride. As the bride is being bound, a dresser tells the groom – who is waiting for instructions – to stand to the right of the bride. Then she arranges the bride's palm lightly over the groom's hand. Holding the bride's other hand, the dresser then leads the couple to the lobby.

In the lobby, bride and groom and the *nakōdo* and his wife are positioned in front of the two rows of their families who have already been arranged by an attendant in front of the shrine. However, on busy days, when one party after another enters the shrine, the wedding party must wait for the preceding party to depart. In such cases, the bride is seated on a sofa designated for this purpose (she uses a different sofa, also in the lobby, in between the Shinto ceremony and the reception) with her relatives and girl friends who are not participating in the Shinto ceremony gathered around her, admiring her appearance and taking pictures.

When the shrine is finally ready for the party, the attendant knocks on its wooden entry doors, which are opened by two shrine maidens (*miko*), usually young students dressed in white and orange formal religious costumes, who are hired on a part-time basis (*arubaito*) and have no religious training. As the whole retinue slowly marches into the shrine, the attendant bows to them and leaves, closing the doors behind her before preparing the next wedding party for this portion of the wedding.

The Shinto ceremony

Although the Shinto ceremony is considered by the wedding parlour's customers as part and parcel of the traditional-Japanese wedding, it did not become a standard part of the wedding until after World War II (Yanagawa 1972:126). In fact, the first Shinto ceremony was held in 1900 at the wedding of the crown prince (Ema 1971:169; Erskine 1925:8).

The shrine in all the parlours run by this company comprises one room of standard design. It is carpeted in red and all its structure and furniture, including the altar, are of wood. The altar is designed to create the atmosphere of an actual Shinto shrine. The 'ancient' (tape-recorded) music played in the background adds another traditional flavour.

The shrine maidens guide the bridal couple to seats in the centre of the room, with the *nakōdo* couple seated behind them. Other wedding participants take seats in order of entrance, following the parents of bride and groom, the groom's relatives on the right side and the bride's on the left. In front of each relative is a small tray containing a cup of sake and tiny pieces of dried cuttlefish (*surume*) and seaweed wrapped in paper (*konbu*).

The ceremony itself is conducted by a Shinto priest dressed in traditional costume.[11] He is not a regular employee of the wedding parlour and is paid by the Princess Palace for each ceremony. The priest greets the participants and then he proceeds to carry out the purification rite done by waving a long stick with strips of white paper attached to its top (*harai-gushi*). The ceremony continues with a prayer (*norito*) and offering – practices which are part of other Shinto rituals. The *san-san-ku-do* ceremony, in which bride and groom exchange nuptial cups of sake is considered another essential component of the ritual, as is the exchange of rings.[12]

While the ceremony conducted in the shrine is strictly for close relatives, other relatives and friends are invited for the reception which follows. However, many of these guests arrive before the reception and watch the Shinto ceremony on videos. Once the ceremony has been conducted, the announcer instructs all wedding guests to gather at the bottom of the stairs leading to the first floor, and from there they are directed by a wedding parlour employee to the hall where the reception will take place.

The reception: dramatic entrances

Among the dramatic scenes which constitute the wedding reception (*hirōen*), the entrances of bride and groom deserve special attention, for the bride leaves the room at least two and sometimes three times to change her outfit (and have a photo taken before she returns). Each of these entrances – for which the groom joins the bride – is highlighted by special effects.

Wedding guests are formally greeted outside the entrance of the reception hall by bride, groom, *nakōdo* couple and parents who stand in a row and bow to each guest in turn. Both bridal and *nakōdo* couples remain outside while the guests are seated in accordance to a seating chart prepared in advance.

Until quite recently, the bride entered the reception hall in the white outfit she wore in the Shinto ceremony. However, in the last few years, the fashion has become for brides to change into a colourful overgarment (*uchikake*), preferably red. This relatively quick costume change, unlike the others which follow, is handled by two dressers on the spot, at the entrance to the reception hall. Another even more recent fashion is to add a 'traditional-like' artificial plait to the already heavy wig. All these fashions are designed to highlight the bride's entrance into the reception hall as well as to add to the wedding parlour's profit.

While at other wedding facilities bride and groom enter directly into the hall (see Edwards 1989:19–20), all Shōchikuden-owned parlours have a curtained stage on which the bridal and nakōdo couples are presented. When all four are positioned on the stage, the curtain is opened and they appear enveloped in a cloud of white smoke created by water and dry ice. Then, as the lights in the main hall dim, the stage lighting, on cue, turns rose-pink, intensifying the astonished hush from the assembled guests. After they have posed for pictures, the four descend from the stage and proceed slowly to their table which is also elevated above the others. The two stages on either side of the reception hall are trademarks of Shōchikuden and add to its distinctly 'showy' image.

The procession down the long aisle, from one side of the room to the other, can take a variety of forms. In the most popular one, described by Edwards (1989:20), the two couples slowly follow the wedding director, usually to the music of Mendelssohn's 'Wedding March'. Other options may add to the drama. For example, in the cases that have recently become quite rare in which the bride changes to another kimono, the bride and groom may walk together under a traditional parasol or the bride may dutifully follow three steps behind the groom.[13] While traditional-Japanese entries are used when the couple is dressed in traditional-Japanese attire, Western-style entrances are employed when they change into Western clothing later on. The flashiest Western style entrance has the couple lowered into the hall in a device called a 'gondola'.[14] The dramatic effect of this entry is usually intensified by accompanying audio-visual aids and is considered particularly appropriate before the Candle Service (see below). All these entrances are carefully documented by wedding guests, many of whom bring cameras, as well as by a video expert, hired for the occasion. The professional studio photographers only take pictures in the photo studio.

The reception: the ceremonial order

After the bride and groom, and the *nakōdo* and his wife have taken their seats, the master of ceremonies – usually a wedding parlour employee[15] – congratulates the bridal couple and their families. Then he introduces the *nakōdo*, who gives the first of the opening speeches. This speech is followed by two speeches, one by a principal guest (*shuhin*) of each side, usually company superiors or former teachers (see Edwards 1989:19–35). All these speeches like that of the *nakōdo* are highly formal and follow a standard pattern.

All the succeeding proceedings also follow a strict 'ceremonial order' (*shiki shidai*) as the wedding programme is termed by its producers.[16] The idea of ceremonial order has been developed with the growth of the wedding industry in an attempt to maximize the use of time and space. This practice is the main reason for the great similarity between all weddings held at commercial facilities, whether wedding parlours, hotels or other public facilities.

To ensure that the proceedings run according to plan, a director is assigned for each wedding, a parlour employee who is directly in charge of all cuing, prompting, setting the stage and the bridal entrances (see Edwards 1989:19–35, passim). Other parlour workers such as waiters and waitresses are in charge of tasks like dimming the lights at the appropriate time, or giving cues to the participants. One or two waitresses stand behind the bride and groom and physically seat them (especially the bride). In other words, there is always an 'anonymous hand' available to help prevent mishaps.

The reception: 'mini-dramas'

After the opening speeches, the bride and groom perform several performances (or mini-dramas) throughout the reception, devised to create climaxes of memorable moments, which are 'framed' in valuable photographs. In the first of these acts, the 'cake-cutting ceremony', the bridal couple inserts a knife into an elaborately decorated cake made of wax, under the close guidance of the director. The well-staged event is accompanied by romantic music, a spotlight beaming on the couple, and yet another white cloud enveloping them.

The next set part of the programme is the toast (*kanpai*), which, as on many such occasions gives guests the cue to relax and begin eating and drinking. This is usually when the bride leaves the room for the first of her costume changes (*ironaoshi*).

The toast is followed by a series of short congratulatory speeches given by company superiors, former teachers, relatives and friends. As in the opening speeches, the congratulatory speakers elaborate on the couple's new role and responsibilities in society. The flow of these speeches does not seem to be hampered by the absence of the bride, who keeps leaving the room for costume changes, each of which takes about twenty-five to thirty minutes. The groom usually has only one costume change which takes only about fifteen minutes, nonetheless, he joins the bride in all her entrances. While Edwards (1989) regards the themes of the speeches as a direct reflection of the ideals and values of Japanese society, and places high importance on their content (pp.20–24, 28–30, 114–127), I view them more sceptically, as having a role very similar to that of the inedible wedding cake, that is, of decoration. For in both cases the form is no less important than the content.

The couple's entrances to the reception hall are always dramatic. The one when they return in Western attire, is followed by the 'candle service' in which each partner enters carrying a long, unlit candle that they light from their respective parents' table. Then, again led by the director, they circle the room together and light the candles placed on their guests' tables. Each candle lighting is greeted by cheers and applause, which is encouraged by the master of ceremonies. When they reach the tables of the groom's friends, their attempts to light the candles are thwarted as the friends have wet the wick to tease the groom. The couple's unsuccessful attempts are accompanied by much cheerful urging and laughter. This apparently 'spontaneous' event (Edwards 1989:31) actually occurs in every wedding, and is apparently encouraged by the wedding producers to slightly alleviate the formality.

After this comic interlude, bride and groom proceed to their own table where they light the Memorial Candle. This central candle, that is heart-shaped, or is a straight long shape with a list of numbers to signify the years the couple has spent in the homes of their parents as well as those they will spend with each other, is said to represent the 'flame of love'. Of course, this scene, too, is documented as the guests at each table snap photos as the couple lights their candle.

At this point the two hours allotted to every reception are almost over. The remaining fifteen or so minutes are filled with light speeches or songs and dances usually performed by friends.

The reception ends with a short 'flower presentation ceremony' in which the bride and groom present bouquets to their partner's parents. Introduced by the master of ceremonies as an expression of the couple's gratitude to their parents for having raised them until their wedding day, the ceremony is usually accompanied by music and some form of narration (see Edwards 1989:33). Shōchikuden adds yet another sentimental element by providing an accompanying 'Happiness' slide show. The slides (photographs are provided in advance by the couple themselves) follow the bride and groom from childhood through their dating period. This event not only signals the end of the reception but also provides an excellent opportunity to bring the participants to shed a tear or two in an emotional outbreak which is considered an appropriate ending. The bride, relieved that her tasks have been completed and less worried about spoiling her make-up, sometimes continues sobbing as she parts from the guests.

After the slide presentation, the bridal couple and parents line up in front of their guests as the master of ceremonies announces that the reception is about to end. He then introduces the two final speakers: the groom's father, who briefly thanks the guests on behalf of the couple's parents, and the groom, who gives an even shorter speech on behalf of himself and his bride.

The master of ceremonies now announces that the reception is over. Then, for the last time, the director leads the bride and groom down the aisle towards the entrance to the room amidst applause and congratulations. At the entrance they are joined by their parents and *nakōdo* and wife. This is a signal to the guests to pack up the untouched food as well as their gifts (*hikidemono*) in large paper bags printed with the company emblem. The final mini-ceremony of the reception is the mutual bows they exchange with the lined-up hosts as they leave the room. Although this ceremony is quite similar to the one at the beginning of the reception, it is much less formal – mainly due to the alcohol drunk – and includes handshakes and sometimes words of thanks.

The reception has now ended, and another wedding party is usually anxiously waiting to enter the reception hall. Thus, additional informal farewells and snapshots with the bride take place in the lobby. Then, bride and groom, and many of the female guests go down to the ground-floor changing rooms to remove their formal attire before leaving the Princess Palace.

While many guests return home directly from the wedding parlour, others, mainly friends and young co-workers of the couple are invited to another party called *Ni-ji-kai* or Second Party. This festivity is usually held at a restaurant or bar and is much more informal than the wedding. It includes friends who were not invited to the wedding parlour. The expenses of this party are sometimes shared by the guests. In this regard, it is interesting that the Princess Palace has recently begun offering rooms for these Second Parties in an attempt to produce the 'total wedding' – and also to increase its profits. However, it is still not clear whether clients will 'buy' this extra service or will stick with the relative freedom of the less formal restaurant party.

Conclusion: reflections on a day at the wedding parlour

I have chosen to use the term 'production' to describe a day at the Kobe Princess Palace in order to emphasize its theatrical aspects, as well as the extremely efficient manner in which weddings are in fact 'produced' there. During my fieldwork, when I first observed these activities on days with many weddings, I had the feeling that I was witnessing a magnificently organized, well-lubricated machine designed for the production of weddings. Watching brides as they run hastily from one 'station' to another, constantly urged by the producers to stick to the strict time-table, brought home to me an image of an assembly line. It reminded me of an insider's account (Kamata 1982:25–26) of a factory floor work in one of Japan's biggest industries:

> The term 'conveyor belt' suggests automation, but actually the work is done by human hands. Only the parts are transferred by automatic power. The first worker, standing at the beginning of the assembly line, feeds the conveyor with parts. The next person assembles the parts, and the man next to him adds still more parts. All this is done in accordance with the line speed. The people working on the line are nothing more than power consumed in the process of assembly. What is achieved at the end of the line is the result of [their] combined energy.

The wedding parlour's work sometimes seems little different from Kamata's description of a car-assembly line. As in that production line, every station at the parlour is responsible for a specific function, and all together are responsible for producing the final result: a series of smoothly flowing weddings. The fact that this entire 'process' takes place in a windowless space only underscores this image.

Indeed, this metaphor of an assembly line is not to be taken lightly. The dressers and bride-makers do indeed love their work, and some of them regard it as a high art. However, they also view the need to maintain a strict time-table and the wedding parlour's efficiency rules as an enemy to their work – one which consciously or unconsciously drives their work to become increasingly standardized and mechanical.

However, the bride-makers and all other producers in the parlour, do not solely manufacture brides and grooms dressed in the perfect manner, but rather are involved in a much broader process of cultural production. Indeed, in any culture, a public ritual such as a wedding reproduces its subjects as symbols and by that objectifies them. However, while other wedding studies (like that of Edwards 1989) are more interested in the production of marital or gender symbols, my main concern here is in other modes of production. I am primarily interested in the production of a 'Japanese' bride and a 'Japanese' wedding, and in fact in the production of Japaneseness.

While Edwards (1989:8) chooses to regard the Japanese commercial wedding as a rite-of-passage that 'everywhere mark[s] the transition of an individual or a group from one social status to another', I have decided to adopt another perspective. In his typology of public events, Handelman (1989) distinguishes between events that model the lived-in world and those which present the lived-in world. Unlike events that

29

model, which are purposive and 'embedded in a means-to-end context', 'events-that-present' have a 'modular' organization in that scenes can be added and subtracted without necessarily altering the story lines of the event. Thus, the incorporation of the three 'new elements' into the Japanese wedding: the cake ceremony, the candle service and the flower presentation (Edwards 1987:61) seems to place the commercial Japanese wedding more in the event-that-presents than the event-that-models category.

The wedding described herein, which presents the lived-in world, is the kind of event that embodies the logic of a 'mirror, the reflecting surface that displays how things are, but that in itself, and through itself, acts directly on nothing' (Handelman 1989:41). It is in this context that the windowlessness of the wedding parlour becomes significant. Like department stores, it is a 'closed system', a space in which people try on various appearances and assess themselves in the mirror of the system. In the department store this means donning and viewing oneself in unobtainable clothing, and at the wedding parlour it consists of allowing oneself to be dressed and re-dressed and immortalized in the mirror of the wedding portrait in traditional-Japanese and Western costumes. However, in both of these spaces, the object of all this attention leaves the closed system in the same style clothing in which he or she entered it. According to Creighton (1992), Japanese department stores offer their customers the opportunity to 'buy themselves'.[17] The mirror offered by both the wedding parlour and the department store is a reflection of the dialectic between Japanese and Western which is part of the Japanese cultural identity.

Another duality which is of interest in relation to the commercial Japanese wedding is that of form and content. Whereas other scholars feel that weddings as rites of passage 'contain ideal images about the status to be entered . . . regardless of [their] form' (Edwards 1989:8), in my view, the form cannot be divorced from the content. Simmel (cited in Tenbruck 1959:72) commented on the two as long ago as 1959:

> In every given social situation, content and societal form constitute a unified reality. A social form can no more attain existence detached from all content than a spatial form can exist without a material of which it is the form. Rather, these are in reality inseparable elements in every social situation and occurrence.

The complex and reciprocal relationship between form and content can be linked to Hobsbawm's interesting distinction between 'custom' and 'tradition' (and the invention thereof): '"Custom" is what judges do; "tradition" (in this instance invented tradition) is the wig, robe and other formal paraphernalia and ritualized practices surrounding their substantial action' (1983b:2–3). Since the present study focuses on tradition or 'traditionalism' (Bestor 1989), it is as concerned with the formal paraphernalia as it is interested in the content of the substantial action. Thus, while for Hobsbawm invented tradition is the wig and the robe, here it is the packaging in which weddings and brides are enveloped.

The individual reality and therefore the equal importance of content and form can be observed in several aspects of the wedding reception described above, for example, in the speeches which go on regardless of whether the couple are present to hear them. This and the fact that no one at the reception really listens to them as all ideas projected are well known (Edwards 1989:20–24) suggests that they are given as a matter of form, in other words, that the 'medium is part of the message' (Moore and Myerhoff 1977:6).

Another, more obvious, example of the complex relationship between content and form is the wedding cake ceremony. The ceremony in which the huge, elaborately decorated – as well as hollow and inedible – cake is cut may be regarded as an example which illustrates that form should not be disregarded. Edwards, however, would not agree with this, as he suggests that the symbolic significance of the cake-cutting ceremony, like that of other ceremonies in the commercial Japanese wedding, may be looked for only in 'values appropriate to the content' (Edwards 1989:37). To his view, in the case of the cake-cutting ceremony, such 'conceptual associations [which are] already present in Japanese culture' (p.109) are images of insemination and fertility. However, Charsley (1992) is not certain that such a clear symbolic significance of the wedding cake does exist. In his study of the history of the wedding cake in various parts of the world, Charsley cites such informants as a hotel manager with a strong wedding trade as describing the cake as symbolic, but without any thought as to what it symbolizes (p.18). He therefore concludes that, although different symbolic meanings have been attached to the cake by a number of those involved, including anthropologists 'looking for pattern and meaning' (p.122), what really influenced the process of the acceptance of the cake in places like Scotland was 'what people would buy' (p.130).

Changes in wedding practices throughout the years support Charsley's – and my – 'market' explanation. This is the case with the custom of throwing rice at the bride. Edwards (1982:707) says that it has not been adopted in Japan because there is 'a tendency for those elements that "make sense" in terms of the symbolic code to be chosen over those that do not'. However, I have witnessed many instances during my fieldwork in which rice was thrown in 'Christian' hotel weddings. This raises the question of whether the custom has become popular because it suddenly made sense in terms of a symbolic code or followed the logic of a market in which the growing popularity of Western 'chapel weddings' has given rise to the adoption of new Western attributes.

The producers' emphasis on form leads to the theatrical aspect of commercial weddings. According to Edwards (1989:137), the 'memorable occasions' manufactured for these weddings have their origin in traditional theatre. While I agree with his depiction of the wedding as a 'series of poses', the stylized gestures and exaggerated poses of the bride and groom – as programmed by wedding producers – would seem to suggest more of a similarity to *Bunraku* puppets than to Kabuki actors.

While, like Edwards, I use the term 'frame' to describe the individual segments and mini-dramas which likens the commercial wedding to the framing scenes of a film (see Moeran 1989a), I disagree with Edwards' interpretation of the term. Edwards grasps the 'frame' in a similar way to writers of literature known as *nihonjinron* (discussions of the Japanese). He uses Nakane's 'organizational frame' to sustain his argument that the concept of self in Japan emanates largely from the social context (Roden 1991:237). In other words, the 'framed' structure of the Japanese wedding is portrayed as yet another supportive argument for what is seen as the uniquely Japanese 'group model' (Mouer and Sugimoto 1986:54–63) enhanced by writers like Nakane (1984) (see also Abbeglen 1958; Rohlen 1974; Clark 1979). I, on the other hand, do not see the use of frames in the wedding production as natural (being uniquely Japanese). Rather, I view the way in which the wedding industry utilizes framing (and form) as enhancing the 'group model'.

Handelman (1990:8) writes that the 'event that presents . . . may be likened to a mirror held up to reflect versions of the organization of society that are *intended* by the *makers* of the occasion' (my emphases). Indeed, it is the makers of the occasion who create the wedding as a mirror, offered to the Japanese customers as a representation of a peculiar thing called Japaneseness. What is of particular interest, then, is this invented form of Japaneseness as a form of cultural identity, and especially its links to commercialization.

2

FROM HOME WEDDINGS TO WEDDING PARLOUR PRODUCTIONS

The extremely well-organized commercial Japanese wedding production, with its elaborate entries, theatrical mini-dramas and frequent changes of attire, has spread from urban centres to most of rural Japan. But the development of this type of wedding is quite recent and is closely linked with the rise of the Japanese wedding industry.

The expansion of the wedding pattern and the growth of the wedding industry both originated when home weddings began to be moved to public spaces, a change which was promoted by agents like the mutual benefit associations known as *gojokai*, which still maintain a major interest in the wedding industry. Although such commercial institutions such as hotels, public centres (mainly municipal) and shrines entered the wedding business in the mid-seventies, the majority of comprehensive wedding parlours are still owned by these associations.

The *gojokai* are associations in which members can accumulate money over a period of time to use for weddings or other ceremonial occasions.[1] Although wedding parlours like the Kobe Princess Palace operate in accordance with a similar scheme, these associations have undergone a shift in ideology with the growth of the wedding industry. Thus, while they were originally set up to provide service for the common good, the emphasis today is more explicitly market-oriented.

In what follows I shall describe and discuss the history and development of the *gojokai* and their evolution into companies like Shōchikuden and Cobella, which owns the Kobe Princess Palace. As a preliminary it is of interest to look briefly at wedding practices in Japan prior to the introduction of commercialized weddings.

Wedding practices in pre-war Japan

If weddings in Japan today are characterized by their uniformity, formality and elaborateness, those in the pre-war period were noted for their diversity, informality and simplicity, especially among commoners and in rural areas. In fact, country weddings were often held only after the birth of a child or the retirement of the groom's parents from active life. Such wedding ceremonies were extremely simple, and generally involving the exchange of sake cups between bride and groom if anything at all.[2]

While the tendency toward uniformity in weddings began after World War II, a few modern wedding practices did have their origins in the Meiji period (1868–1911). One of the main innovations of this period was the introduction of a Shinto ceremony into the wedding. The fashion of incorporating a Shinto ceremony was influenced by the first such ceremony for the Crown Prince (later the Taishō Emperor) only in 1900. Thus, what is being sold today as traditional religious ceremony based on ancient practices is in fact a relatively modern innovation, and according to Ema (1971:169–170) the result of Western influence.

From home weddings to public-space events

If pre-war wedding ceremonies were performed at all, they were commonly held at home (either that of the groom or the bride or even at both) in cities as well as in rural areas.[3] Even when ceremonies were performed in Shinto shrines, it was common practice to hold the reception at home. The home wedding was characterized by the involvement of the larger community (see, e.g. Embree (1939); Cornell and Smith (1956); Beardsley *et al.* (1959)). This included help from close neighbours, especially from the women (Embree 1939:132, 204–205), as well as financial aid from community co-operatives.

It was only after the war that the practice of having the reception in yet another public space – the most popular until the late sixties being Japanese-style restaurants (*ryōtei*) – became a widespread convention, not only for the affluent classes, but for many others too. One of the reasons for this shift was the smaller size of houses, especially in the cities, although some Japanese scholars (e.g. Ema 1971) see it as another result of Western influence.

Conducting the ceremony in a space divorced from the home and surrounding community necessitated the involvement of outsiders to provide the related services. This led to the rise of businesses connected with dressing the bride, arranging for the shrine in which the Shinto ceremony was held and photographing what was fast becoming a 'memorable occasion'. During the transition period, the bride was prepared at home by a beautician, who also dressed her in a rented kimono. It seems that once the wedding entered the public sphere, appearance (or form) became too important for the ordinary festive kimono. On the other hand, the elaborate ones considered appropriate were too expensive to purchase. This was the beginning of the specialized clothing rental shop (*kashi ishōya*). Then shrines began charging money for the use of their premises, and the professional photographic studio came into being to document the occasion. The day usually ended with a reception in a *ryōtei*.

As wedding proceedings became increasingly complicated, involving a growing number of enterprises, it became too difficult for families to arrange weddings by themselves, and the help of relatives and neighbours became irrelevant as the reception was no longer performed at home. It was at this point that the *gojokai* began to act as agents for the families of the bridal couple, and to coordinate the work of the businesses involved in the wedding production.

Thus, the development of the *gojokai* organizations from mutual aid clubs to business enterprises as well as the expansion of the fixed wedding pattern is closely linked to the move from the privacy of the home and close community to public spaces. This shift was part of a broader process generally known as the decline of community solidarity (see Moeran 1984a), in which the community became less involved in the lives of its individual members. The growing wedding industry not only fostered the decline of community solidarity, but also had a vested interest in utilizing this decline for its own purposes. Only when the ceremony came out of the hands of private members of the family and close community could fixed patterns and efficiency routines take over.

The rise of the *gojokai* organizations

The first *gojokai* was founded in 1948, in Yokosuka near Tokyo, by someone who had been involved in organizing funeral services. The organization offered its members (*kaiin*) – who made monthly payments over a period of several years – low-cost wedding and funeral services. Apart from offering a centralized organization for the wedding, the *gojokai* also offered a saving system, an important feature in the economically harsh days of the post-war period. The alleged ideology of the *gojokai* was the provision of services for the 'common good' of its members; however, the fact that most of their initiators were entrepreneurs poses a question as to their stated ideology.

The initiative in Yokosuka was soon followed by member associations offering services related to 'ceremonial occasions' throughout the country. And, as with the initiator of the Yokosuka enterprise, many of those who initiated new *gojokai* were involved in the undertaking business which already operated on a 'membership' basis. They also had the necessary funerary equipment to start with. These organizations were similar to co-operative associations in rural areas where this system seems to have been most developed, although these rural associations were truly built for the common good in that they welcomed new households, and organized festivals, etc. Both the rural associations and their urban counterparts usually owned the equipment which could be used by any member household. In both village and city, these associations grew in importance during the years of acute war and post-war shortages.

The second group to enter the new ceremonial occasions business was kimono-rental shops. These shops already owned the main inventory necessary for the wedding business, whose main service at the beginning was the rental of bridal robes.[4] While the *gojokai* organizations offered other ceremonial occasions in addition to wedding services, their rapid growth in number during the 1950s and early 1960s was strongly connected to weddings. Until the late 1960s, however, they were mainly co-ordinating agents for the various enterprises which took part in organizing the wedding. It was only then that they began to build their own wedding facilities, which led to the immense growth of the wedding industry in the 1970s. Though many of the *gojokai* remained small or medium-sized companies located in one area – like the one studied by Edwards (1989) – a small number expanded into wedding-parlour networks. One of these huge groups of companies is Shōchikuden (literally: 'Pine and Bamboo Palace').

The growth of Shōchikuden

The history of Shōchikuden, one of the largest wedding parlour networks in Japan, is illustrative of the process which began with mutual benefit associations and has grown into the booming comprehensive wedding parlour business. The founder of the company, Utsunomiya Chikajidō, was a vinegar-maker in Kyoto until he went into the undertaking business. His small shop in Kyoto rented out the special altar and decorations used in funerary rites at low prices to residents of the city who became members. These items were necessary for the funeral service, which was conducted at home.[5] A few years after the war had ended, when the kimono-rental businesses boomed because many people had been forced to sell their clothing during the hostilities in order to purchase food, and when many lost their possessions in the bombings and fires, Utsunomiya entered the bridal business by adding a bridal-kimono rental section on one side of his small shop. Offering this wedding service increased the number of members who joined the *gojokai*, which he had established in the Kyoto area. The success of this expansion led him to extend his services to neighbouring areas.

Like other *gojokai* organizations, the growth of Utsunomiya's company was closely linked with his decision to establish wedding parlours. The first Shōchikuden wedding parlour began operation in a Shinto shrine in Kyoto in 1968. A few years later Utsunomiya built a large wedding parlour in the same city.

Today Shōchikuden is a name for a group of ceremonial occasions related companies. The expansion of Shōchikuden involved the diversification of what was originally a business run by Utsunomiya and his three sons into three separate companies (see Figure 2.1). The first son to leave the company was Utsunomiya Hideichi, the youngest son, who established Hanshin Gojokai (later Cobella), the company which owns Kobe Princess Palace, in 1969.

In 1972, Utsunomiya Shiici, the second son, established a company called Ceremo Gojokai in Osaka. Utsunomiya Tadao, the eldest, succeeded his father in 1976 and named his Kyoto branch of the business Cosmo. Cosmo not only operates as an independent company, with its own wedding parlours and funeral centres, but is also the main – although not the sole – supplier of the clothing used in Shōchikuden Group's wedding halls. Utsunomiya's eldest daughter, Sakurai Kumiko, is in charge of the clothing rental section of Shōchikuden. She works out of the Kyoto branch of the business.

Although the three companies now operate as separate stock companies (*kabushiki gaisha*) controlled by Utsunomiya Chikaijidō's three sons, they all remain under the umbrella of the Shōchikuden Group. This means that they are connected to each other not only through their joint activities such as the supply of formal attire, but by their customers as well. Every member of any of the three companies have the right to use any of the Shōchikuden Group's ninety wedding parlours anywhere in Japan.[6]

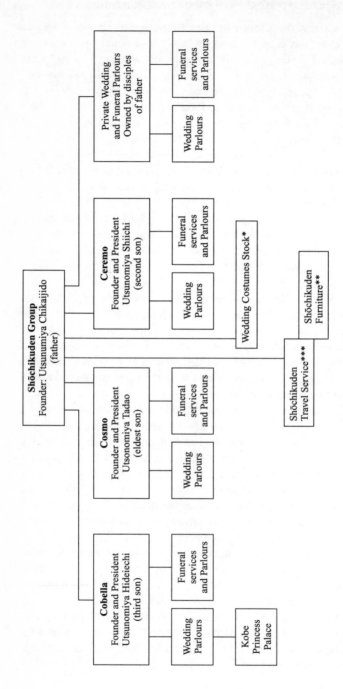

* Wedding Customers Stock belongs to Cosmo and is supplied to all other parlours.
** Shōchikuden Travel Service & Shōchikuden Furniture are sub-companies of the Shōchikuden group and supply services to all parlours.

Figure 2.1 Shōchikuden group structure

The Shōchikuden parlours are of two types: those owned by biological descendants of the founder, and those owned by entrepreneurs to whom the family has given the right (*kenri*) to operate under the Shōchikuden name.[7] But only those who have undergone training with the founder of the original company in Kyoto can buy this right; in other words, it was not extended to just anyone who happened to have the necessary funds. In this way the family has ensured that its reputation will be maintained.[8]

Not every *gojokai* developed as a family business. Some wedding-parlour groups are made up of independent entrepreneurs who agree to use the same name in stipulated areas. But all *gojokai* organizations continue to offer services for ceremonial occasions other than weddings – mostly funerals. Still the phenomenal growth of these organizations – mainly in the late sixties, mid-seventies and early eighties – has been largely related to their wedding business.

The comprehensive wedding parlour and the birth of the 'ceremonial order'

As the *gojokai* entrepreneurs saw the financial potential of the wedding business, they began to use the capital accumulated from their membership fees and wedding profits to build their own facilities. Efficiency also played an important role in the decision to create a single physical space in which to hold every aspect of the ceremony and reception, since the latter enabled better control of all wedding proceedings – and thus greater profits. The new-style wedding parlour thus concentrated enterprises like hair-dressing and dressing salons, clothing rental service, Shinto shrine, photo studio, kitchen and ballrooms, in one place. This facilitated the development of the ceremonial order characteristic of the comprehensive wedding parlour.

With the construction of their own wedding parlours, *gojokai* owners openly shifted their ideology from 'service for the common good' to a 'market ideology' which stressed efficiency and lower prices. This did not happen until the 1960s, because only then had Japan recovered from the disaster of the war, to a point where the situation was good enough to warrant such a change in principle without damaging the companies' reputation.

The profit motive was also a major reason for the development of the all-inclusive fixed wedding offered by the new wedding parlours, for the owners not only wanted to reap the profits from every stage of the wedding day, beginning with the preparation of the bride and ending with the reception. In order to make optimum use of the space, they had to construct a production which left little room for divergence from a pattern whose timing could be calculated in advance.

The problem of obtaining maximum utilization of their facilities was complicated by the limited number of days which Japanese consider to be 'good' for weddings. This meant not only holding weddings mainly on weekends and holidays – in order not to interfere with working life – but also taking into consideration the season and the astrological calendar. For there is a strong preference for spring and autumn weddings, the hot summer months (especially July and August) generally being avoided.[9] The astrological calendar, borrowed from China, is used to distinguish between auspicious and inauspicious days for weddings and funerals as well as for ceremonies connected with building.[10]

Being the 'ceremonial occasions' specialists, the new wedding parlours' owners were bound to be aware of all these factors when seeking a practical way to construct their wedding parlour system. One such specialist, the owner of several new-style wedding parlours who carry the name of Shōchikuden's main competitor, explained it to me. This woman who employs 570 people was very frank in our long conversations on her practical and financial goals: 'If you want to hold a large number of weddings on a "good" day, it is useful to have a programme for the ceremonies. So we developed the ceremonial order (*shiki shidai*) to ensure that the entire operation would take no longer than two hours . . . this was, and still is, better for business.'

The home wedding vis-á-vis *the wedding-parlour production*

According to Embree (1939:209), the home wedding of the late 1930s 'is an extreme example whereby a social gathering begins with stiff formality and ends with orgiastic abandon'. Twenty years later, Beardsley *et al.* (1959:326–327) were still writing that the reception might begin 'stiffly solemn' but that 'conversation warms' during the festivities and that by the end of the evening 'the men wend their jolly, unsteady way home'. In this respect, home weddings were similar to other Japanese ceremonies and parties which always open with a rigid format, but this formality breaks down as people warm to the occasion (Moeran 1986).

Although the end result of today's wedding-parlour reception may seem somewhat similar to that of the home wedding, in that one still sees men (and rarely some women) leave 'unsteady' due to the alcohol they have imbibed, the two-hour limit to every wedding and the strict schedule according to which the guests are shepherded from station to station, not only limits the time available for drinking but seems to put a damper on the 'jollity' of the occasion. As one of Smith's (1978) informants put it: 'No one much likes this way of doing things [in the wedding parlour]. It's really flat and a lot less fun than it used to be' (p.214).

None the less, smaller living spaces and the massive promotion of new-style wedding parlours have convinced a Japanese public with more money to spend of the benefits of a public wedding. Indeed, conspicuous consumption has played a crucial role in the move from the home wedding to the commercial 'production'. Vogel (1967) has noted that the 'conspicuous display of wealth' through the wedding of a child began in the late 1960s, with the rise of the 'new middle class' of Japanese salary men. According to him, it was not 'unusual for the parents of the bride and groom to spend the equivalent of two or three times the young husband's salary on the wedding' (pp.81–82).

This tendency has grown to the point where, today, there is a hierarchy of public spaces available. Thus, parents whose guests are considered to be distinguished (*erai*) will not hold their child's wedding in a wedding parlour, but will hire a hotel, which is even more expensive and therefore more prestigious, even if the economic burden strains their finances. As a bride who married a young scholar and university employee explained: 'This may be a strange way of putting it, but it seems that a hotel is "higher", and when you invite famous professors you just cannot invite them to a wedding parlour.' In most cases, however, the prominent guests considered in the choice of the wedding venue are the groom's company superiors. Although this was never stated clearly in my interviews, it seems that the main consideration here may be the groom's future with his company.

The commercial expansion of the new wedding pattern

The wedding pattern described in Chapter One was originated in the 1970s. Although there have been some innovations throughout the years, these have taken the time constrains necessary for maximum utilization of the parlour's space into consideration. What is surprising is not that a successful pattern has been maintained in particular in parlours or in groups like Shōchikuden, but that every facility offering wedding services offers an identical pattern. Thus, hotels and public halls offering wedding services have imitated the wedding-parlour

41

pattern, and even Shinto shrines have found it appropriate to accommodate themselves to this commercial pattern (Edwards 1989:50).

A leading Japanese wedding entrepreneur explains away this craze for uniformity simplistically: 'Japan is small, so people quickly copy from each other.' Although his explanation does not go far enough, it is true that the pattern became widespread through the network of people and companies involved in the business. First were the wedding-parlour owners themselves, who were related to each other through the *gojokai* organizations and naturally exchanged information on the new features and facilities they were offering.[11] However, the most direct carriers of new practices may be the media, especially women's magazines, which since the 1970s have carried features on weddings. There are some magazines targeted at brides-to-be, but others touch on the subject frequently, in articles as well as through advertisements.[12] In addition, there is quite a large industry producing professional literature for those in the wedding business.[13] Naturally, these magazines are active in promoting wedding-related businesses. In fact, a number of them are published by wedding-related businesses such as bridal make-up companies. These, of course, do more than merely review the industry's practices.

Among the other industries engaged in promoting commercial wedding practices and new features suited to the fixed wedding pattern are those that provide the ingredients and special effects from which these 'productions' (*enshutsu*) are fabricated – for example, the dry-ice machines used to create the white-smoke effect when the wax wedding cake is cut. Clearly, it is in the interest of such companies to promote new ideas which will increase their business.

The decline in popularity of the wedding-parlour ceremony and reception

The 1970s and early 1980s were the 'glamour days' of the specialized wedding parlour. Although these institutions were never the only venues in which wedding services were offered, their great popularity has declined significantly in the past decade.

Tables 2.1 and 2.2 are based on samples of couples living in the urban areas of Tokyo and Osaka, taken annually by the Sanwa Bank beginning in 1976. Table 2.1 describes the places chosen for weddings in 1982 and 1990. A look at the figures indicates that the two main commercial competitors for these services, both in 1982 and in 1990

Table 2.1 Venues in which wedding ceremonies and receptions took place in Tokyo and Osaka, 1982 and 1990*

Place	Ceremony		Reception	
	1982 *(%)*	*1990* *(%)*	*1982* *(%)*	*1990* *(%)*
Wedding parlour	40.5	26.7	41.8	28.2
Hotel	28.0	40.8	30.5	45.3
Public hall	14.9	12.2	15.5	13.3
Restaurant	n.d.	0.7	n.d.	5.3
Shrine/temple	8.3	6.5	5.3	1.3
Church (in Japan)	3.2	7.3	0.7	0.5
Church (abroad)	0.7	2.5	–	–
Home	0.2	–	0.5	–
Other	3.9	1.5	–	2.3
Not held	0.2	1.2	0.5	3.0

* Based on a sample of 410 marriages in 1982 and 600 marriages in 1990.

Sources: Edwards (1989:51); Sanwa ginkō (Sanwa Bank) kyoshiki zengo no suitōbo (A Ledger of Wedding Expenditures) (Tokyo 1982, 1990).

Note: n.d. = no data.

are hotels and wedding parlours (about 70 per cent together). However, between 1982 and 1990 the popularity of wedding parlours versus hotels reversed itself for both ceremonies and receptions. Whereas the proportion for ceremonies in 1982 was 40.5 per cent for parlours and 28 per cent for hotels, in 1990 it was 26.7 per cent for parlours and 40.8 per cent for hotels. With regard to receptions, the change is even more striking: from 41.8 per cent to 28.2 per cent for parlours and from 30.5 per cent to 45.3 per cent for hotels. The last figure reflecting also cases of couples marrying in a church who usually hold their reception in hotels.

Table 2.2, which describes the changes in popularity of venues between 1976 through 1990, indicates that the peak time of wedding parlours was from the late seventies to the mid-eighties. The proportion of weddings in parlours versus hotels between 1978 and 1985 was an average of 40.8 per cent to 26.2 per cent respectively, with a high of 43.6 per cent for parlours in 1979. However, while the popularity of wedding parlours remained almost the same for 1979 and 1980, hotel weddings rose by 5.6 per cent during the same period. This trend continued throughout the time of my research, which was concluded in 1991.

Table 2.2 Changes in wedding venues, 1976–1990

Year	Wedding parlour (%)	Hotel (%)	Public hall (%)	Shrine/ temple (%)	Other* (%)
1976	34.5	20.6	17.5	11.8	14.8
1977	35.5	20.5	19.7	11.5	12.5
1978	39.3	21.7	21.5	7.2	9.6
1979	43.6	20.5	20.0	7.9	8.0
1980	43.5	26.1	16.9	6.1	6.9
1981	39.9	29.2	19.4	4.2	6.8
1982	40.5	28.0	14.9	8.3	8.0
1983	42.7	23.9	15.0	8.2	9.5
1984	37.1	29.3	19.2	4.9	8.7
1985	39.8	30.6	15.1	6.2	6.8
1986	35.2	34.5	16.5	4.9	8.3
1987	32.3	38.4	15.0	5.2	8.9
1988	33.7	35.4	14.9	3.8	10.9
1989	29.9	42.7	11.4	4.5	10.7
1990	26.7	40.8	12.2	6.5	12.0

* 'Other' includes restaurants, churches, as well as the category 'other'.

Sources: Sanwa ginkō (Sanwa Bank) kyoshiki zego no suitōbo (A Ledger of Wedding Expenditures), (Tokyo 1976, 1986, 1990).

Despite the switch in popularity between the two, hotels and wedding parlours together continued to represent 70 per cent of the weddings held in public facilities. But what do Tables 2.1 and 2.2 tell us about the other 30 per cent? They show that, despite a few fluctuations throughout the years, public facilities have remained in third place, and that there is no indication that they will gain in popularity. This is related to the ongoing search for increasingly expensive and elegant venues for weddings.[14] These tables also indicate that ceremonies in shrines and temples have declined in popularity from a high of 11.8 per cent in 1976, when the comprehensive wedding parlour began its growth-spurt and included a shrine within its facility, to an average of 6.8 per cent for years 1978–1985 (the same years discussed above in the wedding parlour versus hotel figures). However, the slight rise in 1990 may possibly indicate a trend towards more 'personal style' weddings. With regard to home weddings, the main venue for these ceremonies in the pre-war period, Table 2.1 verifies that the commercial weddings dealt them their final blow.

The wedding parlours respond to changes in taste

'Young people do not like wedding parlour weddings any more. They prefer hotel weddings just because they are more expensive', complained an experienced saleswoman from Kobe Princess Palace as we were discussing the difficulties she was facing in obtaining clients. This pinpoints the rise in hotel weddings at the expense of wedding parlours as a question of image rather than of prices *per se*.

Targeting the young is not a new practice (see Edwards 1989:90–91), but it does reflect the *gojokai* organizations' change to 'market ideology', and their promotion of weddings more as consumer products than as family affairs. This approach, however, requires keeping a constant finger on the pulse of customer taste. Thus, whereas it used to be enough to offer the young special deals such as reduced honeymoon fares in order to obtain their business, the rise in popularity of hotel weddings and concomitant decline in those held at wedding parlours necessitated additional steps related to image. In other words, the entrepreneurs realized that the 'better ceremonies for less' slogan was no longer serving their purpose. The first thing they had to do was to change their image to match the image of elegance, excellence and costliness which hotels convey through advertising in magazines and public areas like trains and train stations.

A typical hotel advertisement shows a Western model dressed in a spectacular wedding gown, usually white, with a title like 'Simplicity and Elegance', usually in English. The Akasaka Tokyu hotel's slogan – 'Elegance Marieé' – goes a step further to promote the notion of French flair. Hotels, especially luxury hotels, do not advertise inexpensive packages. They concentrate on 'elegance', 'extravagance' and 'modernity', the image they – and some smart wedding parlour entrepreneurs – know will attract upwardly mobile Japanese couples.

Chie Nakane in *Japanese Society* (1984) argues that life in Japan is conceptualized and lived hierarchically and Creighton (1992:43–44) suggests that hierarchy permeates many spheres of social life, including the Japanese system of retailing and distribution. In this regard, having one's wedding in a luxury hotel resembles shopping at a high-class store. In both instances the customers seek status, prestige and respectability as much as the products and the services offered.

This is a major reason why hotel weddings have been gaining popularity and wedding parlours have come to be seen as old-fashioned. One wedding parlour employee told a co-worker when discussing the drop in weddings at the Princess Palace, that young people in Kobe prefer hotel weddings because Kobe had gone through relatively rapid financial progress and was also quick to adapt modern, meaning Western, practices.

One of the ways in which Cobella, one of the Japan's largest and most successful *gojokai* organizations, has endeavoured to cater for these new tastes was by changing name from Hanshin Gojokai to Cobella (*Kobera*) in 1987. 'We have changed our name from Gojokai to Cobella along with the era' (*gojokai kara kobera e no jidai to tomo-ni*), the new promotional stated.[15] In addition, they pointed out that 'Co' stands for the English words 'Ceremonial' and 'Occasions' and that 'Bella', stands for 'beautiful' (*utsukushiku*) in Italian (or 'Belle' in French).[16]

That most of the company's members and customers are not fluent in Italian, French or English can be seen as another example of the importance given to form. Indeed, most customers will probably remember only *Kobera*, the Japanese *katakana* – a phonetic alphabet usually used for loan-words – version of the name. Choosing a word like *Kobera* is an excellent example to Fields' (1988) argument that 'one effective use of *katakana* is in changing a word which has a specific meaning into an abstraction – like International Business Machines becoming IBM' (p.37). According to Fields, this practice reduces the element of confusion in communication, especially regarding foreign words which are the least clear in meaning. However, the most significant role of the foreign sound of the new name is that it has given the Cobella wedding parlours a modern, stylistic image which it previously lacked.[17]

Bridal Fairs are another manifestation of the efforts being made at Kobe Princess Palace, as at all other wedding parlours, to increase business by keeping up with the latest in wedding items and services. They have always been held a few times a year to simplify the process of wedding selection by couples and their families. But in recent years there have been changes in these events which can be seen on several levels. First of all, they have grown from small events aimed mainly at members of the company to grand events open to the general public. In addition, they have become, as has the name of the company, more modern and Western, as evinced for example, in the central place now given to Western-style wedding gowns, as opposed to traditional-Japanese attire.

Cobella's efforts to blur its traditional *gojokai* image and promote that of a modern wedding facility are not that simple, because the company is still supported by a membership system. Thus, to satisfy

46

their older and more traditional clients, Cobella continues to hold small-scale bridal shows for members. These bridal shows are targeted at the parents, mainly mothers, rather than the young.[18] This is another way in which the company continues to exploit its traditional image as long as it continues to contribute to its financial aims.

Cobella: the portrait of a 'ceremonial occasions' company

Cobella was established as Hanshin (Osaka–Kobe) Gojokai in 1969 by Utsunomiya Hideichi, the youngest son of the founder of the Shōchikuden Group. Like his father and eldest brother in Kyoto, Hideichi began by offering wedding services in a shrine in Nishinomiya (a town located between Osaka and Kobe). He did not open his first wedding parlour in the same town until 1975, and this town remains the centre of his operations.[19]

Cobella is not only the largest company in the Shōchikuden Group, but one of the largest *gojokai* businesses in Japan. It owns seventeen wedding parlours and thirty funeral parlours throughout Japan, mainly in the Hanshin (Osaka–Kobe) area.[20] The company has grown from 50,000 members in 1969 to over 1.5 million members in 1989.[21]

Cobella, like all other *gojokai* organizations, is involved in weddings, funerals and other ceremonial occasions. Formally, the company is divided into Shōchikuden for weddings (*konrei*) and Gyokusenin for funerals (*sōshiki*) in an effort to maintain a clear-cut distinction between these two rather contradictory occasions. In addition, weddings and funerals are held in different facilities. However, since the founding father used his original shop in Kyoto for both services, this separation may be seen as a result of modern (Western?) influence. In any event, the capital for both businesses is jointly accumulated.

The *gojokai* system on which Cobella and other such institutions are based does not seem to have changed much since the time these institutions were first established after World War II. Members still pay a monthly fee over a period of several years and use the money accumulated for either a wedding or a funeral. However, even if the *gojokai* were originally altruistic, which I have questioned above, it is certain that altruism or 'the common good' ideology was abandoned in the 1970s.

The membership system

The way the Cobella membership system operates today is yet another illustration of how the business has adjusted to changes in both wedding practices and Japanese society as a whole. It also indicates the sharp business intuition of its management. A more detailed look at the changes the membership system has undergone will help us understand the *gojokai* business in general as well as the 'packaged' wedding pattern offered by their wedding parlours.

Every bride or groom who wishes to be married in Kobe Princess Palace must be a member of Cobella (either directly, or through her or his parents). Every new member signs a contract with the company which stipulates the services to which they are entitled if they maintain their monthly payments over a specific period. A prospective member can choose from three types of membership:(1) The K-type, with a monthly payment of ¥3,000 for a period of 60 months, in which case the sum accumulated will come to ¥180,000 (£720); (2) the P-type with a payment of ¥3,000 but for 90 months in which case the final amount will be ¥270,000 (£1080); or (3) the L-type – the highest rank and recently the most popular type of membership – with a payment of ¥5,000 for 80 month, which accumulates to ¥400,000 (£1600). Several methods of payment are offered as well, including automatic bank transfer, home collection by Cobella saleswomen, remittance, or cash payment at the Cobella offices.[22]

The services increase along with grade of membership, both quantitatively and qualitatively. Thus, according to the contract, brides of the highest rank are entitled to a 'French dress', and their grooms to a special cake-cutting service, even more elaborate than the regular 'Angel Cut'. Members can upgrade to a higher grade at any stage, but can never move down to a lower grade.

Any member is entitled to receive services after 180 days provided that he or she pays the full amount stipulated in the contract 'at once' (*mangaku*). On the other hand, once a member has completed his or her payments (*manki*), their right to use the services is maintained until they claim it.[23]

In addition to the distinction between weddings (*kankon no bu*) and funerals (*sōsai no bu*) in the contract, the wedding category is further divided into services provided for the bride and those provided for the groom. Each member (or any one of the member's family) has the right to one ceremony per membership card. Once that right is used, one must resubscribe for subsequent ceremonies. The member's rights can be used in any of the branches of Cobella and the Shōchikuden Group.[24] It should also be noted that, in neither weddings nor in funerals does the accumulated amount cover all the expenses of the occasion.

The precise specification of the props and services to which members of each rank are entitled goes hand-in-hand with the fixed pattern of weddings (and funerals). Members cannot use the accumulated money as they wish, but must accept the services offered by the company.

The wedding 'package'

Since both bride and groom must be members of Cobella to hold a wedding at Kobe Princess Palace, the 'packages' (*pakku*) of services for each are built so they complement each other.[25] A careful look at the services stipulated makes it clear that while the groom's package includes services connected to the production of the wedding, including the wedding ring, betrothal (*yuinō*) set, the cake-cutting ceremony, wedding portraits as well as his clothing, the bride's package consists mainly of wedding outfits and anything else related to the 'bride making'.

In addition to reflecting the huge difference in the prices of the bride's and the groom's outfits (see 'Wedding costs' below), the clear distinction between the packages has more practical aims which are at least partially related to the new wedding practices.

Because hotel weddings are considered more prestigious and therefore potentially more beneficial to the grooms in terms of the invitation of respectable guests and promotion in their jobs, problems arise when the bride (or her family) is already a member of Cobella and has accumulated a considerable amount of money in one of their packages. The matter is further complicated because in Japan the wedding venue and style is traditionally decided by the groom's family.[26] The construction of separate bride and groom packages allows brides' mothers to begin planning their daughters' wedding day long before the girl knows what kind of wedding a future groom will choose. If the groom agrees to a Princess Palace wedding, he can become a member and pay his lower fee in a lump sum. On the other hand, if the groom does not wish to get married in a wedding parlour, the bride's package is built so that her family can avoid losing money while at the same time complying with the will of the groom's family. In this way, the wedding industry not only avoids interfering with existing gender distinctions but serves a role in maintaining them.[27] The solution in such cases is that, since the bride's package consists mainly of her own rented outfit and make-up, it can be used in a different wedding facility, in most cases at a hotel. In order to keep a not inconsiderable portion of the business in a society tending more and more towards hotel weddings, Cobella even offers to compensate the other facility for its loss of profit from the bride's outfits, which constitutes a considerable amount.[28] Since this is not the optimum arrangement from the wedding parlours' point of view, their managers obviously expend much energy in trying to convince the couple of the parlour's benefits before resorting to this solution.[29]

The membership system: new adjustments

The manipulation of the bride's 'package' is only one of many examples of how the membership system of Cobella – as well as of other *gojokai* – is continually adjusted to respond to changes in society in general and wedding practices in particular. 'Mutual benefit associations' like Cobella understand that a membership system suitable for the harsh times of the early post-war period is no longer relevant in an affluent society.

This process began at the peak of the wedding parlours' success when *gojokai* entrepreneurs realized that their more affluent customers wanted more than a saving system to help them cover wedding costs. An increasing number of clients were interested in using their child's wedding as a 'conspicuous display' of their growing social status, and wealth. This is when Cobella introduced the ranking system.

Later on, when even the possibility of having showy and extravagant weddings no longer seemed to be enough to counter the growing success of hotel weddings, the parlour owners came to the conclusion that it was the system itself that had ceased to be relevant. As the manager of Kobe Princess Palace put it: 'People are rich now, they no longer need to save money for weddings.' This realization, together with the identification of the young as their main customers, has led Cobella to open its parlours – although not formally – to non-members, which means that brides, too, can now become members after they have decided to have their wedding at a Cobella parlour. Other *gojokai* organizations have opened their gates to non-members without even insisting that those who wish to use their services become members at all. They just pay a slightly higher price. But Cobella has chosen again to follow a 'safe' policy, and not to completely ignore the role of parents, who still like to put away money for their children's weddings before the event is upon them. This is the same attitude that had led to the old-fashioned bridal shows for parents and the three-day extravaganza for their upwardly mobile children.

This play between the young and their parents – indeed, between the traditional and the modern-Western – has recently led Cobella to give its membership system a more modern look without really changing the way it operates. The company has issued a Cobella Card for members – after the fashion of club-cards – which entitles card-holders to discounts in a variety of shops not necessarily concerned with wedding-related items. It also offers holders of the card such activities as trips to hot springs and beach resorts as well as lessons in jet-skiing. As the advertisements for these activities state, they are 'for the young'. And anything that will attract the young to the wedding parlour ends up by serving their parents, most of whom – at least of the bride – still enter the *gojokai* system.

Wedding costs

Only those who have paid in a considerable amount of money, either over the years or once they have decided to hold their wedding there, can get married in Kobe Princess Palace. But does the amount accumulated really cover the full cost of a wedding? A look at the prices of wedding-related services, based on the rough estimate which the parlour prepares for its customers (see Table 2.3), and at the amounts accumulated under even the highest-level wedding package plan (¥400,000) shows that the answer to this question is a resounding 'No!'. For the cost of a full package, including a reception for fifty guests, comes to about 1.8 million yen or more than four times the amount paid in.

Let us look at how the cost of a wedding breaks down. In addition to the major expenses, e.g., for food at the reception, the *yuinō*, souvenirs, photographs and video[30] (¥802,000), and clothing for the bride, groom and their families (¥774,000) – which already total more than has been accumulated in the L-type plan mentioned above – are the extras involved in the production of the wedding such as the dry ice for the white smoke, flowers, a memorial heart candle and the master of ceremonies to set the proper tone. Since the wedding parlour charges separately for each element, it is clear that any elaboration in the production is directly translated into increased profits. This explains the inventions and elaborations within the confines of the fixed pattern, which will be discussed in Chapter Six.

Table 2.3 Wedding costs at Kobe Princess Palace 1990–1991 (calculated for 50 guests)*

Service	Individual costs	Subtotals and total
Engagement (*yuinō*):		
betrothal set	35,000	
betrothal receipt set	3,000	
Subtotal		38,000
Ceremony and miscellaneous:		
ceremony fee	15,000	
wedding invitations	9,000	
seating charts	5,500	
video	80,000	
Subtotal		109,500
Reception:		
food	500,000+	
sake	5,600+	
beer	13,400+	
flower arrangements	38,800	
master of ceremonies	40,000	
memorial heart (candle)	12,000	
dry ice	16,000	
karaoke	24,000	
microphone	3,000	
use of facility	25,000	
Subtotal		679,800
Gifts for guests and related miscellaneous:		
souvenirs	90,000	
confectionary (gifts)	30,000	
paper bags	10,500	
tea in waiting rooms	4,000	
flower presentation	6,000	
Subtotal		140,500
Photographs:		
group photograph	15,000	
photograph bridal couple	15,000	
Western bridal couple photo	15,000	
four other poses	52,000	
Subtotal		97,000
Costume rental:		
Bride's attire:		
uchikake (over-garment)	250,000+	
furisode (long-sleeved kimono)	180,000+	
wedding dress	100,000+	
underwear set	3,000	
beauty shop's dressing	48,000	
Subtotal	581,000	

Table 2.3 Contuinued

Service	Individual costs	Subtotals and total
Groom's attire:		
formal Japanese wear	30,000	
tuxedo	30,000	
underwear set	3,000	
Subtotal	63,000	
Family formal costumes:		
6 *tomesode* (short-sleeved kimono)	120,000	
2 morning suits	10,000	
Subtotal	130,000	
Subtotal costume rental:		774,000
Total wedding costs		**1,838,000**

* Costs and the way they are sectioned are taken from a written rough estimate (*gaisan-sho*) which is given to customers. To this rough estimation one should add the bridal bouquet (¥20,000+), wig decorations, etc., which are not included in the estimate.

Since the pattern and services developed in comprehensive wedding parlours established by the *gojokai* organizations have become commonplace in all wedding facilities, it can be assumed that wedding costs at Kobe Princess Palace are roughly similar to those in other facilities, including public facilities and shrines. Although public facilities maintained by municipal governments are usually known to be slightly lower in cost than wedding parlours (see Edwards 1989:50), my own investigations showed that they offer exactly the same services at almost the same price. The same can be said for Shinto shrines. I have also found that the notion that hotel weddings cost twice or even three times more than the same style wedding held at a wedding parlour is due more to image than reality. Sanwa Bank data on this subject show that the difference in price is not that great, for while a few top hotels charge much higher prices, lower hotels – which benefit from the 'hotel' image – charge about the same as the parlours.[31]

According to the Sanwa Bank data for 1990, the average cost of a wedding in Tokyo–Osaka was over ¥2,500,000 (£10,000). The survey pertains to all wedding facilities, including hotels. The Sanwa survey lists the average total expenditure related to marriage, including honeymoon and preparation for marital life (furniture, etc.) as amounting to ¥7,562,000 (£30,000).[32] Here it is important to remember that Cobella and other *gojokai* also profit from these wedding-related services and goods.

Conclusion: the transition from home to public-space weddings, and from the emphasis on weddings to funerals

In very general terms, we can say that the transition from home weddings to more elaborate and formal weddings in a variety of public spaces began a few years after the end of World War II. The agents of change in this transition were *gojokai* organizations and related businesses. The new-style wedding extravaganza reached its peak in the mid-seventies and early eighties, when the Japanese economic miracle brought increased affluence to society in general.

In the above, one can trace the process by which what had been family and community affairs were gradually turned into consumer products. One of the most important steps in this development was removing weddings from the private sphere to public locations. In this connection, one may point to Hobsbawm's link between 'invention of tradition' and the construction of 'formal ritual spaces'(1983a:304). Hobsbawm and others in Hobsbawm and Ranger (1983) locate the importance of 'formal ritual spaces' in the national or rather the political domain. I would like suggest that the use of such public spaces has been profitably and efficiently utilized by economic institutions as well.

Moreover, although Hobsbawm argues that this kind of shift from private to public spaces is typical of a specific historic period – in other words, the transition from traditional to modern society – a quite similar shift from home to public spaces took place as late as the early 1990s in the case of funerals.

Indeed, the ceremonial occasions entrepreneurs' recent view of funerals as 'the future of their enterprise' is another example of the validity of the question raised in the Introduction concerning the possibility of applying a Western way of looking at history to Japan. This perspective as applied by Hobsbawm in his demarcation of the time of a mass production of traditions (1983a), distinguishes one big important break between traditional and modern society.

For the *gojokai* organizations which are fighting what seems to be a losing battle among the young, old people would seem to constitute the perfect market. They tend to have more money to spend and, as I have been informed, 'do not care so much about the name [of the company], as young people. All they care about is quick and reliable service'.

Naturally, Cobella's role – and that of other *gojokai* – in the case of funerals is quite different from that played in weddings. Like large *gojokai* organizations, Cobella maintains a service line twenty-four hours a day. It also has connections and people posted at all large hospitals so they are always available to offer their funeral services immediately. In addition, it owns a fleet of cars to transport corpses from the hospital to the home, as well as specially decorated cars to transport the corpse from the place of the 'last farewell' ceremony (*kokubetsu-shiki*) to the crematorium. While the *gojokai* promote their weddings as 'good value for money', they stress professional efficiency and around-the-clock availability in the case of funerals. This relieves the family of the deceased, who are in a state of shock and despair and therefore incapable of making decisions, from all required arrangements, from the time of death through the funeral ceremony and cremation.

Here, the *gojokai*'s experience as ceremonial occasions experts comes to the fore. In addition to attending to every detail, Cobella gives the family of the deceased clear instructions on how to behave during each part of the mourning services. These directions are given orally, on the spot, as well as in literature prepared for the purpose, and recently in videos marketed by ceremonial occasions entrepreneurs.

In general, the funeral business has followed the same process of development as the wedding business. Whereas most funeral services were carried out at the homes of the deceased until the 1980s, since the early 1990s *gojokai* organizations have been constructing luxury funeral parlours. These offer space and services for the central funeral ceremony (*kokubetsu-shiki*) held on the day of the cremation, as well as for the long wake night (*tsuya*) the night before. Thus, the ceremonial occasions industry has once again benefited from – if not initiated – the move from private to public spaces. Moreover, they use the same kind of argument, i.e., the smaller size of urban houses, used to justify the move to public spaces in the case of weddings. Once this move was made, funeral customers began placing importance on the prestige conveyed through the ceremony as well as on its quality and efficiency. If this is related to the groom's job interests in the case of weddings, it can be related to business interests of the deceased's sons in the case of funerals. This is illustrated by the extremely expensive funerals given to the heads of family businesses.

As with commercial wedding parlours, the construction of funeral parlours led to a 'totalization' of services. Funeral parlours, like wedding parlours, are 'comprehensive'. These new comprehensive parlours have special halls for the services, sell household Buddhist altars (*butsudan*), rent out mourning outfits, and even have displays of gifts given to guests in return for condolence gifts (*kōden-gaeshi*) received. In other words, they have exploited the Japanese tendency to follow the proper 'form', even if it is a form which they have invented.

Among these invented traditions are the extremely elaborate funeral alters (*saidan*) used in the parlours' funeral ceremonies as well as the highly ornate costumes worn by the Buddhist priests who conduct them. Even with mourning outfits, which are basically black and would seem to leave little room for invention compared with wedding attire, ceremonial occasions producers – creative as ever – have begun to promote the tuxedo (with a black tie, rather than the white one used in weddings) for the main mourners. This is also an example of how a modern-Western (or, *Westanese*) elements have been introduced into traditional-Japanese (or, *traditionese*) ceremonies. This trend, which is also manifested in the use of English words such as 'Final Ceremony' to 'decorate' the title of a catalogue for luxury funerals – is all part of the invention and production of tradition.

3

THE KOBE PRINCESS PALACE: WEDDING PRODUCERS AND THEIR CUSTOMERS

'The Japanese cannot decide for themselves. They always need somebody to decide for them', said a young employee of the Kobe Princess Palace in speaking of the parlour's strictly organized wedding plan. Although her remark was made in reference to the Japanese in general, and was obviously addressed to the 'foreign' (or rather Western) researcher, it is revealing of at least part of the wedding industry's attitude towards its customers. That is, the wedding customer is not only seen as passive and indecisive but is also considered ignorant when it comes to weddings and other ceremonial occasions. Thus, owners and employees of comprehensive wedding parlours and more generally, of ceremonial occasions organizations, view themselves as the saviours of an otherwise helpless population.

The maintenance of their image as experts has always been integral to the success of *gojokai* organizations. While this is easier with regard to funerals, where their expertise does, indeed, smooth the way for bereaved families, the image has become more difficult to maintain for weddings, when today even shrines offer comprehensive wedding services, including honeymoon packages and furniture for the couple's new home.

In an effort to illustrate some of the ways in which the wedding parlour and the industry in general strive to maintain, or more correctly to reproduce, their status as ceremonial experts, let us examine the relationship between the comprehensive wedding parlour and its customers. A 'peep' into this aspect of the business, based on my participant observation of the industry, reveals some of the real stories behind the scenes which illustrate how the customer is seen in the parlour. As we shall see, the stories disclose a production so comprehensive that it continues after the actual event has taken place, in an effort to also control the way in which it will be remembered.

However, even in this look at the customer–producer relationship and the reciprocity which this implies, the producers remain at the centre of my observations. Thus, before delving into this relationship, it is necessary to describe the machinery which sets the wheels of the wedding production into motion.

The producers: organization and structure

All wedding parlours in Japan are comprehensive in that all of them provide every service necessary or in any way related to weddings. These services are not only all concentrated under one roof, but in some cases all owned and directly controlled by the company or group which owns the facility. Some, however – including most of those managed by Cobella and many of those owned by the Sōchikuden Group – operate differently: after signing a contract with a customer, Cobella assigns most of the services which make up the full wedding production to small firms which specialize in them.

According to the manager of the Kobe Princess Palace the reasons for using subcontractors as well as a large majority of part-time workers are based on the same logic that created the fixed wedding ceremony: *efficiency*. Since there are many days during the year on which no weddings are performed due to seasonal and other calendrical considerations, the most cost-effective method of offering wedding-related services is to sub-contract them as the need arises. Thus, in addition to meeting this reality by employing part-time staff and by endeavouring to 'stretch' the wedding season, to include June and summer weddings, Cobella attempts to minimize the losses due to 'empty' days through its subcontracting system. The combination of temporary staff and small firms as subcontractors is typical of other Japanese companies who wish to 'retain some degree of flexibility' which will increase their economic success (Clark 1987:47).[1]

One of the few full-time Cobella employees at the Kobe Princess Palace is the manager, who is not only in charge of the small staff employed directly by Cobella, but also coordinates and mediates between the Company and its subcontractors. Although the main reason for subcontracting services is efficiency, this policy results in day-to-day problems which it is the manager's job to try and solve before turning to the head office.

Unlike most parlour managers, the present manager of the Kobe Princess Palace is a university graduate. A man in his late thirties, he accepted this position despite its relatively low pay. Like other parlour managers in Cobella, he began his career with the company, first as a front-desk employee in charge of wedding reservations, and later in the funeral department. He has been the manager of the Princess Palace since it was built in 1981. As a full-time employee he must comply with all decisions made by the Cobella management, but is also encouraged, as are the owners of franchised parlours, to develop his own ideas, especially promotion schemes or new mini-dramas to be added to the wedding reception. The managers of the various parlours have regular meetings in which they discuss these new ideas.

Directly under the manager are the few part-time and fewer full-time employees who work as front desk clerks. Their remarkably varied jobs include wedding reservations, honeymoon bookings and the ordering of furniture.[2] The scope of their tasks differs according to an employee's experience and sex. Male front-desk staff sometimes act as models (*moderu-san*) in bridal fairs and help direct the wedding reception. Only male employees are required to act as models, the female models are outside volunteers who are happy to have the chance to put on wedding outfits. Also, while only men guide the wedding party to the ballroom, the 'anonymous' announcements are always made by females. Both male and female employees wear uniforms, all the men (including the manager) dressing in black suits with a bow tie and the women in two-piece pink suits. Most of part-time employees are young, the women usually not older than 25, and men not more than 30. The two full-time front-desk employees are older men. Although they are considered superior to their part-time counterparts, they participate in most required tasks.

Also hired directly by Cobella on a part-time basis are a few women who serve as waitresses at the reception (although front-desk men help serve if necessary), two or three women who act as attendants and ceremonial guides, as well as the young female students to play the role of shrine-maidens at the Shinto ceremonies.[3] The many other people involved in the wedding production are employed by Cobella's subcontractors.

Subcontractors

Whereas subcontracting in other Japanese companies is handled outside the confines of the 'plant' where items are 'produced', most wedding parlour subcontractors perform their work within its confines. This centralization is necessary for the fluid production of weddings. These subcontractors can be roughly divided into suppliers of goods and suppliers of services. While most suppliers of goods are not personally represented in the parlour, suppliers of services employ their own staff, usually on a part-time basis. Moreover, while suppliers of goods are not confined to offering their products to a single wedding parlour, service suppliers must restrict themselves to one parlour.

The most loosely connected to the parlour are the suppliers of the items given as gifts to wedding guests (*hikidemono*). These shops are given display space at the parlour, where their goods are on consignment. They do not get paid until orders are received for their goods, and until after the wedding parlour has deducted its cut.[4] The same arrangement applies to other suppliers of goods such as the jewellery company. The only ones with a different arrangement are those who supply the Japanese bridal accessories promoted through the beauty shop, in which case the latter – which holds a special position in the parlour and more generally in the 'production of traditions' – also receives a percentage.

The service most tightly connected to the Princess Palace is the catering company, which prepares all the food in a kitchen in the parlour to ensure the smooth flow of the reception. However, in line with cost-efficiency, Cobella does not hire or train cooks, who would be inactive and unproductive on the considerable number of days when there are no weddings scheduled. As the parlour manager explained, it is much more efficient to contract out this service to a company which must, however, agree to work exclusively for the Princess Palace.

The same holds true for the photo studio and the beauty shop, both of which hire and train their own staff, as well as for the coffee shop, where it is considered more profitable to let other companies suffer from the irregular spread of weddings over the week and the year. These three companies, unlike the caterers, are allowed to offer their services to other customers. The fact is, however, that all the parlour's subcontractors receive a majority of their business through this connection. This dependency has a clear effect on their relationship with the parlour, which is emphasized by the Cobella management. For example, the beauty shop owners frequently complain that, 'anytime we ask for better terms, the [parlour] manager has a ready answer: "You should not complain", he says, "since you get customers without moving"'. This same attitude can be seen in the parlour's financial arrangements with its subcontractors, which it reserves the right to change at any time.

The subcontractors are aware of their dependent position and feel that the wedding parlour takes advantage of them. The feeling which is expressed frequently by the owners of these small companies is that, 'No matter what happens, the Company always profits (*mōketeiru*)'. None the less, the subcontractors mostly voice their frustration and complaints to one another and rarely to the parlour management, for they do get their business without having to expend much effort. Thus, the subcontractors who choose to work for the Princess Palace are aware that they are trading off lower profits than those they could charge if they work independently, in exchange for a more or less steady source of customers.

The above is only a glimpse into the complex interdependence between the parlour as the Big Company and its small subcontractors.[5] What is of greater concern to us is how these relations influence the relationship between the customer and the Princess Palace, which the customer views as the supplier of all its wedding services. If the customers of weddings are unaware of these behind the scenes machinations, this is due to the link between the parlour and the customer: the 'sales lady'.

The 'army' of 'sales ladies'

The few hundred '*eigyō-san*' or 'sales ladies'[6] who work with the Kobe Princess Palace are mainly middle-aged. Like the majority of people involved in the wedding production, they are employed neither by the Princess Palace nor by Cobella. Most of them are engaged through local sales agencies (*dairi-ten*), which are another group of Cobella's subcontractors. The main role of these agencies – which operate under the supervision of a local branch of Cobella – is to find new subscribers to Cobella. Their managers, usually men (*ten-chō*), generally work on commission for each member signed up. However, I should note that the relations between Cobella and its sales agencies are one of its best kept secrets. Here, too, Cobella, and other *gojokai* expend nothing until they make a sale.

In turn, most of the women who work for these agencies do not earn a regular salary, but also work on a commission basis. This commission varies from agency to agency. The exact commission is known to be a well-kept secret among the sales ladies, some of whom say that while they do not earn very much, other more experienced and talented women earn very good commissions.

Although sales ladies did not disclose the level of their commission, it is evident that in all agencies the commissions vary in accordance with the grade of the packages contracted for as well as with another inner ranking. This grading which is not disclosed to customers is based on personal characteristics such as the age of the parent who signs the contract and whether the son or daughter is of marriageable age. The reason behind the confidentiality of this ranking is that some of the personal conditions taken into account may embarrass the contracting member. An extreme example is that of the high grading of families which include aged people (with high funeral prospects).

Sales techniques

By bringing new members to the *gojokai*, the sales ladies are the major promoters of weddings (and funerals) produced by Cobella. One of the traditional ways they have tried to do this is by door-to door canvassing (*tobi-komi*, 'jumping in' in Japanese), which employs a very well-organized promotion technique. The agency usually drives groups of women to an area in which their agency holds the right to obtain members, where they work for a day shift from 10 am to 3.30 pm. This timing makes clear that their primary targets are housewives and mothers, who are likely to be found at home during this time. This is not surprising given the widespread assumption that it is the women in Japan who 'hold the household purse strings' (Lebra 1984a:134–135) and who ultimately decide about subscribing to a *gojokai*. The best prospect for membership is a mother who is worried about the wedding costs of her daughter since they are far higher than the son's share of the wedding package.

Some less aggressive promotion techniques include telephone marketing and direct mail. In the latter, postcards advertising Cobella are placed in people's letter boxes. When I lived in an area covered by one of Cobella's branches, I occasionally found a pre-stamped postcard from the company in my letter box. This postcard promoted not only Cobella's ceremonial occasion-related services but also part-time work for women (*okusama pāto boshū*) as saleswomen. It included a short questionnaire concerning the potential subscriber's general knowledge about the costs involved in ceremonial occasions, particularly weddings and funerals, and was so designed as to extract information on whether anyone in the family is a candidate for a ceremonial event (such as wedding, 'coming of age ceremony' (*seijin shiki*) or '7–5–3').[7] The postcard concluded with: 'you just have to write your name and address and send the already stamped postcard to hear more about our services', and by reminding the addressee that a small gift would be sent to those who filled in the questionnaire.

Although the main promotion technique remains door-to-door soliciting, the technique is becoming less efficient, especially in the case of weddings, as increasing number of couples are becoming members only after they have decided to get married. At first this trend was partially solved by having agency sales ladies promoting Cobella's service in the parlour itself. To ensure that every woman had an equal chance to secure new members, the women worked in shifts on the busy weekends, taking turns, standing at the entrance to the Princess Palace where prospective customers could be approached. Most women agreed to this solution, especially those who were finding it increasingly difficult to solicit members in their homes. Indeed, some of them told me that they had signed up most of their customers at the parlour itself in recent years.

It did not take long for the Cobella management to decide that they should reap the profits from these in-house package sales. Thus, beginning in 1991, the sales ladies were told they could no longer stand at the entrance. Instead, the parlour began to utilize its own full-time and part-time front-desk female as well as male staff to promote its services. As in other instances where the Company changed its agreements with its subcontractors unilaterally, the order was sudden and naturally brought about the objection of the sales ladies as well as their agencies. As one of them complained: 'We lost our best spot for getting customers. From now on we will have to find our customers all by ourselves.' This was another example of how Cobella – in its efforts to maintain its image as the dominant one in the relationship – showed the subcontractors 'who's the boss'. All they could do was hope there would be enough work outside the parlour. If there was less work for weddings, they would concentrate on the growing funeral market.

The sales lady and 'her customers'

Although the main task of a sales lady is to sign up new subscribers for the ceremonial-occasion-packaging industry, her role does not usually end when she makes a sale; she is considered responsible for her customers until they have exercised their rights as members. Thus, she also attends them from their preparatory visits to the parlour and throughout the wedding. A good sales lady also keeps in touch with her subscribers to make certain that she does not miss any additional business opportunities, such as the 'coming of age ceremony' at the twentieth birthday of a daughter. And when a family has used their rights, she tries to convince them to re-subscribe for another package.

Sales ladies stand out from other wedding parlour employees, for, unlike most other employees they do not wear a uniform and have relative freedom of movement inside the wedding parlour. In addition, they are usually older than other female Cobella employees since most of them are middle aged.[8] Seeing themselves as being in charge of 'their customers' – as they refer to brides and grooms whom they do their best to serve faithfully – they feel free to enter any department in the parlour. Although the other departments often regard this behaviour as importunate (*urusai*), it seems that a certain amount of persistence is almost a requirement if the sales lady is to fulfil her role. A brief portrait of one of the veteran sales ladies, perhaps the most visible one in the Princess Palace, will illustrate this point.

A portrait of Mrs Suzuki

Mrs Suzuki has worked as a sales lady for Cobella for fifteen years. She works through one of its agencies and has 'married' over eight hundred couples. She is over sixty and everyone thinks she is a widow.[9] It is difficult to imagine a busy working day at the Princess Palace without Mrs Suzuki, guiding her customers in her loud voice. She is always there on time to take photographs of the bride as she is being prepared for the ceremony in the beauty shop. Later on she will take care of other snap shots of the wedding guests before the ceremony starts. She then accompanies the bride, groom and their families throughout the rest of the day, taking care of any request or question that might arise. She does not leave the parlour until she has seen 'her bride' back to the beauty shop, where the latter gets ready to leave the parlour.

Mrs Suzuki surely knows how to make new customers, which sometimes requires a certain boldness. I have witnessed instances when she literally snatched a customer away from an employee of the wedding parlour to get the commission on the bride's package. At one of the bridal fairs, a uniformed front desk clerk was guiding a bride-to-be and her mother through the wedding dress display when Suzuki approached him saying something like 'please pass [them] to me (*watashi-ni kudasai*)'. Before the poor fellow could protest, she had guided the customers through the dress display in her self-assured way. While it is clear that in this case experience won out, it is important to note that while Mrs Suzuki had to 'fight' in order to get her salary, the front desk employee had less incentive to do so since his (relatively low) pay would not change in any event. But what about the client being shunted from one person to another? This incident demonstrates the passivity or 'objectified' position of the customers as they are passed from one 'producer' to another.

Her persistence and aggressive attitude within the parlour not withstanding, Mrs Suzuki manages to maintain good relations with all its departments. Thus, while other sales ladies are not usually welcomed in the beauty shop – especially when they interfere with the beauticians' professional work – she is allowed to enter the beauty shop almost at will. Mrs Suzuki's handling of both her clients and her counterparts in the parlour, with persistence but also with just the right amount of politeness, makes her a successful 'sales lady'.

Producers and customers: interaction

The first contact between the Princess Palace and its customers is usually through the sales lady either in one of her door-to-door solicitations, or at the parlour itself. Although referred to as 'the customer', the potential member is not always the mother of a prospective bride or groom, for the child may or may not decide to get married at the parlour. Thus, although wedding producers tend to regard the family as the 'customer', it is the couple whom the sales lady must convince to have their ceremony at the Princess Palace. In recent years, therefore, more attention is given to the young couple, mainly the bride.

Once the couple does decide to marry at the parlour, the preparations for their wedding production entail several visits to the Princess Palace, usually more on the part of the bride since her appearance in the wedding has to be more carefully prepared. The process also involves decisions regarding the attire to be worn, the number of guests to be invited, and how they should be seated, as well as the gifts they are to receive. Then there is the location of the honeymoon and perhaps even furniture for the new home to be considered. Although the first visit to the parlour may be of the couple alone, later visits in which the outfits are chosen usually include other family members, especially the bride's mother, who is usually active throughout the preparations, particularly in the choice of Japanese costumes. Other family members such as the groom's mother and both fathers may join in the visits to the parlour, mainly on weekends when bridal fairs are being held.

Despite the new emphasis on the bridal couple, their families, especially the mothers, have not abandoned their traditional role in preparing their children's weddings.[10] However, this role has diminished considerably from the time when weddings were held in the home with the assistance of the close community. Indeed, today's comprehensive wedding parlour not only offers 'total planning' for the wedding itself, the honeymoon and the newlyweds' furniture, but even includes the formal outfit required for the *miyamairi* ceremony, in which the baby, who is yet to be born, is presented to the local deity.

Some of the preparatory stages for the wedding, such as the betrothal ceremony (*yuinō shiki*), are still generally performed in private, after consulting the appropriate books on etiquette. However, in their continual efforts to broaden their control of the production (and its profits) some wedding parlours offer special private rooms in which this ceremony, too, may be performed. The only reason these are not available in the Princess Palace is the lack of space.

The 'ignorant' customer vis-á-vis *the 'experts'*

The young parlour employee's view of the customer as passive and indecisive is typical of everyone involved in the production of weddings. Another pervasive notion is that '[Japanese] people nowadays do not know much about ceremony'. This is part of the philosophy which underlines the 'total wedding'. For, if today's Japanese are generally considered ignorant when it comes to manners and ceremonies, the 'unrefined true middle-class' who constitute the wedding parlour's clientele are considered extremely unfamiliar with the necessary details and in need of guidance and advice from the time they are signed up as members through the ceremony and reception, and even after the production itself has taken place. Especially when dealing with non-elite clients, the parlour is wary of working with what its employees regard as 'troublesome' customers. However, the well-lubricated machinery of parlours like the Kobe Princess Palace is set up to deal with both 'ignorant' and 'troublesome' customers.

The process through which weddings left the home and became public events accompanied a general process of migration of rural youth to cities and their concomitant separation from the seniors who served as the repository of traditional knowledge and ritual procedure in the villages (Edwards 1989:77–78). Those involved in the ceremonial occasions industry have not only exploited this unfamiliarity for their own interests, but have also played a role in propagating this alienation and ignorance. This, together with the elaborate preparations and instructions on the part of the wedding experts, has itself resulted in an even greater dependency of the customer on the producer or expert.

That the ceremonial occasions *gojokai* emphasize their role as experts can be clearly seen in the everyday interaction between producers and consumers of wedding services. But it is evident in other ways as well. One interesting example is that of a comic book (*manga*) which sales ladies distributed to prospective members.[11] This comic book, published by the national organization of all *gojokai* is called *Make the Best of Living* (*Kurashi ni Ikasō*). It introduces the *gojokai* system through the experience of an ordinary Japanese family which is ignorant about the help *gojokai* can offer them until one day a salesman comes to the house and tries to convince the housewife to join the association. One of the main characters in the book is the 'doctor' (*hakushi*), in a suit and scholar's hat, who acts as the expert and answers all the housewife's questions about the *gojokai*. The fact that both the salesman and the expert are men can be explained as an attempt to emphasize their authority. Of course the happy end is that the wife, thinking of her daughter's wedding, decides to become a *gojokai* member. The alleged purpose of this comic book is to supply important information concerning such *gojokai* offerings as weddings, funerals and costume rental. However, the paternalistic way in which the doctor explains everything to the woman emphasizes her ignorance in ceremonial occasions at the same time as it expands on the *gojokai* role as experts in this field.

Another example of how the industry promotes its image as 'the experts' may be seen in the small brochure which all Shōchikuden customers received for a period of time. This leaflet which had the shape and the colour of a Japanese passport, carried the title 'A Life Care Passport Presented to a "Mrs" – Shōchikuden'. However, in the place of customs stamps, the 'passport' gave details on the manners required for prospective brides own weddings, for weddings of friends, as well as funerals and other Japanese and even some Western occasions. In addition to emphasizing the wedding producers' position as ceremonial experts, the 'passport' also gives us an insight into what a woman must do to exemplify 'real Japaneseness'. As such, it once again points to the importance of form to the Japanese, especially to the Japanese woman. In this context, the question also arises as to whether ignorance in Japanese manners implies a flaw in one's cultural or national identity. It is clear that wedding producers strive to convey this impression in order to enhance themselves as the preservers of 'real Japaneseness'.

Just as I do not suggest a 'conspiracy' theory regarding wedding producers as inventors of tradition, I do not see the 'experts' as deliberately producing or reproducing 'ignorant' customers, although it is clear that ignorance does facilitate invention. However, it is also clear that the customers/clients do seek close guidance from those who have become known as experts.

The search for advice begins before the wedding, with preliminaries such as the betrothal ceremony (*yuinō*). Although the parlour may suggest that it help in this regard, the *yuinō* is still generally conducted outside the parlour. Indeed, many of my informants prefer to rely on what the immensely popular modern etiquette manuals have to say about its conduct. None the less, the importance accorded to what these experts say illustrates the Japanese reliance on 'experts' in general. Shiotsuki Yaeko's best seller, *Introduction to Ceremonial Occasions* (*Kankon sōsai Nyūmon*), originally published in 1970, is said to have sold over seven million copies by 1991. The Japanese tendency to consult formal sources and etiquette manuals is not, of course, limited to weddings. As we have seen, the customers for funerals feel even more insecure, which has led to an industry of guides and videos produced to help them.[12]

This inclination to seek guidance and direction manifests itself constantly in the Kobe Princess Palace. Among the multitude of examples is a tour of the wedding parlour organized by one of the sales ladies during a bridal fair to introduce prospective customers to the services available. Upon arriving at the Shinto shrine, the groom's mother was very impressed by the traditional-Japanese ambience but uncertain as to precisely what kind of ceremony was conducted therein. Her question – 'Is this the place where the priest waves that white paper stick?' (referring to the purification ceremony) – reveals not only the distant relationship most Japanese have with religion, but, more relevant to our interest here, a stated ignorance about formalities. This woman was not in the least embarrassed to ask this question because she accepted the sales lady as a representative of the ceremonial occasions expert. Her next words even before she heard the sales lady's reply indicate the importance accorded to form in the Japanese ceremonies: the woman said that they wanted this kind of ceremony because it seemed the most beautiful and most popular.

'First there is the bow . . .' repeated a groom, memorizing his part in the opening of the reception at his hotel wedding when the female attendant (*kaizoe*) was instructing the couple on the proper behaviour for the coming moments. While the Princess Palace usually has two attendants on duty, who must go back and forth between couples at various stages of the festivities, hotels assign each couple an attendant who remains with them throughout the day. In this particular case, the couple was very nervous because the promised rehearsal had not taken place. Even the attendant's reassurance that she would be by their side to instruct them before every part of the day was not enough to calm the groom. He was still worried that he would fail to play his part well.

A certain amount of passivity is typical of all wedding participants including parents and guests. Many of them, especially women, get dressed in the parlour, placing themselves in the hands of the kimono experts who are also considered specialists in formalities. These customers will often ask kimono dressers questions regarding the proper etiquette for Japanese as well as Western attire, and slavishly follow the instructions received.

All wedding facilities, well aware of this tendency, take full advantage of it to enhance their image as experts and thereby to increase business. Full guidance is considered a necessary service and thus more prestigious wedding venues offer an image of closer guidance. The wedding parlour, on the other hand, efficient as ever, moves the wedding principals through directing hands along the 'assembly line' of the production process.

One of the wedding parlours' routines to help alleviate their customers' anxiety is the Bridal Schedule given to every couple when they sign up for a wedding. This carefully planned six-month programme begins with the application and ends with the honeymoon. It is a month-by-month schedule informing the bride and groom when they are supposed to perform the betrothal ceremony, order furniture, sign up for their honeymoon, and so on. This programme is also included in the parlours' wedding catalogues which generally open with the image of a couple in love and close with an exotic photograph of them in the Hawaiian islands on their honeymoon – clear manifestation of the total wedding supplied by the parlour in question.

The 'troublesome' customer

While wedding producers usually benefit from their customers' ignorance regarding ceremonial occasions, some customers are not that easy to satisfy. All those involved in the wedding production, from those at the front desk to the beauticians and kimono dressers, are constantly on the look-out for 'troublesome' (*yayakoshi*) customers who may pose a threat on the smooth flow of the production. One of the main ways of dealing with these customers is to identify them as soon as possible and try to make certain that they remain content. In other words, a troublesome customer gets better treatment.

It usually takes only one remark by one of those involved in the wedding production for the rest of the workers to get the point that a customer is potentially 'troublesome'. Moreover, in the Princess Palace there is a code-word to signify 'troublesome' on the application form itself, so that everyone involved in the production process will give that customer special attention. The confidential code word is the Chinese character for congratulations and long life (*kotobuki*), which is used frequently in the wedding industry and is unlikely to be recognized for what it implies. It remains a question whether perhaps this ironic code word is part of the meagre stock of humour in the production of weddings.

Despite the efforts to identify troublesome customers, this sometimes fails to be done until the day of the wedding. In these cases unusual behaviour or mode of speech or dress may attract attention. Such was a case with a bride who – very untypically of brides – smoked in the brides' room while waiting for her dresser. This was enough to make the beauty shop manager check the bride's registration forms for further clues. In this instance, as in many others, the clue was that the bride lived in a neighbourhood characterized as *urusai*, which has connotations of noisy, fastidious and hard to please. The manager's next step was to pour the bride a cup of Japanese tea and send me into the room to deliver it, instructing me to be extremely polite while serving it to her. The manager went so far as to tell me the exact Japanese phrase to be used: 'It is hot, but please have some tea.' This is just one example in which the troublesome customer received better care even though (and maybe because) she broke the rule against smoking in the brides' room. However, instead of requesting that this bride put out her cigarette, she was served tea, a gesture which I had never witnessed before. Her improper behaviour was therefore rewarded because she had been identified as *urusai*.

This was far from the only case in which beauty shop employees were instructed by the manager to treat a customer with special care, or even in which the beauty shop manager found it necessary to offer a special service herself. In one such instance she decided to do an outside (dressing) job in a hotel herself even though it involved long hours of travelling. She did this because she knew the customers involved were 'difficult' and knew it would be better if she was there in person.

One of the explanations for this way of dealing with difficult cases is the uneasiness felt by the Japanese when confronted with unconventional situations and people. More specifically, there was usually a real concern that troublesome customers might refuse to pay for the services if they were not satisfied with every aspect of them.

There is a special category of customers considered to require special attention: the *yakuza* or people who belong to the Japanese mafia. In every case of even a suspected *yakuza* wedding during my fieldwork at the Kobe Princess Palace, it was obvious that the customers involved were accorded special treatment.[13] While this is not the place to describe a *yakuza* wedding in detail, one in which I took part as an employee will serve to show how these weddings differ from 'ordinary' weddings with regards to the deference with which their participants are treated. Unusual care was taken in all the departments and through every stage of the wedding production. This included the dressing of the groom by the beauty-shop manager herself and the dressing of the bride at her home by the head bride dresser. Home dressing has become very rare, let alone by the head bride dresser herself. In this case it may suggest the importance, or rather power, of the bride's family.

With regard to the special role accorded the groom, this was the only groom in my two-and-half years of fieldwork who had more costume changes than his bride. This, and the unusually elaborate traditional-Japanese costume he wore may be related to aspects of masculinity and 'Japaneseness' attributed to the *yakuza*. According to Raz (1992:220), the kimono worn by *yakuza* on special occasions serves to denote the 'Japaneseness' of its wearer. On the other hand, the kimono's rarity (for men) also signifies the opposite – exclusivity – a duality typical of the way in which the *yakuza* present themselves to fellow *yakuza* and to the common Japanese: a variety of sign-sets which are both inclusive and exclusive (Raz 1992:213).[14]

The *yakuza* couple were accompanied through the various stages of the wedding day by the head of the largest sales agency – a man – instead of the usual female sales lady – which may also be related to aspects of masculinity associated with the *yakuza*. The most extreme act of favouritism was the extension of the time allotted to the wedding reception – over five hours or more than double the usual time. The producers' attitude towards these 'special' customers – which I view as reflecting an ambiguous combination of fear and latent adoration[15] – also reveals the attitude towards 'ordinary' customers, who do not 'deserve' the same consideration.

'Claims' as the customers' sole weapon

Although the wedding parlour client/customer is basically passive, directed and manipulated by the wedding producers, even 'ordinary' customers have some power. This begins, of course, in the efforts shown to make them choose the services of a particular parlour over others. However, this is also true after money has been paid and even after the event is over. Customer 'claims' (the English word is used) against the parlour are one of the parlour's great concerns, even though the parlour usually passes any complaints to the relevant subcontractor. This is because although wedding productions are divided so that each subcontracting company is responsible for a specific part of the production, it is at the many meeting points among different subcontractors where the question of liability generally arises.

The Kobe Princess Palace has devised a few organizational mechanisms in an effort to eliminate these problematic points, for example, the strict time-table for each part of the production. There is a pre-printed form, with copies for each subcontractor and wedding parlour department, for every day on which weddings are held. Each producer fills in the necessary details about each wedding to be held on that day. Thus, the beauty shop fills in details on the outfits and hair styles; the photo studio adds the number and types of photographs to be taken for each customer and so forth. This form is used as a 'time-watcher', in that every 'act' of the production must not exceed the time filled in on the form. In the event that a customer submits a claim against the parlour, or even if the parlour suspects that one may be submitted, the management goes back to this form to find the 'guilty' party. As one beauty shop employee explained: 'In some cases we finish the bride's costume change (*ironaoshi*) on time, but the photograph takes longer than usual, so then we have this [record] to show that *we* were OK.' This worker was referring to the possibility that the bride's late return to the reception room after a change of costume might result in a claim against the parlour and the consequent demand for reimbursement on the part of the customer.

In the cases observed during my fieldwork, it was clear that such customer claims are considered a real threat by everyone connected with the wedding production. None the less, it was also clear that even this alleged power of the customer is in fact limited because the producers have the power to manipulate the event at any given time, even after it has taken place.

The case of the fallen tiara, or the importance of video recording

The incident

Towards the end of a reception, after the bride and groom left their seats and had taken a few steps towards the door, the bride, already in Western dress, lost her head decoration. Luckily, her groom succeeded in catching it, and they proceeded to the door where they were to stand with the *nakōdo* couple and both parents for the final bowing ceremony (*hiraki*). One of the reception workers (a Cobella employee) noticed the incident and used the time before the guests left the room to quickly re-fix the tiara on the bride's forehead. But because of the haste with which this was done and because the person who did it was not a professional in this area, the tiara fell off again during one of the bride's bows. As a result, the bride was forced to complete the ceremony without her Western crown.

The manipulation

Despite the fact that no claim was made by the customer in this instance, the parlour decided that it should cover itself in the event that one might be submitted. Since the producers felt that no claim could be made before the customers had seen the reception video, they agreed to 'fix' the video in order to prevent any possible problems. However, there were disagreements regarding the 'correction' to be made.

The negotiations over the editing of the video are interesting since they represent the manipulation of an event that has taken place supposedly to protect the parlour from the power of the customer, but in fact – as in any form of manipulation – to ensure that the manipulator is the 'winner'. The disagreements between the subcontractors also illustrate conflicts of interest between the different 'players' in the production, in this case between the beauty shop represented by its manager, Keiko, and a young freelance cameraman employed by Cobella.

As the person responsible for the mishap, Keiko was invited by the cameraman to watch the video. It was clear to both that something had to be done before presenting the video to the family. The disagreements arose over what and how much to cut. Here, there were clearly two opposing interests. While Keiko wanted to remove all parts that might be used against her shop, including the mishap itself – suggesting that the video end just before the tiara fell off for the first time – the cameraman had a different view. Representing both the wedding parlour and the general artistic value of continuity, he wanted the video to remain as close as possible to the general length and content. In his opinion, the video given to the family had to include the final ceremony for its deletion would also be the cause of a possible claim against the video and himself.

Finally, a compromise was reached. It was agreed that the video would be cut twice: once just before the tiara fell off for the first time and again when it fell off for the second time. This meant omitting scenes of the reception worker attaching the tiara to the bride's forehead (a scene which would have been cut in any case, since preparatory activities are not usually shown in the video). The video would conclude with the final scene at the door. Keiko did not agree to this, however, until after she had been convinced that the missing tiara would be barely noticeable since this was not a close-up.

The case of the forgotten arm

The incident

A few days after their daughter's wedding, the family of a bride married at the Princess Palace gathered to look at the precious wedding photographs when suddenly one of the family members discovered something disastrous: while one of the bride's arms was appropriately painted in white – the correct colour for traditional-Japanese costume – by the beauty-shop employees, the other one was as brown as it would normally be in the warm Japanese summer when the wedding took place. Not only were the family aghast to see a tanned 'Japanese' bride, but a bride with arms of different colour was obviously unacceptable. The family demanded that the wedding parlour reimburse them for at least the sum they had paid for the studio photographs where the catastrophe was the most obviously observed. While the customers were apt to win financially in this case, their main loss could not be recovered since the dozens of photographs taken by guests could not possibly be restored. It is interesting to observe the way in which this claim was processed by the parlour.

Processing the claim

As usual in cases like this, the wedding parlour passed the claim on to the responsible party. This time it was obviously the beauty shop. The manager of the parlour summoned Keiko, the beauty shop manager, and relayed the incident, handing her photographs taken by wedding guests as proof. Keiko could not evade her shop's responsibility and reproved the dressers involved. She also decided to leave the 'convicting' pictures in the shop so every employee would see them and be more careful in the future.

However, reproaching her employees neither resolved the problem, nor answered the parlour's demand that the beauty shop pay for the studio photographs. Although at the internal level of the beauty shop the manager accepted full responsibility, she could not possibly do so at the general parlour level. There were two dimensions of the problem: the financial issue and the prestige of her shop and its position in the parlour. Thus, after consultation with her mother-in-law, who is the owner of the shop, the beauty shop's position was that it was willing to share the cost with the photo studio. After all, said Keiko, the studio workers were negligent in failing to notice the problem during their long preparations for the bride's photographs.

In the end, after fierce negotiations via the parlour manager rather than directly between the two subcontractors, the photo studio consented to share the cost if the beauty shop paid a larger part. This is how the matter was resolved.

The case of the insulted model, or the power of the prospective customer

The incident

This case illustrates the relative power of a customer who has not yet paid for a wedding at the parlour. It occurred at the fashion show in one of the bridal fairs, at which the models are always non-professionals. This time, one of the models was a girl who had already signed up to have her wedding at the parlour in a few months. She viewed the opportunity to wear wedding costume before her real wedding as an excellent rehearsal for the real event. However, in the confusion and rush of the beauty shop preparing ten models for the show, she was neglected and did not receive appropriate attention. This future bride, mortified by what she felt was mis-treatment, ran home crying before the show began.

The threat

If the incident had ended there it would not have been so terrible. However, the real problem occurred when a few days later the girl's father stormed into the parlour, reproached the parlour manager severely and threatened to cancel her wedding ceremony. Only after the manager assured him that he would take steps to punish the guilty personnel did the man calm down. Next the manager summoned Keiko of the beauty shop, reprimanded her personally and ordered her to fire the employees involved in the incident. Although Keiko did not fire those at fault since the parlour does not generally interfere with subcontractors' personnel and since she herself was personally responsible, she and her mother-and-law, the shop owner, did take the incident very seriously and not only severely reproached the other persons involved in the incident, but also decided on a new working procedure for future bridal fairs. The parlour manager's and Keiko's extreme reactions in this case illustrates the power of those who have signed up for weddings but have not paid yet. An interesting note in this case is that the customer who succeeds in exercising power over the producers as this father did is defined as 'troublesome'. In this case the beauty shop later found out that the family was said to have already cancelled a wedding somewhere else to the parlour manager's great concern.

The above three incidents vividly demonstrate the variety and complexity of the relationships between the producers of weddings and their customers. Although I related the incidents from the point of view of the producers, they also indicate that there is some degree of reciprocity in the producer-customer relationship. For these cases also represent stories of power relations which are negotiable. However, while they show that the customer appears to have some power, they also indicate that it is usually the producers who end up winning – or at least not loosing very much – whenever there is a clash of interest between the two sides.

This is best illustrated in the first case, where the producers manipulated their 'product' to the extreme point of changing 'reality'. They believed – and perhaps rightly so – that they can control or even create the customer's reaction by changing the representation of the event. The first two cases indicate that both customer and producer consider the representation of an event as being at least as important as the event itself. Indeed, in the case of the fallen tiara, the borderline between the event and its representation seems to have been completely abolished. By controlling reality in this manner the producers reproduce the 'objectified' position of their customers without the consent of the latter. This objectification begins with the offer to provide a total wedding and continues through the wedding day, when the customers allow themselves to be passed on from one production point to another.

Although the cases of the forgotten arm and the insulted model might be seen as evidence that some wronged customers are given satisfaction, the question one must ask is how strong a customer has to be in order to prevail. The answer seems to be that it is generally only the 'troublesome' customer who pose any real financial threat to the parlour. This became clear in the case of the young model, when the producers discovered that they were dealing with a troublesome family which had already 'dared' to cancel a wedding elsewhere. In the case of the fallen tiara, one of Keiko's strongest arguments in her controversy over how much of the video should be cut was that the customer was 'troublesome' (*yayakoshii*). It would appear that if this had not been the case, the wedding parlour might have considered it enough to make a few minor changes in the video instead of 'major surgery', before presenting it to the family.

Conclusion

In an effort to connect areas not usually considered together, I began this chapter by describing the organization and structure of the wedding parlour in general and the Kobe Princess Palace in particular and then expanded on the link between this internal structure and its operating mechanisms and the producer–customer relationship.

The internal organization of the Princess Palace along what can be termed an 'employment system' of individual employees, both temporary and part-time, as well as subcontractors, has been constructed to produce maximum efficiency, flexibility and profits. Cobella's reliance on small companies which specialize in a particular aspect of the ceremonial occasions business is certainly not uncommon to large Japanese companies, such as those in the automobile industry. The literature tends to correlate between company size and measures of its quality,[16] while the small companies are frequently expected to be dependent on the large company. However, a look at the wedding industry indicates that there may be much more variation in those relations than has been assumed. In fact, there is a continuum which runs from mutual trust through to exploitation. Moreover, the stories told in this chapter may be seen to indicate only the 'tip' of a relationship which is replete with conflict and mechanisms of conflict resolution.

Elsewhere (Goldstein-Gidoni 1993) I have argued that this challenges notions concerning the 'harmonious' Japanese company and society. Here, however, where I am more interested in relationships between 'companies' and their customers, I have discovered that there is a striking lack of literature on this area of Japanese studies. The existing literature on Japanese customers or consumers either views them in terms of their prospective business and therefore from the perspective of customer satisfaction, or relates to general trends such as standardization or the antithetical and more recent individualization. While these concerns are indeed important and relevant to my general discussion of the success of the unified wedding pattern, I have tried herein to offer something else: an inside look at the real relationship between 'live' people. This 'human' angle will facilitate my examination of the production of culture and of tradition in the rest of the text and especially in Chapter Six. For there I shall suggest that 'needs' and 'demands', following Appadurai (1986), are 'socially regulated' and based on the reciprocal relationship between producers and consumers.

4

BRIDAL DRESSERS AS CARRIERS OF 'TRADITION'

Prior to the age of commercialized weddings, the Japanese beautician performed her role in preparing the bride at the home of the latter. Today, however, with the advent of the 'total wedding', a beauty shop within the confines of the wedding facility is an absolute necessity. This is true of wedding parlours as well as of hotels and public facilities. As the department responsible for creating the bride's appearance throughout every stage of a wedding, the beauty shop plays a central role in both the preparations for and the production of the wedding day.

Being in charge of preparing female wedding guests as well as the bride and family, the beauty shop is responsible for the production of 'appearance', with an emphasis on 'bridal appearance' (*hanayome sugata*). As has been implied, the importance of expertise in this area should not be underestimated in the context of a ceremonial occasion like a wedding.

In addition, the beauty shop's work in kimono dressing also gives it a role in re-producing (or producing) 'traditionality'. This traditional image of the beauty shop's dressers is constantly stressed by the shop and the wedding parlour because it contributes to the general process of invention and production of traditions which underlies the wedding parlour's work.

The beautician's role: from hair-dresser to dresser

The history of the wedding industry and the ceremonial pattern of weddings may be described as a process of elaboration, invention and centralization (of services). Changes in the role of the beautician-dresser at weddings are closely related to two crucial stages in this history: (1) the late 1940s and early 1950s, when the wedding ceremony began to be moved from the home, and (2) the 1970s, when comprehensive wedding parlours began to be established.

The professional hairdresser (*kamiyui-san*) was mentioned as part of the relatively simple home wedding already in pre-war Japan. In those days, however, her role was limited to arranging special hairstyles for the bride and female relatives (Embree 1939:205). It was only after the war, and later in the 1970s, when the kimono was no longer worn in everyday life and the costumes for ceremonial occasions began to include reproduction of traditional dress, that hairdressers began to assume the role of dresser which they still retain.

Accounts of rural home weddings after the war describe a professional hairdresser, as she was still called, as responsible for making up and dressing the bride as well as for her coiffure, which had by then become a wig (e.g., Beardsley *et al.* 1959:325). In some instances, the hairdresser also served as the bride's attendant throughout the ceremony, sometimes even having a small ceremonial role in the affair (Norbeck 1954:179–183).

With the establishment of the comprehensive wedding parlour and its centralization of services, dressers, being employed by the subcontracted beauty shop, started working in the confines of the wedding parlour.[1] Although nowadays they no longer attend upon the bride during the ceremony, since this role has been taken over by other wedding parlour employees, they do attend upon the bride's costume changes that accompany every wedding production.[2] As an increasing number of wedding guests required professional help in kimono dressing, their role as 'dressers' (*kitsuke no hito*) became more and more important.[3] In the process of elaboration and invention, the dressers' role has been expanded to include Japanese and Western styles of dressing and make-up. The story of one such hairdresser – Sakamoto Sachiko, who owns The Cinderella Beauty Shop in the Kobe Princess Palace – illustrates this process of elaboration.

Sakamoto Sachiko: personal background

Sakamoto Sachiko, the daughter of a successful merchant from the Osaka area, married into another 'good' family. The Sakamoto family men had been physicians for generations. Sachiko's husband followed the family tradition until he was killed during the war in the Pacific. Thirty-three years old and pregnant with her third child, Sachiko, received little help from her family, and felt she had to start working to support her young children. After she closed her late husband's clinic, she decided to study to become a beautician. She recalls that her family was very much against the idea that she would work at all, especially in such a low-status profession.[4] However, despite her own distaste for working with what she, too, saw as 'low-class' women, she enjoyed this kind of work. After graduating in 1950, Sakamoto Sachiko opened her own beauty shop at a time when the beauty business was booming due to the permanent-wave craze in Japan. She recalls times like the New Year when she was so busy that she did not have time to sleep. In time, her talent, ambition, and hard work gained her the highest rank among beauticians – that of bride-maker.[5]

Sakamoto Sachiko's contact with the Cobella wedding parlour chain began in the mid seventies, the heyday of the wedding industry. With her excellent business intuition, Sakamoto Sachiko, who already owned two small beauty shops, understood that she could do much better if she could become involved in the business of weddings.[6] After all, she had attained the rank of bride-maker and prepared brides in their homes – business that was gradually disappearing along with home weddings. Thus, in 1979, when Cobella decided to open a wedding parlour in Sakai, in the southern part of Osaka where Sakamoto Sachiko lived and worked, and wanted a beautician to open a shop within its confines, Sakamoto's expertise in kimono dressing and bride-making made her an obvious choice (and, to this day, the Cobella management still admires her high proficiency in this art).[7]

From the time Sakamoto Sachiko decided to close her shops and move into the Sakai wedding parlour, she allied herself exclusively to Cobella. In 1980, when the company expanded its business to Tokyo, she opened a shop there for her eldest child and only daughter, who moved to Tokyo with her husband to manage it. This shop was not located in one of Cobella's wedding parlours, but in a small hotel in which the company had purchased the right to run the beauty shop and costume department. (This shop was closed due to a fire and reopened in a different location.) The Cinderella Beauty Shop at the Kobe Princess Palace which opened in 1981 was Sakamoto's third shop in a Cobella facility. Three years later, her last and seemingly favourite shop was opened in Himeji (see Figure 4.1).

A family business

The business which Sakamoto Sachiko has built through the years is a family-run enterprise (*dōzoku gaisha*, see Dore 1958:105–106; Hamabata 1990:87–89) even though it may be unique in that it involves only female members of the family.[8] Sakamoto's elder daughter managed the Tokyo shop until it was handed over to another

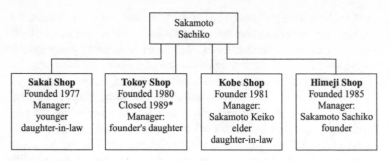

* The Tokyo shop was closed due to Sakamoto's daughter's health condition.

Figure 4.1 Sakamoto's beauty business

company due to the daughter's 'physical condition'.[9] The youngest of Sakamoto Sachiko's daughters-in-law manages the Sakai shop, and the Cinderella Beauty shop in the Kobe Princess Palace[10] is run by her elder daughter-in-law, Sakamoto Keiko.

The story of Sakamoto Keiko may help illuminate the way in which the family business has expanded. Keiko, the wife of Sakamoto Sachiko's eldest son, did not attend beauty school until she was 36. She is a graduate of a music university who moved to Hiroshima after marrying Sakamoto's son and was content to be a housewife and mother to her two children. When her younger daughter was in elementary school, the family returned to Osaka and moved into the family home while Sakamoto Sachiko took a smaller apartment near by. When her mother-in-law (whom she refers to as 'mother', as is common in Japan) decided to open the Kobe shop for her to manage, Keiko still knew nothing about the business. So Sakamoto Sachiko, who until then worked with her younger daughter-in-law in Sakai, left the Sakai shop in the hands of the latter, and managed the Kobe shop for a year while Keiko went to a beauty school. Keiko remembers this as a difficult period. She not only attended classes for eight hours every day, but continued to run the house and take care of her husband and children. She also recalls feeling uncomfortable that most of her classmates were young enough to be her daughters; but since she had no other choice, she knew she had better study hard. Keiko took it for granted that she had no choice but to join her mother-in-law's business once having been asked. 'She was my husband's mother so we had to work together.'

Obtaining a beautician's licence was necessary not only in order to succeed her mother-in-law, but also to become the formal manager and employer of the Cinderella Beauty Shop and to be able to sign a contract with Cobella – which the Sakamotos always refer to as 'The Company' (*kaisha*). Keiko repeated the phrase 'succeed to the house' (*ie o tsugu*) several times as we spoke about her becoming a beautician at the age of thirty-six. She also told me that there were several other women like her in her class who had no choice but to succeed to their family business.

Apart from family commitment, Keiko also saw joining the beauty shop business as a good financial opportunity to increase her family income. She said that she knew she could allow herself things, such as sending her children to a private school, that she could not otherwise afford. After a year of internship in the shop itself, she became its formal manager. She is now the one who signs a contract with Cobella every year (as do her younger sister-in-law in Sakai and her mother-in-law in Himeji).

The Cinderella Beauty Shop's position at the Kobe Princess Palace

If the relationship between the parlour and its subcontractors runs the gamut from exploitation to mutual trust and interdependence, the Cinderella Beauty Shop's relations with the Kobe Princess Palace may be considered as closer to the latter. Among the reasons for this is its unique position as the representative and repository of 'Japanese-tradition'. However, before we investigate this aspect of the beauty shop's position in the wedding parlour, it is of interest to consider briefly the financial aspects of the relationship.

The beauty shop is a private business. Its owners pay Cobella a monthly rent of ¥250,000. Like other businesses on the premises, its status as a private business is compromised by its being almost completely dependent on the wedding parlour for its survival. For, although the shop offers hair-setting and permanent-wave services to the general public, its clientele is mostly limited to people who take part in the weddings held there.

The beauty shop's income is based on the fees it receives from the parlour for preparing brides, from what it charges wedding guests for its services to them (see Table 4.1), and from commissions earned for promoting special accessories like traditional wig decorations. Thus, while the shop receives ¥10,000 from the parlour for each bride it prepares, this amount can vary depending upon the 'extra' accessories it succeeds in selling to enhance the bride's appearance. As these

Table 4.1 Costs of service offered by the beauty shop

Service	Cost (in ¥)
Tomesode[a] dressing	2,000
Furisode[b] dressing	2,500
Men's dressing (*montsuki*)	1,500
Hair setting	3,500+
Permanent wave	5,100–10,000
Facial[c]	5,000
Depilation	3,000+
Manicure	1,500

a *Tomesode* is the formal kimono worn by married women.
b *Furisode* is a long-sleeved formal kimono worn by unmarried women.
c This cosmetic treatment is mainly given to brides as preparation for their wedding. It is sometimes given by the beauty shop free as a service for the bride.

'extras' are suggested for the two or three changes in outfit and appearance that every bride undergoes during her wedding, they can be an excellent source of additional income.

As the traditional-Japanese costume is the most complicated it lends itself to the largest number of possible additions and elaborations, for example, higher quality wig ornaments (*kanzashi*) than those provided in the bridal package. This is how it works: special wig decorations made by the famous pearl company Mikimoto are rented for ¥20,000 to ¥30,000. From the amount the customer pays to the wedding parlour, Mikimoto receives only 30 per cent, the beauty shop gets another 30 per cent, and the wedding parlour 40 per cent.

The clothing department

The rental of wedding costumes always has been and still is one of the main activities of *gojokai* organizations. This historical fact, together with the fact that the outfits worn at weddings constitute a central part of income generated, may explain why the costumes for rent in all the parlours owned by Cobella – and Shōchikuden – are owned by the parlour rather than by a subcontractor. Although all the wedding parlours of the Shōchikuden Group have their own stock of outfits, they do not all handle their clothing departments (*ishōbu*) the same way. In most parlours the department is either managed by the parlour itself or by a subcontractor. In the Kobe Princes Palace, however, this department is managed by the beauty shop manager, Sakamoto Keiko, a quite unusual arrangement.

As manager of the clothing department, Keiko hires and pays the salaries of the (mostly part-time) female staff who work there.[11] She is also in charge of choosing new outfits and costumes as well as the way in which they are presented to customers. For her efforts she receives a commission of 5 per cent of the proceeds from the costumes and accessories that are rented out.

Although the policy of having the same manager for both the clothing department and the beauty shop is still rare among wedding parlours in general, Utsunomiya Hideichi, the head of Cobella, tries to initiate this arrangement in every instance where this is possible. In his view, not only is the work of both departments closely connected, but the 'ignorant' customers (mainly brides) are more likely to accept advice concerning attire when it is proffered by a beautician. Although the women employed in the clothing department are neither beauticians nor kimono dressers, in the eyes of the head of Cobella the fact that they are directed by a beautician creates the right image.

The Cinderella Beauty Shop's position at the Princess Palace benefited from this double management. Towards the end of my fieldwork there was a meeting between the wedding parlour manager and all subcontractors to prepare for an upcoming bridal fair. However, this time, unlike previous fairs, the manager did not want representatives of all the companies concerned with the bride's appearance (e.g., the producers and sellers of dresses, accessories, bouquets, etc.) to attend the fair in person; he suggested (in fact, ordered) that the beauty shop and its part-timers manage everything. Although at first Keiko felt that this arrangement would put too much pressure on her and her staff, she (and her mother-in-law) later found that the new practice strengthened the beauty shop's position at the parlour, making it possible for them to make additional demands of its management. For the Cinderella Beauty Shop was the only one to be paid for the bridal fair (an amount of ¥100,000), while other shops in the Cobella chain were never paid for their participation in this kind of event. This illustrates how, in some instances, relations with subcontractors can supersede dependence and approach interdependence, especially when the parlour is trying to find ways to keep a subcontractor from breaking their relationship.

The Cinderella Beauty Shop: setting

The Cinderella Beauty Shop is located on the ground floor of the wedding parlour, although its work extends to other areas. It has two entrances, one opening into the parlour, and the other on to the parking lot, used by beauty shop employees and by such customers as brides on their wedding day. The centre of the shop is the Western-style beauty salon, which includes a reception desk and is arranged like an ordinary hairdresser's salon.[12] The biggest room used by the beauty shop is the brides' room (*hanayome no heya*), which is attached to the beauty salon and can be entered only through the shop.[13]

The brides' room is a Japanese style room that is used for making up and dressing the bride for her first and most elaborate appearance (a Japanese outfit of *uchikake* and wig). The room, which is lined with eight tatami mats, has mirrors on two sides – half-sized ones for make-up and full-sized ones for dressing – a show-case of Japanese wigs on the third wall and shelves used to hold the brides' *uchikake* for the day (divided into the times of ceremonies) on the fourth side. In one corner, on top of a cabinet, is a glass show-case with two white horses. This case is treated like a shrine, with the horses referred to as deities (*kami-sama*). Keiko does not neglect to offer them water and food and prays in front of them by clapping her hands and shutting her eyes for a short moment each time she comes to the shop.[14] The special ceremonial envelopes[15] containing money given as a tip (*oshūgi*) are also put in the box until they are collected by the beauty shop owner at the end of each weddings day. Next to the horses is a door leading to a lavatory for the exclusive use of brides and the beauty shop owners.

While the brides are dressed in the brides' room, the grooms are dressed in a smaller room just opposite, which other male guests may also use to change into their formal attire. Female wedding guests are dressed by the beauty shop's part-time dressers in two connecting rooms located at the back of the ground floor. Since these rooms are mainly used for kimono dressing, they are called *tomesode* rooms (*tomesode* is the formal kimono worn by married wedding guests). Both rooms are lined with tatami mats and have full-sized mirrors on all their walls.

Completely separated from the beauty shop is the *ironaoshi* room. Literally meaning colour (*iro*) change (*naosu*), *ironaoshi* refers to the bride's change of outfits during the reception. This small room (three mats) is located on the main floor, inside the photo studio. Since it is used for all the bride's costume changes during the reception, its location inside the photo studio makes the bride's absences from the reception room shorter than they would be if she had to go to the photo studio after each change of clothing for the mandatory photographs. Its location also means that dressers are always on hand to arrange the brides' (and other guests') costumes for the photographers.[16]

The *ironaoshi* room has two mirrors, in front of which are two stools for the bride to sit on while being made-up, and a third mirror for Western dressing. Its floor is elevated and its entrance (*genkan*) is lined with white brides' shoes. On a partition in the entrance, the workers hang the artificial-flower bouquets for all the brides to be wed on that day.

The beauty shop work: structure and organization

All the beauty shop workers, full and part-time, are women who have graduated from kimono school.[17] There are three full-time employees – all middle-aged women who work every day from nine to six and longer on busy weekends – and (between 1989 and 1991) about thirty part-time workers. Although Sakamoto Keiko is the official manager of the shop, the ultimate authority is Sakamoto Sachiko. As Keiko herself puts it: 'with regard to management, mother is the ultimate person responsible. She is the owner and she is the one who has given (invested) the money'.[18]

Although Keiko is the direct manager of the shop, she comes to the shop mainly on weekends or when weddings take place. Then she works at the beauty salon and in the *ironaoshi* room doing Western dressing and make-up. She also oversees the shop's finances. However, she leaves the every-day management to her three full-time employees: Yamada, the shop chief; Tomiyama, the head 'dresser'; and Tanaka, who is their all-around assistant.

The shop chief (or *chiifu* as she is called by everybody) joined the shop one year after it opened in 1981. From then on she has worked nine hours every day and up to thirteen hours a day on weekends – sometimes until as late as 10 pm. Like the other two full-time employees, she has four free days a month.

One cannot mistake the chief for a regular worker. Though kind, she is a tough woman who controls everything that goes on, from the shop itself to the brides' room, through the *tomesode* and to the *ironaoshi* rooms. Since her expertise is Western make-up and hair-setting she spends most of the day in the *ironaoshi* room. She is also in charge of the daily book-keeping and of dealing with part-time employees.

While the chief is in charge of the technical and administrative side of the shop, Tomiyama – who is considered the shop's expert in kimono dressing – may be described as responsible for the more aesthetic side of the work. Another 'division of labour' between Tomiyama and the chief is that between Western (*yō*) and Japanese (*wa*). Tomiyama's expertise in kimono dressing is second only to that of Sakamoto Sachiko herself.

87

As the one in charge of the brides' room, Tomiyama sees herself as being responsible for every bride who leaves that room. Although she is more tender in character than the chief, she is not forgiving when a mistake is made in preparing a bride. She does not hesitate to order a dresser to remove all the make-up or clothing from a bride and re-do it herself from scratch. Tomiyama, unlike the two other full-time employees, is not a licensed beautician.[19]

Tanaka does not have expertise in either Japanese or Western bride-making. She can accomplish a Western hair-setting and handle a kimono, but not a 'full' bride. A very quiet person, she is quite different in nature from her counterparts. What makes her a good worker is her sense of responsibility and order. Thus, she is in charge of opening the shop in the mornings (sometimes as early as seven) and closing it at the end of the working day. In her quiet and compliant way (especially towards the shop's owner), Tanaka complements her two workmates. Together the three make a reliable working team which can operate the beauty shop quite independently. A core of veteran part-timers help them run the shop; among them is the head of the *tomesode* room.

'Divisions of labour' and hierarchies

The more than thirty women employed by the Cinderella Beauty Shop prepare brides and their families, dress guests, and do Western and Japanese style make-up, among other things. All these tasks are clearly ranked, as are the people who carry them out. Hierarchies even exist in the single area of Japanese dressing (which is considered higher than Western dressing), the most apparent one being that between ordinary dressers and 'bride-makers'. Another ranking manifests itself in the area of kimono dressing. There is also a definite hierarchy based on length of employment.

However, before we describe these distinctions and hierarchies and their meanings, we must first examine the role and position of the person who stands at the top of the whole structure: Cinderella Beauty Shop founder and owner Sakamoto Sachiko.

The ō-sensei

'Good morning, the *ō-sensei* is here today' was the *aisatsu* or day's greeting[20] which welcomed me on some of the busy Sundays at the Kobe Princess Palace and the Cinderella Beauty Shop. These were the special occasions on which Sakamoto Sachiko came to the Kobe shop for the day. Although she usually spent weekends working at the Himeji shop which was then under her direct management, she also visited her other shops on working days as well as for special training sessions. In this way she not only affirmed the affiliation between the shops, but also maintained her claim to dominance.

The title *ō-sensei* says much more than that Sakamoto Sachiko is the shop's ultimate owner. The term *ō-sensei* can be translated as 'great master (mistress)' of a certain art.[21] Although the term is now used to refer to masters of many spheres of life, from university professors to prestigious hairdressers, it none the less has a special flavour in the wedding parlour context. Whereas other managers and subcontractors in the parlour carry 'modern' titles such as *shachō* (head, company president, for the photo studio owner) and *shihainin* (general manager of the wedding parlour) Sakamoto is considered a great *sensei* of the traditional art of kimono dressing.[22]

A visit by the *ō-sensei* usually had a great impact on the atmosphere of the beauty shop, especially if she was in one of her angry moods in which not a single employee (or anthropologist, for that matter) could escape being scolded. Her presence was felt most of all in the brides' room, where she would prepare a bride or two while supervising other bride-makers.[23] If the atmosphere in the brides' room can be described as generally quite severe, it usually became an almost frightening place in the *ō-sensei's* presence – especially (but not only) for new bride-makers who tried their best to stay as far away from her as possible.

The brides' room was not, however, the only part of the beauty shop where the *ō-sensei* exercised her authority. She would always pay quick visits to other rooms, where she gave a hand when necessary, or just made her presence known by giving some general orders.[24] Moreover, she never failed to make her presence known in every department of the wedding parlour, re-emphasizing her status not only in front of her direct employees but to the wedding parlour's employees and management as well.

A day at work in the Cinderella Beauty Shop

Like the wedding parlour in general, the beauty shop does not seem to be the same place during the week that it is on weekends. On weekdays the shop is usually very quiet, its full-time employees mainly occupied with preparing for the weekend and ordering the necessary number of part-timers for the weekend (usually two dressers per wedding). On Sundays, however, the shop is as active as a beehive. Brides, wedding guests, sales ladies and uniformed part-timers are all bustling around.

The brides' room is the heart of the beauty shop work. Not only it is located inside the beauty salon, which also contains the reception desk, but this is the room where the bride begins and ends her 'journey' between costumes on her wedding day. Moreover, it is the place where workers meet to take their afternoon tea and, on slow days, where training sessions in kimono dressing are given. Finally, it is central in a more symbolic way, since it is where the 'mini-shrine' is located.

While the more experienced beauty shop employees carry out their appointed tasks in the brides' room, most of the part-time dressers work in the *tomesode* room, where they dress wedding guests in kimono. The latter takes ten to fifteen minutes, a relatively short time in comparison with the more than two hours which it takes to prepare a bride. This, together with the number of customers (which can easily reach one hundred on a busy day with about fifteen weddings), gives the *tomesode* room a very different character from that of the brides' room: the pressure of work in the *tomesode* room is more periodic, peaking in the thirty minutes or so before each ceremony with customers usually arriving in family groups rather than singly. These groups typically include three generations: grandmother, mother and daughter (the bride's sister), as well as some aunts (possibly with their daughters). Then there may be a group of more remote female relatives and, of course, the female go-between (*nakōdo*) who always wears a formal kimono. Often, the whole party can not be dressed simultaneously, even when full-time dressers and other bride-makers lend a hand. When this happens, customers have to wait as long as thirty minutes, wearing only their special kimono underwear, until they are fully 'kimonoed'.

What characterizes the *ironaoshi* room is its air of efficiency. Since this is where brides change in the midst of their wedding party, the work must be accomplished as quickly as possible. Thus, a single bride may be taken care of by six or even eight hands simultaneously. While one expert is setting her hair, another is busy with her make-up; at the same time, a part-timer is putting on her earrings and yet another is slipping on her gloves. After all this has been completed, the bride is 'inserted' into her wedding dress, which is prepared in advance.

The necessary efficiency of the *ironaoshi* room is aided by formal mechanisms. It is connected by intercom, not only with the other rooms used by the beauty shop (in order to divide working hands in the most productive manner at each moment), but also with the reception halls. Whenever a bride leaves the room for one of these reception rooms, the room in question is notified so that its director can make certain that the programme there will be ready for her return. Another way in which efficiency is maintained is by the strict rule that employees must fill in the exact time of each bride's entrance and departure.

Distinctions: Japanese and Western in the beauty shop context

It is the beauty shop that sets the standard for the traditional-Japanese and Western style elements that comprise the modern Japanese wedding, and it is in the beauty shop that the distinction between these two styles is felt most. The distinction marks a clear division of labour in the beauty shop. Although some workers can handle both tasks, they are still differentiated as we have seen in the case of the chief and her counterpart, Tomiyama. The same division exists between Sakamoto Sachiko and her daughter-in-law, Keiko.

In addition to the division of labour and ranking in the shop's hierarchy, there is also a special quality attached to each of the two styles. This can best be illustrated by comparing the atmosphere in the brides' room with that of the *ironaoshi* room and the beauty salon. In the brides' room where the bride is prepared for her most traditional-Japanese appearance, the work is carried out silently and an atmosphere of seriousness permeates the room. Bride-makers are strictly forbidden to have a private or informal conversation with the brides. Even among themselves, the dressers are much more reserved in the brides' room than in the *ironaoshi* room, where the atmosphere is usually much more relaxed even though the dressers must work more quickly.

In Chapter One the activities at the wedding parlour are divided into preparatory and formal activities. However, although the brides' room is situated on the ground floor which is generally given over to preparatory and behind-the-scene activities, the work done there takes on the character of on stage activity. Female family members and friends can enter this room and take photographs of the dressing process. When there is only one bride in the room, the groom and male relatives may also take photographs or make a video of the preparations. Unlike the Western dressing carried out in the *ironaoshi* room, which is judged by its efficiency and run in accordance with time-saving rules, Japanese dressing is considered an art because it is viewed as traditional craftsmanship. This lends the process of kimono dressing the qualities of a performance.

This distinction, like the others that distinguish Japanese from Western, is related to a much more pervasive attitude towards the two

91

styles, which will be discussed below. First, let us take a deeper look at the distinctions between the two and at the way the dressers of each view their work.

The uniqueness of kimono dressing

The seriousness or rather uniqueness of kimono dressing extends beyond the brides' room into the *tomesode* room, where relatives and friends are dressed. Although this room is characterized by much more pressure and consideration of efficiency, there seem to be some rules which kimono experts are usually unwilling to break. One of them is the holistic nature of the dressing. For kimono dressing is not seen as merely helping a woman dress in her own (or a rented) kimono; the kimono dressers see it as a specialist task, which should be done entirely by themselves. This means that even when a woman comes to the wedding parlour half-dressed in a kimono and asks (for the full price) to have the work completed, the dressers will insist that she remove the kimono and the work be done afresh (*yarinaosu*). In this way, they maintain their image as repositories of unique knowledge rather than mere providers of a service, and thereby justify their expert (*sensei*) status throughout the wedding parlour.

Moreover, whereas Western beauty work is usually discussed in terms of professional efficiency, Japanese bride-making is accorded an entirely different vocabulary. Tomiyama, the brides-making expert, explicitly refers to her work as creative, 'like art'. Thus, she regards each bride that she has 'made' as a piece of (art) work (*sakuhin*) and every beautiful bride as her own achievement. Sakamoto Sachiko, the beauty shop owner was more careful when asked to define the work of kimono dressing and bride-making:

> To say it is art is a bit too much. On the other hand, it cannot be defined as a hobby, as that is too light. It is the unique (*dokutoku*) work of a beautician. However, when people do it really beautifully, it can reach art, even though there are many conditions [like the bride's body]. Yes, if someone does it perfectly it can perhaps be seen as an art. But, after all, it is the Japanese beautician's unique job. It is pleasant work, but work which goes through hardships (*kurō*).

Although the shop owner was hesitant to define kimono dressing and bride-making as art, her observations do reveal her view of the nature of these pursuits. What became obvious as she continued to speak was that 'Japanese' is not only distinguished from 'Western', but also has special qualities which lend it its uniqueness. It was these qualities, clearly 'Japanese', to which she alluded when she remarked of the 'hardships' involved in kimono dressing. As we shall see, hardship is strongly associated with traditional Japanese notions regarding apprenticeship and craftsmanship.

One of the characteristics which preserves the 'Japaneseness' of kimono dressing is the strict observance of one's proper place. A recurrent phrase used by the ō-sensei is 'Top is top, bottom is bottom'(ue wa ue, shita wa shita). She uses this phrase time and time again in all her visits to the shop, thereby instilling in the workers the idea that they should all know their proper place. This goes for all the divisions: between veterans and beginners; between bride-makers and ordinary kimono dressers; and even among the furisode and tomesode kimono dressers. It also means that no worker is allowed to criticize the kimono dressing of the ō-sensei (when she is present) or the head dresser Tomiyama, when Sakamoto Sachiko is not around. This attitude is closely connected with the way in which know-how is transferred from top to bottom in the shop.

Knowing one's proper place also has very clear implications for the very process of dressing. Here 'top' is analogous to 'front' (mae), and 'bottom' to 'back' (ushiro). As a rule, the more experienced dresser stands in front of the client being dressed, and the less experienced at the back. The 'front' work – actually the main work of adjusting the kimono – is considered more complicated. Indeed, a particularly experienced dresser can do without an assistant (joshu) to do the 'back' work. The assistant, always a beginner, is also responsible for preparing all the small items (komono) necessary before the actual dressing and for helping the customer don the special kimono underwear.

The almost ritualistic distinctions between 'up' and 'down' and 'front' and 'back' are characteristic of the attitude towards kimono dressing in modern Japan as well as in the wedding parlour. It is similar to the attitude towards bridal dressing as performance in that the art of kimono dressing is often presented in terms borrowed from dance. In this connection, it is of interest that one of the most respected part-time employees at the Cinderella Beauty Shop was an experienced teacher of traditional Japanese dancing. This expert in dance executed her dressing almost as a dance. As such a highly regarded dresser, she worked only on special occasions, because the beauty shop had to pay her more than other dressers. A good performer, she was considered an ideal dresser by the others.

The work force: veterans and beginners

The beauty shop's part-time work force is divided into two distinct groups: the veterans (the English term is used), who have worked at the shop (as part-timers) since it opened or from its early years, and all the others, a segment of whom work for a brief period and then move on. Most of the veterans are now bride-makers, a rank they have reached after years of training.

Motivations for working at the beauty shop

All the part-timers, regardless of length of service, are paid by the hour, at a very low rate, beginning at ¥550 (£2.2) per hour and going up to ¥700 (£2.8) for some of the more experienced women.[25] The low pay, and the fact that they work no more (and usually less) than eight days a month forces one to ask what on earth it is that draws these women to work at the beauty shop.

Keiko, the beauty shop manager is aware of the low wages; but she also knows that whenever the shop recruits new part-timers, many more women apply for the jobs than are needed, and most of them do not leave when they hear the rate being offered. She admits that there is a small population which works for a short time and leaves, but this does not seem to bother her. It is Keiko's (as well as Sakamoto Sachiko's) understanding of what motivates women to work in their beauty shop which helps them determine the salaries they offer. As Keiko put it:

> Women who come to work as dressers are people who do not have to work for the money. Most of them are ladies (*okusan*) from middle [-class] houses. These women have taken dressing classes as a hobby, not for money, but so they can dress their daughters and themselves. Then [when they realize how little they have learned], they come to a place like ours to be taught at least the basics. In this way they make the most of their hobby and keep it alive. They get reimbursed for transportation as well as their hourly payment. And finally this gives them the opportunity to earn money for their own pleasures (*asobi*). There are plenty women of this kind.

Keiko (and the *ō-sensei*) are indeed correct. Most of the women who come to work at the shop are middle-aged with grown-up children who have time for themselves and are looking for a new interest in life. After graduating from the kimono schools, some of them discover that

94

the short (and expensive)[26] time they spent there did not teach them very much. Since there are no longer enough private ceremonial occasions at which to practise, they consider themselves lucky to receive any pay at all for putting what they did learn into practice and polishing up the skills they should have acquired along with their dressing license. Many of these women appreciate the opportunity of doing this under the supervision of the *ō-sensei* and other senior (*senpai*) workers.

For those women who do need the money, kimono dressing is considered preferable to secretarial work or retailing. They only have to work a few hours a week, and that is much better than other common 'part-time' jobs which often require going into work five or six days a week (Saso 1990:145). This way, their work does not interfere with their housework and allows them to feel that their devotion to husband and children is not impaired. In fact, the beauty shop part-timers view their work as an additional 'channel' of their role as women and wives. One of the more obvious links between the worlds of household and of work may be seen in the relatively high number of mothers to daughters. 'If I had had boys', one of the new dressers told me, 'I don't think I would have gone to study kimono. But, I have two girls, and they are almost twenty years old.' This novice dresser was referring to the 'coming of age ceremony', celebrated in Japan at the age of twenty, in which wearing a kimono for girls has become very popular.

As Keiko explained, some of the women saw the job as a mere hobby but soon said they found the work too difficult and left. In fact, these women rarely complained of the pressure of work; what usually disturbed them more was the others' attitudes towards them. They could not accept being treated as novices at the age of 45–55, did not find it proper always to be reproached by their seniors (in expertise), and having to do tasks like cleaning in addition to dressing.

The veteran part-timers

Not all women feel discontent at being treated as novices. Indeed, some women regard being scolded by their superiors and the lowly tasks they are assigned as essential to the skills they have come to learn. These women view kimono dressing as an art or craft which must be acquired through a traditional apprenticeship. This is the way most of the veterans, most of whom are bride-makers, feel.

The veterans' salaries are not much higher than those of beginners (a difference of ¥200 at most). Even the tips they sometimes receive do not make their income large enough to live on.[27] While some of them need no more than they earn at the shop, others (mainly widows) work elsewhere during the week, in secretarial work or by giving kimono lessons, or live on a pension. As one of them put it, 'My work here is not for subsistence (*seikatsu*) but more for pleasure (*dōraku*)'. These women get their gratification not only from making a beautiful bride, but also from being acknowledged by their *sensei*.

Aspects of artisan apprenticeship

Beauticians and kimono dressers did not always require the formal training that is *de rigueur* today. Hairdressers of the past – the forerunners of today's dressers – were trained under a Japanese apprenticeship system called *totei seido* (Dore 1973:376–378, 386; Clark 1987:15–17). Although some vestiges of the 'master' (*sensei*)–disciples (*deshi*) relationship may still be seen at the Cinderella Beauty Shop, they were much more in evidence in earlier days of the *ō-sensei*'s work, when the women from the country-side whom she trained lived in her house until they were ready to return to their home towns and open their own shops. Indeed, the *ō-sensei* still keeps in touch with her disciples.[28]

Having to acquire skills far from the natal home (Kondo 1990:235–236)[29] and the long-lasting relationship with one's master (Lebra 1984a:240) are characteristic of the traditional relations between the *sensei* and his/her disciples. Although modern dressers are not trained in the same strict pattern of the traditional *totei seido* (or its current 'nostalgic' version), aspects of the *totei seido* can be found in the beauty shop in the way knowledge and concepts are transferred to novices by the beauty shop owner and dressers, especially the veterans. These features are part of the attempt to establish a 'traditional' image.

The acquisition of specific dressing skills

While it is true that all the women who come to work at the beauty shop are licensed dressers, they must acquire the shop's 'own way of doing things' (*uchi no yarikata*) before they can be productive workers. *Uchi no yarikata* is repeated over and over again by the *ō-sensei* and her senior workers. Indeed, new workers are even told to forget what they have learned at the kimono school and to pay careful attention to the way the work is carried out in the shop. Obviously, kimono school graduates are not meant to take this literally. But it does remind new workers that they must adjust their knowledge to the ways of the shop, or rather of the *ō-sensei*. It also implies and encourages these workers to feel solidarity with the shop.

Acquiring dressing skills also means an ongoing process of learning. This view was explicitly expressed by the *ō-sensei* when she said that it takes ten full years of study to learn how to 'make a bride' perfectly: 'After a year one can learn the outline, but when the work of a one-year apprentice is compared with that of a ten-year veteran bride-maker, it looks like the work of an elementary school student.' The *ō-sensei* never stops studying herself. She participates in training sessions and competitions with other dressers of her level and brings the new knowledge acquired to her disciples at her shops. In line with the hierarchical 'chain of knowledge', she transfers this knowledge mainly to senior employees (or disciples), who then pass it on to their inferiors.

Training at the shop

When younger employees complain that they are not being properly taught by their superiors, the answer they always receive is that they must observe and study. Keiko has said that these young workers are ignorant of their own culture in which 'There is a system of master–disciple (*sensei-deshi*), which is not teaching but watching the master at work and learning through work.' Learning through observation (*minarai*; literally, seeing and learning) was traditionally the primary mode of master-instruction. Put more vividly, apprentices had to steal knowledge (*nusunde oboeru*), since they could not necessarily count on being taught formally. The art of kimono dressing, especially that of bride-making, is one of those which are not supposed to be taught orally. Thus, the *ō-sensei* would become particularly angry when a bride-maker asked how to accomplish a specific task. 'One should first do. And then, if necessary, her superior will tell her to do it all over again (*yarinaosu*)', she would tell her apprentices, thereby, emphasizing learning through training.

However, although apprenticeship is stressed in some aspects of the beauty shop's work, perfection demands that its owners do not rely only on learning through observation. Since most of the employees work only a few times a month, they need some kind of formal teaching in order to acquire the proper dressing skills. This formal teaching is usually conducted by the *ō-sensei* mainly during a short summer training course (*kōshū*). It is supplemented by sessions throughout the year given either by her or by one of the seniors.

The summer course

The summer course is an eighteen-hour, three-day training session given in the brides' room. Every employee of the shop is supposed to participate in the training session, although part-timers are not paid for their time since they are meant to regard this as a rare opportunity to learn directly from the *ō-sensei*. The first part of the course is comprised of demonstrations of bride-making and ordinary kimono dressing by the *ō-sensei*. The second part, which usually takes up half of the second day and the entire third day, is dedicated to individual training by shop seniors and by the great teacher herself, in which the employees take turns being dresser and model.

The *ō-sensei's* 'performance' of bride-making on the first day sometimes attracts female employees from other departments of the wedding parlour. The make-up and dressing of the model (usually a young girl) are carried out very carefully, with explanations of every step. The reason for all employees having to attend, even though only a few of them make brides, is that every employee should know something about bride-making, not only because it represents the ultimate in kimono dressing, but also so they can assist when necessary. The instruction in both bride-making and other dressing includes practical information related to the peculiarities of the Kobe Princess Palace. Thus, it is not 'a bride' who is being prepared, but a bride in that wedding parlour, which means, for example, that the length and tightness of her gown must be adjusted to accommodate the fact that the parlour has no lift. In other words, here as in other areas of Japanese craftsmanship, practical and aesthetic factors are combined.[30] For those who do not 'make' brides, the *ō-sensei* also utilizes the summer course to teach dressers 'tricks' which can help them in dressing, as well as how to be better promoters of their own work and the shop's work and goods (mainly kimono accessories). 'It is not enough to do good work with one's hands', she tells them, 'One should also be good in "mouth-work" (*kuchi no shigoto*)'.

A typical example of mouth-work is inventing names for kimono ties. For example, the long-sleeved kimono (*furisode*) for unmarried girls requires a more complicated tie than the *tomesode* for married women. To create a professional image, the dresser should invent a name for the particular tie which she does. Names such as 'flower' or 'butterfly' will usually be appreciated by the girls and their mothers. Mouth-work also includes being polite and kind to the customers.[31]

Another aim of the summer training course seems to be to create solidarity between staff and owner as well as a spirit of 'group' identity among workers who join at different times and work on different weekends. Except during the occasional short afternoon teas, employees have few chances to meet informally. Nor do they have formal meetings where they can get to know each other. The opportunity to get to know each other during the three-day course is therefore of great importance. The course opens formally, with all the employees sitting in a circle around the *ō-sensei* in the middle. Sakamoto Sachiko then proceed to interview each employee, introducing the veterans to the others. Whereas the course opens formally, the closing session is an informal tea with the owners, which is nevertheless led by the *ō-sensei*. The atmosphere of this session is meant to create the illusion that the course has facilitated familiarity not only among the workers, but between them and the *ō-sensei* as well.

The making of a bride-maker

The summer course is a decisive point in the process of becoming a 'full' bride-maker. Not all part-timers aspire to or succeed in becoming bride-makers due to the arduous work and devotion this entails. After a year or so of working in the *tomesode* room, a talented and hard-working part-timer may be promoted to assistant (*joshu*) in the brides' room. There she will work long days – as she must not leave until the last bride returns to the room prior to leaving the wedding parlour – doing all kinds of menial tasks. During her months as an assistant she might have some opportunities to observe one of the expert bride-makers at work, or even to get some general explanations from the head dresser. But her main learning does not begin until the summer course, when she has her first chance to practise bridal make-up and dressing.

After the summer course, the novice bride-maker continues to work as an assistant. From time to time she will be asked to join one of the experts on an 'outside job' (*shutchō*).[32]

The day a 'fresh' bride-maker is told that she has been assigned to 'do' a bride by herself usually falls on a day when the *ō-sensei* herself is in attendance.

Becoming a bride-maker: a veteran's story

Although today the *ō-sensei* is less involved in the everyday work of the shop including promoting the dressers, she did promote the veterans who worked with her in the early days. According to veterans, the atmosphere in the shop was much stricter then than it is today. For them, becoming a bride-maker was regarded as becoming a mature practitioner of the art of dressing (*ichinin-mae*). Here is the story of such veteran.

> It was in the summer of my third year, the time of the summer course, when the *sensei* approached me and said that I should state whether I wanted to make brides, . . . but I did not say I did. I never thought that I would ever make brides. I was over 50 years old. . . . . It seemed too high to me, too great a stretch to that level. I was satisfied with dressing *tomesode* and *furisode*. But, when the *ō-sensei* saw this, she said: 'Kawamura-san does not have the heart [will] to follow me.'

At the *ō-sensei's* reaction, this middle-aged woman determined that she would learn bride-making. She not only took the three-day course, but studied throughout the year while working as an assistant in the brides' room and observing the *ō-sensei* at work. She spent additional money on a kimono expert, whom she and a few other beginners (some of them still working today) paid to teach them in their houses. When they found that this training was not good enough, three of them came to the shop every day to practise, one of them acting as a model. For at the shop they had the *ō-sensei* and the head dresser to check and correct their work.

> So, in this way, I steadily improved my skill (*te ga agaru*) until in my fourth year [at the shop], I became able to make brides . . . if the *ō-sensei* had not uttered those stern (*kibishii*) words, I would not be doing [brides] even now . . . After all, severe words are better . . ., and it was *the sensei* who uttered those words. Now it makes me very happy and grateful . . . After all, if you work in such a place and can not reach *hanayome* [bride] you are not a full person (*ichi-nin-mae*). At last I became like everyone else . . .

The Cinderella Beauty Shop: past, present and future

The beauty shop's old hands frequently recall nostalgically the 'old days' (actually only ten years ago) when the shop had just opened and the *ō-sensei* trained them herself almost every day. Another veteran, who began working there when the shop first opened, put it this way:

> When I started working in the shop, I worked in the *ironaoshi* room, but I also did *tomesode* as everyone had to do this. We

100

studied every day, at that time the *sensei* taught us by herself.
Now there are seniors (*senpai*) like Tomiyama-san who teach.
But then, at the beginning, it was the *sensei* herself. It was
frightening. . . . You know what I mean . . . I studied with all my
might. I was scolded by the *sensei*. There were many days when I
went home crying. It was different from now.

What the veterans miss most of all is the severe (*kibishii*) teaching of
the *ō-sensei*. 'Now', they say, 'even the *sensei* is not so severe any
more. She has become gentle (*yasashiku narimashita*)'. Moreover, they
go on to complain, the women who come to work as dressers today do
not even need a licence, and they are not as rigorously trained as they
were in 'those days (*mukashi*)'.[33]

The veterans' complaints about the incompetence of today's new
workers are not really well-based, as newcomers still need a licence
before they can begin work, and are trained rather stringently by their
seniors, especially the head of the *tomesode* room who tries to maintain
the *ō-sensei*'s strict ways. Their view at least in part is a result of a mere
nostalgic image of the past. Nevertheless, it seems that the present
atmosphere in the shop is, indeed, less severe than it was in the past. No
doubt one of the reasons for this is the fact that the *ō-sensei* is not at the
shop regularly, having been replaced by her daughter-in-law, Keiko,
who – as a beautician rather than kimono dresser – is viewed, and views
herself, as an artisan (*shokunin*) rather than as an artist.[34] It is clear that
when the *ō-sensei* managed the shop, her direct control had a stronger
influence on the work and the atmosphere.[35]

The trend towards simplification in hiring and the less stringent
training at the Cinderella Beauty Shop is also a function of larger
structural processes involving the shop's relationship with the wedding
parlour. The wedding parlour was much more involved in the beauty
shop's work when the shop first opened. Potential shop employees were
interviewed by the parlour manager as well as by Sakamoto Sachiko
and the shop chief. In addition, no woman could apply for work in the
shop who had not already proven her ability in three months of sales
work, after having taken a sales course. During these months, the
aspiring shop worker – who also had to be a licensed dresser – had to
sign up fifteen members to the *gojokai* in order to qualify for an
interview. In other words, when the wedding parlour and the beauty
shop were both newly established, the employees' first loyalty was to
the wedding parlour. Today, however, the wedding parlour does not
usually interfere in the work of the beauty shop, especially not in the

recruitment of employees. This way of running things results from several processes in both the wedding parlour and the beauty shop.

As described above, when the wedding parlour was established its management decided to lease out the work of its various departments to subcontractors whose internal work it did not interfere with. Moreover, Sakamoto Sachiko has always been respected for her great knowledge in kimono dressing, and the confidence that the parlour has come to have in the shop, its owner and her daughter-in-law Keiko should not be underestimated. However, although the beauty shop's position in the wedding parlour as essential to the production of a wedding ceremony is an established fact, its founder and owner still worries about its future. For she views the future of her business as connected with the future of Japanese bride-making.

At age 75, the *ō-sensei* has started talking about her retirement. 'I will leave in about five years', she told me. 'I want to have some fun before I die.'[36] She has begun to prepare for this by intensifying the training in her shops. She started conducting more short courses during week days. She has also decided to teach Keiko the art of Japanese bride-making.

The *ō-sensei*'s belief in the continuity of the business reflects her belief in the continuity of the prevailing style. According to her, weddings will not become only Western, and the bride (at least in the near future) will continue wearing a Japanese outfit. 'The Japanese have this love for delicate work,' she told me. 'It is in their nature (*nihonjin jishin*).' This view is not limited to the *ō-sensei*, but promoted by the whole wedding industry which has a vested interest in seeing that this remains the case.

What is left for her, as the *ō-sensei* sees it, is to continue passing her knowledge firmly (*hishi de*) on to her disciples so they will be able to guard (*mamoru*) her business after she leaves. She genuinely believes that her disciples will continue to follow her artistic craftsmanship. Like many other Japanese (and other) women who have had careers, when the *ō-sensei* looks back she does not regret her life. Like them, she is firmly convinced that she chose the best possible life course (Lebra 1984a:240). 'When I look back, I feel content', she says. 'I am not like a salary-man (*sarariman*). I have created something'.

The *ō-sensei* can retire in peace. She knows that her two daughters-in-law will maintain the business she established, although she hopes that they will be able to acquire the necessary knowledge in Japanese bride-making. As for future generations, the daughter of her own daughter was attending beauty school during my fieldwork, perhaps in penance for her mother, who failed to make the grade. Although other granddaughters have not yet evinced interest in the family business,[37] they cannot be discounted. After all, their mothers also began late. But whoever comes in or takes over in the end, there is no doubt that the shop will not be the same without the great *sensei*'s presence and air of 'traditional' authority.

Conclusion: Japanese women and dressers as the repositories of 'tradition'

Following the history of the Cinderella Beauty Shop, its founder and its employees has allowed us to follow the process of creation of a new vocation. The beauty shop of the Kobe Princess Palace has come to play a crucial role in the production of weddings held there. We have seen that, however modern its inception, the profession of dresser is still considered a traditional craft. This aura of 'traditionality' is granted to the profession due to its occupation with the kimono and the Japanese bride – which are viewed as uniquely 'Japanese'. We have also seen how the beauty shop and its owner strive continuously to recreate this traditional image, which adds to its importance in the context of the wedding parlour. And finally, we have seen how decisive this image is in the production and commercialization of tradition, from which the wedding industry makes considerable profits.

One of the ways in which Sakamoto Sachiko, the beauty shop owner, endeavours to promote this image is to retain some vestiges of the traditional master-disciple relationship. This includes the promotion and maintenance of the image of the shop as a 'family' and the workers as members of a special group. She does this by emphasizing the beauty shop's – that is, her own – unique way of doing things (*uchi no yarikata*), which she has developed through years of non-stop learning. The significance attached to the development of a particular style of artisanship in the shop is similar to that in other Japanese arts and crafts (see Kondo 1990:231–230).

When newcomers to the shop are told to forget what they have learned previously and study the shop's way of doing things, a 'we/they', 'in/out' (*uchi/soto*) dichotomy is created which is closely connected with the attempt to create a 'group' distinction. This 'we' and 'in' atmosphere can be identified in many areas. One example is the summer course, which is an attempt to create an imagined 'solidarity' with the beauty shop and its owner. The 'we/they', 'in/out' aspect of the session is graphically illustrated in the circle around the *ō-*

sensei. For although every beauty shop employee, whether full or part-time, veteran or newcomer, is included in the circle, the clothing department staff is seated on the periphery (even though it is managed by the shop).

This attempt to create a 'family like' atmosphere is related to the effort to construct a so-called traditional-Japanese company. Much has been written about the Japanese company as a family (e.g., Abegglen 1958, Rohlen 1974, Vogel 1979:157, Nakane 1984, Clark 1987). According to this explanation, work-based groups constitute an intimate environment which 'has indeed a very similar function and role as that of a *mura*, a traditional rural village community' (Nakane 1984:126).

Among the activities which can be seen as part of the Japanese company's attempt to impart a 'family flavour' (*kazoku no aji o tsukeru*; Kondo 1990:203) are 'informal' end-year and New Year parties, as well as company trips to resorts such as hot springs. The beauty shop endeavours to promote the 'family flavour' in these activities by always having at least one member of the Sakamoto family participate in them. Thus, Sakamoto's elder daughter came to one of the New Year parties in Kobe from Tokyo, despite her deteriorating physical condition, to 'show her face' for a few minutes. A summer hot-spring trip attempted to create a fictive family rapport by importing members of the Sakamoto family who live in America to serve as guests of honour.

Another contribution to the 'Japaneseness' and 'traditionality' of the beauty shop can be seen in the discourse of the employees when they speak of their experience in the shop. They (especially the veterans) keep alluding to 'traditional' artisanship and they speak nostalgically of the earlier strict training in reference to an ideal past (*mukashi*) which is often related to the concept of tradition (*dentō*) (Moeran 1984a:165). Another recurrent term in the *ō-sensei*'s and the veterans' descriptions of their training and work is the *kurō* or hardship involved in becoming a full practitioner of the art (*ichinin mae*) (see Frager and Rohlen 1976:263, 265).

The emphasis on tradition is exemplified in the special atmosphere which surrounds the Japanese as opposed to Western bridal-making, especially in the brides' room. Kondo (1990:231–232) found a similar atmosphere of strictness (*kibishisa*) and silence in the division of Japanese sweets in a Japanese factory. But this is not really surprising because Japanese confectionaries, like the brides' room, are seen as traditional (*dentōteki*) by outsiders.

Despite my comparison between the artisans who produce Japanese confectionary and the beauty shop dressers, it is clear that while Kondo's Ohara-san, head of a Japanese confection department, created himself as a 'living stereotype of the traditional artisan' (Kondo 1990:232), this definition can not be unequivocally applied to the dressers at the Cinderella Beauty Shop. For, in Japan, part-timers, especially if they are women, can never be fully regarded as artisans. Indeed, for many of the part-timers in the beauty shop the work is not much more than a hobby which gives them a new purpose in life (*ikigai*) after their children have grown up.

Interestingly enough, the choice of a feminine pursuit is not limited to women who take up part-time work late in life. Lebra (1984a:226) found that women who are forced to go to work early in their life because they are single, widowed, separated or divorced also choose 'female' occupations, mostly in businesses they set up by themselves. Thus, the young widow Sakamoto Sachiko decided to become a beautician even though the profession did not seem to suit her social status, and despite her family disapproval. Another woman who is now a successful businesswoman in the ceremonial occasion industry (see note 6), and who became a beautician at the age of fifteen out of financial need, opened her own kimono rental and dressing business when she divorced her husband in the age of twenty-three.

While there is some tension for the women involved, between kimono dressing as a hobby and as a traditional craft, the traditional characteristics of the kimono cannot be ignored. It seems that the link between Japanese women and kimono, which began to be forged in the Meiji era, is closely related to the role of women in Japanese society.[38] It is paradoxical that in a period characterized by huge changes in traditional customs, the Japanese government through its policies on women relayed a 'symbolic message to Japan's women to become repositories of the past' (Sievers 1983:15).[39] This is not surprising if we accept Hanna Papanek's (1977:15) explanation regarding societies undergoing rapid development:

> In societies that are changing very rapidly, ambiguous signals are presented to women. Fears are often translated into attempts to prevent changes in their roles. They become the repositories of 'traditional' values imputed to them by men in order to reduce the stresses men face . . .

If Japanese women are repositories of 'traditional' values, what are the 'traditions' they are being asked to preserve? Elsewhere (Goldstein-Gidoni 1993, ch. 5), I have described how the study of the art of kimono dressing has come to be seen as a traditional Japanese art like the tea ceremony and flower arrangement – which are also considered extremely female pursuits. Ironically, women were banned from practising the tea ceremony when it was first invented in the sixteenth century (Beard 1953:97). Does this mean that women's status or role has been radically changed, or does it instead reflect the decreasing aesthetic importance of an art? The answer to this question is found in the way in which these arts are practised by women. Just as many dressers regard their work as a hobby rather than serious artisanship, women engaged in similar pursuits do not generally aspire to a mastery of these arts. Instead, they sporadically pick up courses which they think will lend them a touch of refinement.

The patterns through which women try to perpetuate their position in society can be observed in the relationship between mothers and daughters. Thus, mothers attach great importance to being able to dress their daughters in kimono. In this connection, Lebra (1984a:42–46) comments on the significance of 'femininity training', which was part of the socialization of girls in pre-war and wartime Japan. This kind of training included learning elegance, modesty and tidiness, which were all connected with wearing the kimono (properly). It is interesting how mothers of today perpetuate similar values in the socialization of their daughters even though these values are strongly combined with women's compliance and inferiority.

We have seen how professional women perpetuate this condition in society by exploiting those in their employ because 'there are plenty of them'. It is also true that when bride-makers create the 'ideal Japanese bride' they are in fact 'bargaining with patriarchy', which is '[women's] active collusion in the reproduction of their own subordination' (Kandiyoti 1988:280).

It should, however, be stressed that in viewing women as subordinate and as repositories of tradition, we must avoid adopting the image of women as passive. For, although 'repository' implies storing or maintaining something that already exists, the dressers play a much more active role than the mere 'storage' of tradition. In fact, they are involved in the invention, construction and production of these new traditions.

Finally, it is important to emphasize that the invention and production of tradition in which the dressers, like other wedding producers, are involved, is dynamic and the relationship between producer and customer reciprocal. Thus, just as the bride-makers in the beauty shop are the producers of tradition, they are also consumers who willingly buy traditions. The best example of this is the amount of money they spend on acquiring the traditional-Japanese art of kimono dressing and 'Japanese manners' in the modern kimono schools. In both activities they manifest their involvement in the ongoing process of the construction of a Japanese cultural identity.

5

THE JAPANESE BRIDE AS A PACKAGED PRODUCT

A good deal of the groomed beauty of the women in glamour portraits comes from the fact that they are 'made-up', in the immediate sense that cosmetics have been applied to their bodies in order to enhance their existing qualities. But they are also 'made-up' in the sense that the images, rather than the women, are put together, constructed, even fabricated or falsified in the sense that we might say a story is made up if it is a fiction.

(Kuhn 1985:13)

By viewing the commercial wedding parlour's 'total wedding' from the producers' perspective, rather than from the perspective of the bride and groom as the main actors, we can see the relationship between the bridal couple and the suppliers of wedding services as one between 'consumers' and 'entrepreneurs'. From this point of view – of the ceremonial occasions industry – it becomes clear that the bridal couple are 'objects', processed by the industry. And the main 'object' of this 'manufacturing process' by the wedding parlour as well as by a whole range of subsidiary businesses, is the bride.

My discussion of the work carried out in the Cinderella Beauty Shop highlighted the special place of the kimono in both the wedding parlour context and Japanese society in general. The kimono and the pursuit of kimono dressing is part of today's feminine world; it is done by women, and for women. The ultimate symbol of this world is 'The Bride'. Not only is 'making' a bride (the verb *tsukuru* – to make – is used) the highest level a dresser can reach at the beauty shop, but wearing the Japanese bridal costume (*hanayome ishō*) is considered the *ne plus ultra* of kimono wearing. Thus donning the 'bridal appearance' (*hanayome sugata*) is considered and promoted as the climax of a Japanese woman's life. None the less, the 'Western appearance' which every wedding parlour includes, should not be denigrated. It, too, is regarded as every girl's lifetime dream. In this chapter I shall examine the creation of both the *traditionese* and *Westanese* appearances, as well as the bridal image.

Deciding on wedding costumes

After the wedding day has been set and arrangements made for the engagement ceremony, the honeymoon and the bridal furniture made, the wedding parlour suggests that the bride and her mother choose the wedding outfits. This is usually done no less than three months before the great day. The bride is not only asked to choose her outfits, she is also expected to use the time between then and the day itself to prepare herself, her face, hair and body for the 'greatest moment' in her life.

Before she arrives at the wedding parlour to choose the actual attire she will wear on her wedding day, the bride must make some initial decisions. Since every bride who marries in a Shōchikuden facility changes outfits during her wedding,[1] and I did not witness a single instance when the *uchikake* (long, elaborate overcoat) was not worn, the choice of not changing costumes does not exist. Not only does she want to be a beautiful bride – which means showing herself in several different lights (see Hendry 1981:160) – or different colours, as the term for costume changes (*ironaoshi*) implies – but, as one bride told me, it seems 'natural' (*atarimae*) for her since 'all brides today are doing this'.

Although wearing the *uchikake* is pre-ordained, most brides consider the *uchikake* an integral part of being a bride. I have heard more than one bride say: 'When I was dressed in the white *uchikake*, I felt like a bride.' Moreover, since it is regarded as the most 'traditional' form of Japanese bridal attire, wearing the *uchikake* also means being 'Japanese'. The *uchikake* has not gained its prominent place in the wedding ceremony on the basis of custom alone. The wedding industry made a concerted effort to create the notion that there is a 'genuine' bond between it and young Japanese women. As the *ō-sensei* put it: 'Even an unattractive Japanese bride mysteriously becomes transformed into a beautiful bride with *uchikake* and wig.' Then she added, reflectively: 'The *uchikake* and wig have been made to suit all the Japanese, haven't they?'

Although wearing the *uchikake* seems 'natural', an increasing number of brides are doing away with the Japanese *furisode* or long-sleeved kimono. The decision to forego the *furisode* is also generally made before a bride has seen it in the wedding parlour. When I asked the head of the brides' room why today's brides are choosing to omit this costume change, at first all she could do was express her regret that they were relinquishing this beautiful and 'traditionally Japanese' item of clothing. Her subsequent explanation – that the *furisode* appearance requires a smaller wig than that worn with the *uchikake*, and that modern young women usually wear bangs which do not lend themselves to being tucked into a wig – seemed quite practical. But it turns out that there is more to it than that, for today's brides are forsaking the *furisode* for Western party dress which calls for a hair style more in line with the one they wear habitually. What the head of the brides' room was actually saying, then, was that the younger generation does not appreciate real Japanese beauty. A female owner and president of several wedding parlours reacted to this question in a similar, though more pessimistic, tone: 'Young girls have just stopped loving kimono, you see . . .'[2]

Both the bride-making expert and the entrepreneur regretted the loss of the *furisode*, but accepted it as part of the new generation (*shin jinrui*) which does not respect the same values as the older generation. Indeed, beauty shop dressers sometimes strongly express their criticism of the 'new generation' to which their brides-*cum*-customers belong. Like when one dresser called 'the students of today . . . worse than the *yakuza* (the Japanese mafia)'. Another told her counterparts that when she was riding the train she was sometimes shocked to hear a 'girl's voice' spouting language which would be more natural coming from a mouth of a boy. Thus, the dressers knew that trying to convince this young generation of brides to wear the furisode would be fighting a loosing battle.

The *ō-sensei* provided an explanation for the decline of *furisode* which is very interesting from our 'production' point of view. While the beauty shop owner agreed that the bride's own preferences and considerations or wishes (*kibō*) come into play here, in her opinion the main reason for its decline is to be found in the increasing showiness (*hanayaka*) of the wedding production (*enshutsu*) which seems to almost demand a Western wedding dress instead of a kimono. 'In a *furisode* the bride can only walk straight and sit', Sakamoto Sachiko told me. 'In a dress she can do many things, and it is possible to put on a production.' What the *ō-sensei* was referring to here were the Western mini-dramas which the wedding parlour endeavours to sell its customers. This last remark not only bolsters the 'production' argument pursued herein, but also manifests once again the clear and deliberate distinction between Japanese and Western. In Western dress the bride seems to be much more active and can move around – at least enough to light some candles at the special candle service. However, in Japanese costumes her passive role is accentuated. This distinction between passive Japaneseness and active Westernness can be seen as another example of the 'self-Orientalization' (Miller 1982:209–11) or 'self-Japanization' in which the wedding industry is involved.

Returning to the bridal *furisode*, one reason brides give for omitting it is that it is too difficult and tiring (*shindoi*) to wear it and the *uchikake*, both of which are very tight and heavy. The older generation merely say that 'young girls are no longer used to kimono and do not, in general, know how to endure' (*gaman dekinai*).

But this rationalization seems to cover a quite different reason. As young women are marrying later than in the past, some of them see it as inappropriate to wear *furisode* at their age. As one bride, a school teacher, put it: 'I did not wear *furisode*, not only because it is wearying and heavy after the *uchikake*, but even more so for age reasons (*nen rei teki-ni*). *Furisode* has the image of a 20–year-old (*hatachi*), of the coming of age ceremony. I am already 26, and I felt it was not proper for me any more'.

Age has always been important in Japanese tradition, there is an appropriate age for almost every occasion in a person's life history. A girl is usually presented to the deities of the local shrine when she is 30 days old. She is dressed in her first kimono at the age of three. She probably wears her first *furisode* at age 20 at the 'coming-of-age ceremony' (*seijin shiki*) celebrated in every city and town on January 15th for young men and women who have reached this age.[3]

Finally, a few years after the coming of age, girls reach *tekireiki*, literally 'the right age', but meaning marriageable age.[4] The school teacher was not the only 'old' bride who felt she would look ridiculous in the *furisode*, and younger brides decided to discard it as they already had pictures of themselves in *furisode* from their coming-of-age ceremony.

In sum, it seems that whereas the *uchikake* is taken for granted as bridal wear, when it comes to more aesthetic and practical decisions, an additional Western outfit has replaced the *furisode*. Reaffirming the categorized role of the two different attires, one of the brides who chose not to wear the *furisode* said: 'I don't like any kimono but the *uchikake* is more bridal wear while *furisode* is merely kimono.'

The bridal fair as an exhibition of bride's attire

After the bride has decided on the kinds of outfits she will wear on her wedding day, she comes to the wedding parlour to choose the specific attire for each one. Although she may do this on any day of the week, or during weekends when she is not working, most wedding outfits are chosen at the grand events called bridal fairs. These fairs, are, in fact, the first step in what I term the 'production process' of the bridal appearance. Although the bride is allegedly the 'star' of the bridal fair as well as of the wedding, in both cases she is really the 'object' being 'manufactured' by the wedding producers.

Bridal fairs take place in wedding parlours and hotels. In Cobella, they constitute an important promotion device as well as a convenient way to centralize bridal preparations. The bridal fair is usually divided into two parts: a display of bridal items and a theatrical production which includes a fashion show. The display of bridal items – from wedding costumes to furniture – is located on the parlour's lower floors. Aside from presenting the latest in Western and Japanese fashions, the show presents the mini-dramas available for the reception, and takes place in one of the reception rooms on the top floor.

Both the display and the show are obviously aimed at the bride as the main consumer of the products being offered, whether fashions or other bridal items. For example, the grooms' outfits are tucked away in a relatively narrow corner near the display of outfits for wedding guests (*tomesode*), while the brides' Japanese and Western clothing take up most of the lobby. This is not surprising if we bear in mind that the rental of bridal costumes is at least ten times higher than that of the groom's outfits, and that the bride's outfits constitute a considerable part of the general wedding costs.

A prospective bride never attends the bridal fair on her own, but is usually accompanied by her future husband, her mother, or both her parents, and sometimes (on Sundays, when the fair becomes more of a leisure activity), by the groom's mother or both his parents. Another item that is never missing at the fair is the camera. The bride is photographed as she tries on wedding dresses, and the pictures are usually developed on the same day so they can be used as an aid for choosing outfits which will look good through the lens of the camera.

The bridal fair held at the Kobe Princess Palace in September 1990, which also celebrated the tenth anniversary of the hall's inauguration, will illuminate the way a bride being married there is treated. For this event, it was decided to construct a large stage at one side of the lobby, with wedding dresses on display all around it (all the way to the coffee shop). In comparison with previous fairs, it was quite apparent that the Western wedding dresses received much more space and attention than the *uchikake* and *furisode*, which did, however, occupy a considerable space on the opposite side of the lobby, which visitors had to pass as they made their way up from the ground floor. Thus, according to the wedding hall's plan, Japanese wear was to be chosen first.

Japanese attire

Before deciding on her Western wedding dress, the wedding parlour management advises the bride to choose her Japanese attire. Whereas she tries on the wedding dress, Japanese wear cannot be fully worn since it takes too much time and effort to do this. So in order to create the outline of the *uchikake*, the prospective bride is invited to have a cone-shaped pillow tied to her back, which resembles the curve created by the obi under the outer coat. This gives her a very general impression as the *uchikake* is not tied, but just put over her body. However, this is sufficient since *uchikake*, like kimono in general, does not have to fit the body, on the contrary, the body is adapted and 'corrected' to fit the attire. The main considerations in choosing the *uchikake* are colour, pattern and grade.

Uchikake are offered at various prices (or grades). After the bride and her mother have decided on the amount to be spent, they move on to choose the colour. Although all brides wear white *uchikake* for the ceremony, they have recently begun to wear a coloured *uchikake* for the studio photograph, and often for their dramatic entrance to the reception hall (*nyūjō*).[5] Although the coloured *uchikake* used to be red, which is still the most popular colour, green, black and silver have been promoted recently. Since the bride is the one who ultimately chooses, 'gaudy' (*hade*) and 'luxurious' (*gōka*) colours and designs are shown in order to appeal to her. As for the bride's mother, she might find in the 'luxurious' *uchikake* yet another way of displaying her family's affluence to the wedding guests.

Purple, blue and green are popular colours for the *furisode*. Although pink is a popular choice for coming-of-age *furisode*, it is not used for bridal *furisode*, or *uchikake*, being considered too childish for a bride. The choice of colours in the cases of both the second *uchikake* and the *furisode* may disclose something about the way 'tradition' is dealt with and manipulated. For it is obvious that considerations foreign to tradition such as the desire of the industry to satisfy its young clientele play a role in the colours offered. In this regard, the popularity of purple is particularly interesting because traditionally, purple and violet were avoided by brides and grooms since they fade soonest and may bring about a divorce (Bishop 1900:254).

The *uchikake* and *furisode* background colours are adorned with bright patterns in a variety of colours. Whereas the *furisode* is usually decorated with flowers or geometrical patterns, the *uchikake* has more 'traditional style' designs. These are patterns considered good or lucky omens (*kishō, zuisshō*), for example, pine trees, plums or cranes, which are usually connected to longevity or other positive aspects of life. The crane has traditionally been considered a sign of long life, victory in battle and good tidings, so it is often used for happy occasions such as weddings and births. The crane is sometimes combined with a pine-bamboo-plum (*shōchikubai*) pattern (Niwa 1990:80) for the engage-ment (*yuinō*) presents, as this combination represents happiness (Hendry 1981:159). Thus, not only is the traditional-Japanese trait of the *uchikake* manifested, but also its 'eternal' bond with Japanese weddings.

Western attire

In contrast with Japanese attire, Western wedding and party gowns are tried on, and the bride's hair is set to create a full Western appearance before a final choice is made. The dresses on display are extremely elaborate, of materials like velvet and taffeta, often trimmed with lace or other decorations. The party dresses are also offered in elegant colours like dark green, purple, dark red and glamorous gold. The elaborate style is further exaggerated by the huge crinolines generally worn under the skirts. However, the 'luxurious' (or 'gorgeous' – a popular term at the Kobe Princess Palace) character of the dresses is not found only in their colours or fabrics. What marks the special quality of these dresses is the crucial distinction between them and everyday wear.

It seems that this unique quality of the wedding dress is searched for not only by Japanese brides and their mothers but also by brides in other parts of the world. Charsley (1991:66), who studied the contemporary Scottish wedding industry, summarizes the bride's attitude towards the wedding dress:

> A wedding dress is therefore not simply a dress in which a woman
> is married; it is a dress uniquely associated with her as a bride on

that occasion, a dress which is a key part of the way in which she embodies the idea of a bride.[6]

Interestingly, the white wedding gown plays a similar role in other parts of Asia. As a manager of wedding services in the Republic of Korea explained the choice of a wedding dress and a veil as bridal attire: 'This is how they want to see themselves; its a one opportunity in a lifetime to wear a wedding dress' (Kendall 1994:177). In Korea, like in Japan, brides who wear a wedding dress and a veil feel (or are made to feel) that in this they 'participate in a romantic image of nascent womanhood purveyed through the media, as in the West' (Kendall 1994:177).

Aside from making every effort to ensure that the wedding dresses on offer are 'gorgeous' and 'romantic' enough to suit a bride, the wedding parlour must keep in touch with the very latest in fashion as dresses considered extremely popular in one year may lose all their charm in the next. This was the case with a particular party dress – black velvet with yellow sunflowers – which was deemed quite elegant in 1989 but which one bride's mother at the 1990 fair criticized as too casual, 'like everyday wear', even though it fit her better than any other dress. Thus, even though the wedding dress is 'invented' from different 'materials' than the Japanese attire, it too has to be as different as possible from everyday attire.

What then, are the materials from which the dresses are invented? It is clear that they are from other periods and other worlds, and that the 'other world' is always the 'West'. But this is an abstract West, as it is seen through Japanese eyes (or the eyes of wedding producers and their customers). It is also important to note that these dresses are said to be fabricated of materials which will 'make dreams come true', will ensure that she is not only a 'Japanese bride' but also a 'Western' princess. The Japanese girl and woman-to-be is supposed to be satisfied with this 'dream come true', as it will probably be her first and last chance to appear in such 'daring' clothing.

The main stage: commercial 'fight' over the bride

While the selection of Japanese attire involves mainly the bride and her mother, choosing the Western dress involves other family members as well as the groom. After selecting one of the dozen dresses on display around the main stage at the 1990 bridal fair, the bride was invited to put it on in the provisional changing room before ascending to the stage, where only brides and their attendants are allowed, while her family looked on and took photographs of her from below. (Even the sales ladies, who accompany the brides throughout, are restricted from the stage.) The stage is symbolically separated from the rest of the lobby by a red carpet which leads the brides to it, and by the fact that all shoes, except the bridal shoes supplied by the wedding parlour, must be removed before going up to it.

However, the stage is not merely the bride's. It is also a live display of the competition among companies offering bridal accessories which takes place literally over the bride's body. Since most bridal accessories are not included in the 'bridal package', and require extra payment, the competition here is much tougher than it is in, for example, services like catering which are provided by one company at each wedding parlour.

Elaborate as it may be, the wedding dress can not be worn without accessories. The white dress must be adorned with a tiara, a necklace (and matching earrings) as well as a veil. And the coloured party dress also requires some type of hair adornment as well as necklace and earrings. Finally, the Western bridal appearance is considered incomplete without a bouquet of (in the majority of the cases) artificial flowers. Among all the costumes and accessories only the bouquet (*buke*) is purchased instead of rented, and may be taken home after the wedding. It is usually the last item chosen, and in most cases is selected to suit both 'Western-style' dresses.

The competition between the companies taking part in the bridal fair is sometimes quite stormy. The several dress companies who participate must compete with each other. Even Mikimoto, the only accessory company to participate, has to compete with the less expensive accessories offered by the clothing department and the Cinderella Beauty Shop. This competition goes on without the customer being aware of it. A recurrent scene at the 1990 fair struck me as providing a vivid demonstration of this 'invisible' competition.

Two different bouquet companies participated at the fair, each of them represented by one female employee. After a bride had decided on her dresses and accessories, the woman who was more alert or happened to be free at that moment would approach the girl and offer her what she considered a suitable bouquet. While the bride and her dresser were deciding on that bouquet's suitability to her general appearance, the woman from the competing company would be waiting for her opportunity 'to attack' the bride. At the first slight hesitation of the bride, the second woman[7] would immediately proffer her

116

'merchandise'. This process repeated itself until the bride and her attendant made a final decision. Although this competition was quite visible to me as an informed observer, the main 'object' of the competition – the bride – did not seem aware of the existence of two competing companies. Since they pay the wedding parlour for everything, they do not usually realize that competing companies are involved in their choices.[8]

Producing the bride's body for the great day

The bridal fair is only the starting point in the 'bridal production' preparation process. The bride is urged by the wedding parlour to come in to the beauty shop a month before her wedding, to consult on wedding-day preparations, have wig fittings and also, perhaps, to sign up for its 'Bridal Beauty Plan'. This plan includes a month of work on her face, hair and body in preparation for her wedding day. The cost of these extra cosmetic and hair treatments is paid directly to the beauty shop, and this entitles her to a free paraffin mask treatment two days after her face and neck have been shaved, and two days before the great day, which the pamphlet issued by the beauty shop claims will make the young lady (ojōsama) more beautiful for the 'once-in-a-life-time ceremonial [formal] day (hare no hi) for which she has always been waiting.'

Preparing the bride's body, especially her face, for the wedding, is not a new practice. Reports of rural home weddings describe the shaving of the bride's face and neck to prepare her for the heavy make up. Nevertheless, these preparations were usually accomplished on the day of the wedding or the night before. Thus, the drawn-out cosmetic and aesthetic treatment offered to today's prospective brides seems to result more from modern attitudes towards women's beauty, than to represent continuity with past practices. The general Western (which is always parallel to 'modern') character of such kinds of 'bridal aesthetic' plans lends support to this conjecture.

'Bridal aesthetic' plans are offered by beauty salons as well as wedding parlour beauty shops. Thus, a large chain called TBC (Tokyo Beauty Salon) offers 'Bridal Aesthetic' treatments in its 139 shops throughout Japan. The advertisements[9] for these treatments convey the same message as that utilized in clothing promotion, i.e.: 'Get ready for your once-in-a-lifetime day.'

Since most of these beauty salons aim at producing the modern Western image, the treatments they offer are given Western names, such

as '*hando kea kōsu*' (hand care course) and '*hea resu*' (hair less).
Moreover, they are strongly connected with the Western parts of the
wedding ceremony. Thus, the advertisements promise to take care of
'each finger of the bride's hands – which 'hold the bouquet, light the
candle in the candle service, and exchange rings in the wedding climax
(*kuraimakusu*)'. They also guarantee to make these bridal hands –
which 'attracts the attention of all the participants' – 'smooth'
(*nameraka*) and 'fresh-looking (*mizumizushii*)'.

The female body plays a very important role in Bridal Aesthetic
Plans. Beauty salons offer to prepare the bride's body not only for the
wedding day, but also for 'him' (*kare*). As one salon puts it in its
promotional literature: 'Marriage is to say goodbye (*sayonara*) to the
up-to-now you, and to begin a second life with him.'[10]

In today's Japan young working women between the ages of eighteen
and the late twenties form a vary large and lucrative sector of the
consumer market. These girls – referred to by the catchy phrase 'Yenjoy
girls' (Moeran 1989a:23) – are constantly urged to spend what they
earn on entertainment, clothing and on their bodies. The 'joyful' yenjoy
period comes to a close when the 'office lady' turns into a 'wife'
(*okusan*) and mother. Thus, it is no wonder that a whole range of
'aesthetic' and 'feminine' industries do their outmost to extract as
much as possible from what they present as the 'peak' of the girl's life,
but which is also usually the last splurging episode of her life.

The comprehensive bodily treatment which will prepare the bride's
hands, hair and face for the roles she has to fulfil in her wedding, also
characterizes the wedding parlour's attitude. Whether the part the bride
has to perform is Western or Japanese, the concept is that of
production. The beauty shop not only prepares the bride for her
wedding, it also – and even more so – produces a 'perfect bride', one
who will be bodily prepared for her wedding day acting role.

Manufacturing the bride's face: the 'final touch'

The wedding day is a long and arduous one for the bride. She must
arrive at the wedding parlour two-and-a-half hours before the ceremony
is scheduled. Entering directly into the beauty shop, which she knows
well from her previous visits for advice and treatment, she is led to the
Japanese-style room she has probably never seen before, the room for
brides on their wedding day. This will be her first and last 'station'
during the five or so hours ahead of her. Here, she hands herself over to
the expert dressers who will take care of her throughout the day. The

initial preparations for the elaborate *uchikake* appearance are the most time-consuming and exacting of all the make-up and costume changes she will undergo in her journey from traditional-Japanese to Western bride.

After a brief exchange of greetings (*aisatsu*) between the dresser and the 'young lady' (*ojōsan*, as the bride is referred to throughout the day),[11] the make-up process begins. Although there may be other brides in different stages of preparation sharing the same room, they do not exchange greetings or converse among themselves.

Donning the white mask

Separated from her familiar Western clothes, the bride – already in white kimono underwear (*hadajuban*) and white Japanese socks (*tabi*) – sits demurely in front of one of the mirrors to watch herself as she is transformed into a 'Japanese bride'. The make-up process which takes more than an hour, includes the painting of face, neck, arms and hands.[12] Although the bride's make-up (at least that of upper class brides) was white in the past (Tamura 1904:47), the old-style white powder known as *oshiroi* has been replaced by modern style make-up. Several companies specialize in bridal make-up which (according to their advertising materials) supply the 'colour of Japanese ceremony' (*nihon no gishiki no iro*).

This make-up is accomplished in several stages, including painting, brushing and powdering the face with a special powder to keep the paint from fading in the event of sweating or crying. Although the colour of the face is much whiter and the make-up considerably heavier than Western make-up, veteran dressers say that it is not as white as it used to be. One of the reasons given for this is that it is a response to the new generation's preferences – another implicit criticism of the new generation (*shin jinrui*) for not appreciating the 'real' Japanese beauty which is equated with white skin. In this vein, beauty shop workers also complained among themselves of the difficulties presented by brides with darker skins.[13]

The dresser's expertise is tested by her ability to form the desirable bridal image by a skilful play with make-up. She uses mainly white and red (and some black). Red is used near the bride's eyes and ears to give the impression of bashfulness (*hazukashii kanji*) through the illusion of blushing. The whiter liquid paint used to paint the front of the bride's neck and her nape is used not only to make the face more distinct, but, even more so, to give it a feeling of naivety (*uiuishiisa*) and freshness (*shinsen*).

After painting a very thin black line over the bride's eyes and attaching artificial eyelashes comes the most delicate task: painting the mouth, which completes the make-up process. The mouth, which is considered to be the *pointo* (focal point) of the bride's face, is painted a deep red colour, but only over part of the lips, the rest of which have been covered in white. This creates a smaller mouth in a shape of a 'mountain' (*yama*).[14]

The overall aim of bridal make-up is to create a face that is completely unrecognizable. One of the points to be taken seriously during the make-up process is that none of the 'real' face (or skin) should be revealed. Just as Liza Dalby's geisha 'mother' (*okasan*) found it disturbing to have those 'untouched spots' on either side of her 'foreign' nose when she made her up (Dalby 1983:131–133), the dresser fights against any stubborn spot on the bride's face. One of the most serious flaws in the make-up work is for a bride to find even the tiniest spot of 'her own face' (*jibun no kao*) emerging underneath the white mask.

It seems that this heavy make-up plays a crucial role in allowing the bride to become detached from herself as a person, and to become 'the bride' as a symbol. The most common reaction of brides as the make-up process reaches its final steps is the feeling that they look different from usual. Many of them comment that they look 'like a completely different person'. Some merely laugh or giggle with surprise; others react by associating their different look with that of a Kabuki actor, for example, as one bride referred to her image in the mirror.

The next complicated stage of completing the facial 'mask' is arrangement of the traditional Japanese wig and its traditional decorations (*kanzashi*).[15] When added, these objects, also completely detached from everyday life, help create the desired image of the 'Japanese Bride'.

Completing the 'package'

The last stage in the production of the 'traditional bridal appearance' consists of dressing the bride in the *uchikake*. The process (*kitsuke*), like any kimono dressing, requires two dressers: the expert who made up the bride in the front (*mae*) position, and an assistant who helps in the less important back (*ura*) position and who makes all the preparations for the actual dressing. The donning of the *uchikake* follows the basic rules of kimono dressing. However, since bride-making (*hanayome o tsukuru*)[16] is considered the highest form of kimono dressing, more attention is given to the smallest details and an air of extreme seriousness adds another layer of 'traditionality' and formality.

The first stage in any modern kimono dressing is 'correcting' the woman's body by padding it to achieve the kimono figure. The same padding to 'correct' such flaws as too large breasts or uneven shoulders is carried out in dressing brides. However, in the case of brides, the 'correcting'(*hosei*) materials have been commercialized to include an expensive set of pads and bandages.[17] An under-robe (*nagajuban*) in the recurrent colours – red over white – is tightly wrapped under the white kimono and over the 'correction'. This set of under-robes and kimono with white obi tied in a special knot for brides is not seen as it is covered by the *uchikake*.

The additional accessories (all in white) necessary to complete the 'traditional bridal appearance', include a fan which is used for the studio photograph, and an empty purse, tucked into the bride's kimono. Their role seems to refer symbolically to objects which brides in the past carried on their journey to the place where the ceremony was held.[18] The last item to be attached – either the *tsunokakushi* (horn cover) or *watabōshi* head covering (see Chapter Six) – has a symbolic[19] as well as an aesthetic role.

The final 'packing'

The bride is now ready for her ultimate 'bridal appearance' (in which she will be photographed), but the long *uchikake* worn over the white kimono creates a practical obstacle. While a trailing garment may have been suitable for the living space of the traditional (mainly rich) Japanese home – where much of the everyday activity was conducted close to the floor, where people knelt not sat (on chairs) to accomplish tasks, and where the tatami mat floors were clean enough to permit trailing garments – today such garments are not appropriate for the modern-style wedding parlour.[20] For the bride is about to climb staircases on her way to the photo studio and reception hall, and the carpets are not clean enough to ensure that the expensive rented attire remains unsoiled. Moreover, as inexperienced kimono wearers, brides find it difficult enough to walk in a folded kimono let alone in a full flowing one. Finally, there are considerations of efficiency and timing which make up to a dozen brides mincing their way around the parlour impossible. Thus, the bride is 'packed up', as the term defining the act, *karage*, literally means, in a set of red and white elastic bands which will be untied for the studio photographs and tied up again for the reception.

Although she is now completely ready to be exposed to the wedding guests, the bride still has to go through a last-minute lesson in kimono manners in general and in wearing the kimono as a bride. Kimono wearing requires a special way of walking, with the toes always turned inwards and the *zōri* (Japanese sandals) dragged along the ground rather than lifted.[21] The bride is also instructed to walk very slowly, not only because of the weight of wig and costume, but also in order to allow herself to be seen and photographed to her best advantage as she proceeds.[22] The dresser also instructs the bride on how to hold her hands and her fan and reminds her to keep her chin lowered to keep the heavy wig from falling off. Finally, she is instructed to move only when told, and no more than necessary to accomplish the act in question.

The bride as passive object

This passive characteristic of the bridal role is embodied in the bridal costume itself. When one bride complained that she could not raise her hands because the *uchikake* was so tight, her dresser replied with a smile: 'You are not supposed to do your exercises in it. You only have to raise your hands high enough to do the *san-san-ku-do* (sake exchange in the Shinto ceremony).'

This passive and object-like role seems to be generally accepted by the brides themselves, who tend to become like automatons from the moment the make-up process begins. One bride waiting to be taken upstairs got something in her eye and was told by the dressers to try to remove it herself because they had failed to do so, she asked 'Is that OK?' (for me to treat my own eye?). I have observed many similar situations that illustrate the brides' detachment from themselves. Afraid to spoil the 'creation' produced by the dresser they are willing to accept – even ask for – specific instructions on minute points. Thus another bride, who had a thirty-minute wait in the brides' room before going upstairs, suddenly looked at her empty (painted) hands, as she had not yet been given her fan, and asked what was she supposed to do with them. This bride looked at her own hands as if they did not really belong to her and asked the question in a way that revealed not only her detachment from the 'creation' she had been made into through the production process, but also clear readiness to submit herself to the bridal role.

The bride at her wedding

'Mild jollity flows around the stiff, doll-like figure of the bride without touching her, for she must sit expressionless and motionless.' So wrote Beardsley, Hall and Ward (p.326) of a bride at a village wedding. We find that the bride's demeanour at today's wedding parlour has changed very little.[23] She sits with the groom and the *nakōdo* couple, separated from the wedding guests. However, while the two men may take a bite of the food now and then (the female *nakōdo* also eats very little and does not speak), the bride strictly refrains from eating or speaking. As instructed by her dresser, she sits quietly and unsmilingly, her eyes downcast. For she must exhibit the 'self discipline' and endurance (*gaman*) expected from Japanese women in general.

> Self discipline keeps the emotional pitch low even in the most critical moments of life. Throughout her wedding day, though it be her greatest occasion, the bride is expected to look neither joyous nor sad but, instead, aloof and unmoved.
>
> (Beardsley *et al.* 1959:67)

Although a certain amount of physical endurance is expected of any woman, especially an inexperienced girl, who wears kimono, there is another kind of endurance required of the bride. Like the 'home bride', the wedding parlour bride is expected to display self-discipline and hide her emotions. Brides do not usually cry until a very late stage of the reception, when crying is encouraged by the wedding producers because it can no longer do too much harm to their appearances. There are, however, some rare instances in which brides have not been able to restrain their emotions under the tension. This was the case with a pregnant bride, who seemed so tense that both her mother and sister spent time with her in the brides' room trying to cheer her up by repeating how 'charming' (*kawaii*) she looked. This bride – not unlike other brides – did not say much while she was being made up. However, as she was being led to her family waiting room, she suddenly burst into tears and was unable to stop sobbing for several minutes. Her mother manifested the self-discipline she expected her daughter to have. 'Kiko, Kiko', she repeated her daughter's name in a severe voice, 'Pull yourself together.' Then she left the waiting room to greet wedding guests in the lobby. The dresser, worried about the bride's make-up and artificial eyelashes, rushed downstairs to bring her another small tissue to dry her tears.

The bride does not sit on her raised seat at the reception for much of the festivities, spending a considerable part of her own wedding either in the costume changing (*ironaoshi*) room or the photo studio. Indeed, she usually spends more time out of the reception room than in it. This aspect of the wedding production frequently results in a feeling of 'busyness'. As one bride put it: 'Instead of hearing the [wedding guests'] speeches I had to leave, so my feeling was more of hustling or being busy (*awatadashisa*) than of palpitation (*doki-doki*).'

The 'Western-style' bride vs the 'traditional-Japanese' bride

Although there seems to be some continuity in the bride's role from earlier home weddings to the contemporary commercial wedding, in the modern wedding the bride must play two roles: she is not only 'The Japanese Bride', but also a 'Western Bride'. In other words, just as she is 'packed' into the *uchikake*, she is also 'packaged' into her Western appearance.

The bride arrives at the wedding parlour in her everyday Western clothes (*yōfuku*), from which she is soon to be detached when turned into a 'Japanese bride'. Then, once she has completed the Japanese role assigned for her by the wedding producers, she returns to Western outfit, albeit one quite different from her everyday Western clothing. None the less, elaborate as it may be, her Western gown is much more comfortable than the confining kimono. Not only is it much lighter and more comfortable than the heavy *uchikake* and wig, but there is a distinct difference in her mental feeling. Having removed the *uchikake*, wig and 'white mask', she has at least partially returned to her real self. Although the Western appearance requires heavy make-up, this 'mask' is not as unfamiliar to most Japanese girls[24] as the traditional-Japanese make-up.

One of the characteristics of the 'Japanese bride' is that she feels 'different' or even 'unrecognizable' to herself. Many brides report feeling like 'a completely different person'. They also speak of wedding guests, mainly children, who do not recognize them in their 'Japanese bridal appearance'. On the other hand, in Western attire, especially in the coloured dress with the looser hair style that goes with it (instead of the chignon required by the white gown) they look much more like themselves. As one bride told me: 'The first time that my face could shine with pride was after I changed to the blue party dress. My feeling also became much lighter and more cheerful.'

Another attribute of the Western appearance is a certain air of 'Western individuality'. Although the term used, '*kosei-teki*' is translated as 'individuality', it has other interesting connotations in Japan, especially in connection with femininity and women as elitist cosmopolitan consumers. Wedding-parlour owners attempt to inflate the connection between 'Westernness' and 'individuality', in order to create the impression that the Western appearance allows more freedom of choice than the Japanese one. Although those who 'produce' the bride create her Western appearance, they try to give her some feeling of participation when time permits, she is allowed to choose the shade of lipstick used and even allowed to apply it.

It seems, then, that the wedding producers are actively involved in creating the distinction between Western and Japanese. One of the fascinating points about this process is that, at the same time that the Western is presented as more familiar, the traditional-Japanese is exoticized and thus becomes more detached.

The packaged bride: further layers of packaging

The bride is 'packaged' not only by the elaborate layers of her *uchikake* but also by the more general and symbolic modes of 'packaging' and 'repackaging' delineated in advertising materials, in the generally accepted images of Japanese brides and women, in concepts of fashion and aesthetics, in colours and in language.

Packaging in colours: 'a touch of scarlet' on a 'pure' white

One of the most obvious symbolic forms of 'packaging' is seen in colours used. Among the colours which create the total bridal appearance, two seem to be of particular significance: white and red. The first costume to be worn by the bride is usually a white *uchikake* considered *de rigueur* for the Shinto wedding ceremony. There are several interpretations of the white colour worn by the bride. It is sometimes seen as representing purity, in the same manner that the white wedding gown of the West does. Aside from this Western influence, however, in Japan white traditionally refers to the white in which babies and the dead are dressed, symbolic of the *tabula rasa* which starts a new period in life (or death; Hendry 1981:170). The fact that white has a similar meaning at weddings and funerals was also implied by rites used for the departure of the bride which were performed at home weddings, such as breaking the bride's tea cup and lighting a bonfire. The meaning attached to this symbolism is that the bride is dead to her own household; from now on she lives only for her husband.

Although the interpretations or references to white which I heard from brides at the Kobe Princess Palace were not directly connected to death, the notion of white as *tabula rasa* or non-colour was expressed. Thus, one bride said that for her, wearing the white *uchikake* (called *shiromuku*), represented the move to her husband's house; dressed in white she could be 'dyed' (*somaru*) into his house. Many other brides felt that being dressed in a white *uchikake* gave them the feeling of getting married, of entering another house, and of being and yet becoming a different person. As one of them put it: 'I had a feeling of being a different self from what I was until now.'

Similar to the red colour of the bride's lips on the white mask is a woman in a crowd of men, adding a touch of beauty. 'A touch of scarlet' (*kō itten*) is the phrase used to denote a woman in a group of men (Cherry 1987:26–27). Red is 'pretty', an attribute females are supposed to seek. Red also signals happy occasions. Thus it has become a popular colour for the second *uchikake*. In addition, Japanese women of the past used to wear red undergarments beneath the kimono, a glimpse of which men considered quite erotic. Red was also thought to ward off menstrual pain and keep the female reproductive system running smoothly. Although white undergarments are usually used today, a touch of that red has been left in the bride's under-robe, which is patterned in red over a white background. The touch of red over the 'pure' white background is a symbol of beauty. As one of the advertisements which uses this colour effect explains: 'A splendid day, looking beautiful' (*yokihi, utsukushiku*).[25]

'Packaging' in images: the bride as a doll

The Japanese bride is not only wrapped in the appropriate colours, but is also made up to fit the complementary images of brides (and women) in Japanese society. Needless to say, the wedding industry perpetuates those images.

'How beautiful, like a [Ms.] doll' (*kirei ne, ningyō-san mitai*) is the greatest compliment that can be given to a Japanese bride at the wedding parlour. In many ways this compliment, although attributed to the bride, is praise for the dresser who created her.[26] The bride as a doll is a very common image in the literature on Japanese brides of different periods. Not only was there the 'doll-like' of Beardsley *et al.* (1959:326), but Norbeck (1954:181) also likens the 'short measured steps' of a village bride of about the same period to an 'animated doll'. In her letters, Bird, a nineteenth-century female visitor to Japan, described the make-up and dressing of a bride which she saw by chance. Of the final result, she wrote: 'She looked as if a very unmeaning looking wooden doll had been dressed up with the exquisite of good taste, harmony, and quietness which characterize the dress of Japanese women (Bird 1984 (1880):206–207).

It is not only foreign visitors and anthropologists who view the Japanese bride as a doll. The Japanese themselves see her as such. Indeed, the image of a (confined) doll is found in other spheres of life relating to Japanese girls and women. The term 'daughter in a box' (*hako-iri musume*) refers to a sheltered maiden who is protected by her family from the outside world. Since the Japanese use wooden or glass boxes to protect pottery, tea bowls and, precious dolls, they see a parallel between caring for these treasured possessions and for their daughters. Some view the notion in a negative way, as over-protection of a painfully shy girl who can do nothing but sit prettily within the confines of her box-like Japanese home (Sievers 1983:34). However, most middle-class Japanese consider this term as a compliment for loving protection.[27] Whether this Japanese attitude towards girls is a result of 'reverse Orientalism' (Miller 1982:209–211) or 'self-exoticism', or an 'authentic' Japanese attitude has become hard to tell.

Another connecting line between daughters and dolls is found in the 3 March Girls' Day. Although it was formally decided in 1948 to consolidate Boys' Day and Girls' Day into a single national holiday – 'Children Day' – to be held on 5 May (previously Boys' Day), Japanese families still celebrate the two holidays separately. Girls' Day is commonly known as *hinna matsuri* or 'Doll Festival'. About a week before the festival a display of miniature dolls is set up in the house to be admired by everybody. This set includes the imperial couple on top, with court ladies, musicians and warriors on the descending steps along with miniature furniture and a bridal trousseau. When finances permit, the dolls are dressed in ancient brocade kimono. (Such sets range from ¥800,000 to ¥1,000,000.) Very fine dolls are usually stored in glass cases like the '*daughter in a box*' whom they honour. The parallel between girls and miniature dolls goes even further: it is common belief that the longer the dolls remain out after 3 March, the longer it will take the daughter of the house to find a husband.

Japanese girls and young women are fond of dolls. They decorate their rooms and their small cars (*Minica*) with cute (*kawaii*) dolls.[28] Like their dolls, Japanese girls strive to achieve 'cutie' (*kawaiko-chan*) image. *Kawaiko-chan* is only one of the terms which describe girls who pretend to be dumb and act childishly (*burikko* or 'pretending kid' is another term; Cherry 1987:39). In sharp contrast to the erotic feminine image promoted by Western stars like Madonna, the pop idols of Japanese females are childish, and always 'cute'.[29] Even Barbie dolls did not sell well in Japan until toy makers re-designed them to portray a childish cute naive image. While American girls pretend to be women (like their Barbies) in order to attract boyfriends, Japanese women pretend to be childish and cute, like their dolls. This image is widely utilized in the wedding industry's promotional materials, and in the manner in which it creates brides. Thus, one Shōchikuden wedding parlour uses a girlish first-person voice throughout its catalogue, and dressers in the beauty shop use make-up in shades of white and red to create a 'fresh' (*shinsen*) 'naive' (*uiuishii*) 'doll-like' bride.

Commercial packaging: images and language in wedding advertising

The decorative brochure entitled 'Wedding Sketch' (in English), which every prospective couple receives at the Kobe Princess Palace, has the bride as its main character. An illustration showing a large picture of a (Western-style) bride, with a very small groom figure at the corner of the page, is accompanied by the following text: 'The bridal appearance of which I have always dreamt. I wish to get married [or 'be a bride'] in the most wonderful me' (*ichiban sutekina watashi de totsugitai*). The text goes on to describe the bridal costumes 'for which every girl yearns (*josei nara dare mo ga akogareru hanayome ishō*)'. The emphasis on this 'natural' longing (*akogare*) for wearing particular costumes is typical not only of wedding advertisements but also of advertisements for kimono to be worn at the coming-of-age-ceremony, and for kimono dressing in general. This advertising strategy can be summarized as telling girls that, as girls, they should 'naturally' long to wear a kimono, as well as that their highest wish should be to don bridal attire.

The catalogue goes on to promise the bride that the Kobe Princess Palace will provide her with outfits, both Japanese and Western, which will 'paint' (*irodoru*) her beautifully. In other words, it promises the bride two packages: traditional-Japanese and Western.

Placing the bride in the centre is not unique to the Kobe Princess Palace or to wedding parlours in general. It is one of the main advertising techniques for all weddings, no matter where they are held. An elegant brochure from a shrine which became a comprehensive wedding parlour opens with a double-page picture of a traditional Japanese bride in *uchikake* and *tsunokakushi* (head covering) whose caption reads: 'I [am], becoming a bride (*watashi, yukimasu*).' It is of interest that the character for bride (*yome*) is accompanied by a special phonetic reading invented for that text (*yukimasu*). This 'play' with language (called *ateji*) is an example of the way in which symbolism is used in the language of wedding advertising.

The bride is also the main 'object' of wedding advertisements in the mass media. Advertisements at train stations and on trains often show pictures of brides, either in Japanese or Western wear (in the latter case, a foreign model is often used). Viewing girls as the main 'consumers' of weddings also reveals itself in women's magazines, all of which have many wedding advertisements. In these magazines brides are always presented in their wedding costumes, but without their grooms. Like the brochure mentioned above, the short text accompanying the pictures repeats the 'longing' (*akogare*) a Japanese girl should 'naturally' have for donning her bridal costumes.

This emphasis on The Bride is meant to confer more importance on the bride than on other participants in the wedding. This, of course encourages the bride to be a consumer of more wedding-related goods and services. Since unmarried young women are the best consumers in modern Japan, they are re-created as consumers at the same time as they are objectified and 'packaged' by the producers of these goods and services.

The bride as a flower

'Flower Bride' (*hana*-flower, *yome*-bride) is the term used for the bride at the wedding parlour and in the wedding industry in general. Flowery language is used to describe Japanese women beginning when they are still 'buds' (*tsubomi*), a synonym for virgins (Cherry 1987:35). Many girls' names contain floral characters, such as *Hanako* (flower child), although boys are often named by their birth order. Just as a woman is viewed as adding a 'touch of scarlet' (*kō itten*), like a red flower, to a crowd of men, so a man seated between two women is said to have 'flowers in both hands' (*ryōte ni hana*). This same concept of women as decoration prevails in the male-dominated work place, where fresh young 'office ladies' (OL) are called *shokuba no hana* or 'office flowers'. However, unlike the artificial flowers in the bridal bouquet, which maintain their blossoms forever, office flowers are replaced at the first signs of aging (or at marriage).

While the doll image occurs mainly in descriptions of the 'Japanese-style' bride, the bride-as-flower image is also used in reference to the 'Western-style' bride. 'Y-o-u, like a flower' (*hana no yōna a-na-ta*) claims the advertisement for a famous Tokyo hotel, which has a

'Western-style' bride (represented by a foreign model) sitting in her white dress next to a huge array of fresh roses. The paradigm of the idea is found in an advertisement of a beauty and costume rental shop for brides on the Ginza, Tokyo's most up-market street. This advertisement features two brides who fill the page: the fair-skinned Japanese bride is wearing a kimono,[30] and the (foreign) Western bride is in a white dress and veil. The caption says it all: 'A Flower of Japan. A Flower of the West. A Ginza-made Bride (*nihon no hana. seiō no hana. ginza de tsukuru hanayome*)' (see Plate 12).

Conclusion

The slogan chosen by the exclusive Ginza shop to promote its business is much more telling than it may seem at first. It not only refers to the widespread image of the bride as a flower, but involves the 'dual' bride – Japanese and Western – and finally, it makes use of the verb *tsukuru* with its connotations of 'making' and 'manufacturing'. Clearly, the process through which the traditional and the Western bridal appearances are manufactured is part and parcel of the whole process of manufacturing weddings – and brides.

'The bride' has become the main object of an enormous industry, with a vast number of related bridal services and products. As weddings and the preparation of brides becomes increasingly commercialized, the promotion techniques of the wedding industry have grown increasingly similar to the general promotional techniques for any other commercial commodity.

The emphasis on the bride as an 'object' is exemplified by the bridal fair, which usually takes place on weekends when they serve as family entertainment. The sales techniques at these bridal fairs with their emphasis on entertainment is also similar to that of commodities. In line with this 'philosophy of commerce', 'One must not confront the buyers brusquely with a commodity but 'guide them into the "entertainment"' (Haug 1986:68).

Nor is the device of the stage, designed for brides alone to try on the Western wedding dresses, unfamiliar to the promotion of commodities:

Thus the sales room is designed as a stage, purpose-built to convey entertainment to its audience that will stimulate a heightened desire to spend. 'On this stage the sale is initiated. This stage is the most important element in sales promotionon.'

(Haug 1986:69)

What is being sold on the stage and at the bridal fair in general is more than the commodity itself: it is also the fulfilment of a life-long dream. Indeed, the 'Once-in-a-Lifetime-Dream' is one of the main concepts in the promotion of weddings. This emphasis is closely connected with growing affluence in Japan. It was articulated by the wedding parlour manager as follows:

> For a girl it [wearing wedding costumes] is a once-in-a-lifetime event, a moment to cherish, a supreme moment that she will have as a memory forever. And now that there is money to spare, she can afford this. Twenty years ago people could not even afford a honeymoon abroad.

Of course the fulfilment of this dream is an illusion, for the girl is given the special status of star for only one day. Nevertheless, it seems that the wedding industry is aiming (and quite successfully) at one of the 'commodity aesthetic' ideals which 'would be to invent something which enters one's consciousness unlike anything else; something which is talked about, which catches the eye and which cannot be forgotten; something which everyone wants and has always wanted' (Haug 1986:152).

Let us look more carefully into the nature of the role which the bridal fair and other promotional schemes really confer on the bride. For her predominant position has two aspects which are linked in a fascinating manner. On the one hand, the wedding industry targets the female half of the young couple as the heavy consumer. However, although she may be treated as the more 'favourable' consumer, this comes at the cost of being objectified. Moreover, this process of objectification has at least two faces: objectification as a female consumer and as a symbol of Japaneseness.

In the several dozens of advertisements which I have collected from various magazines, brides usually appear alone and in Western attire. When the latter is the case, she is often represented by a Western model. In the two cases where Japanese costume is mentioned or shown, the bride is accompanied either by a Western bride, or – when she is portrayed trying on the *uchikake* – by her mother.

In her analysis of advertising Judith Williamson (1978:13) has written that 'Advertisements are selling us something else besides consumer goods: in providing us with a structure in which we, and those goods, are interchangeable, they are selling us ourselves' (1978:13). Like British and American advertisements, Japanese wedding advertisements sell more than the goods and services they offer, or even the 'lifetime dream'; they also sell a sense of cultural identity to the young brides and others involved in the wedding. However, this 'Japanese' identity is not at all simple. There seems to be an ongoing negotiation between its two aspects: the Western, which is to some extent presented as the more familiar, but is often represented by the Other, and the traditional-Japanese, which gives the illusion of roots by having the mother in the picture even though it is only being tried on, as if it has not yet been definitely accepted, or appears next to the Western bride, as if it only has meaning in reference to the Other.

The detached attitude towards the traditional-Japanese shows up as the young woman is being transformed into a 'Japanese bride'. This may be related to a feeling of stasis because she has left the house of her parents and not yet entered that of her husband. But 'I felt as if a different hand is involved and I am gradually becoming a different person' denotes more than this. The 'different person' referred to by this bride was unrecognizable not only to herself but to some of the wedding guests. This feeling is enhanced, if not created, by the white mask painted on the face and neck of the 'Japanese-style' bride.

The same device is used in Kabuki, and Earle Ernst (1974:195) writes about it as follows: 'The detachment of the actor from his role is further marked in his make-up. The face of the actor on stage is a compromise between the human face and the mask.' Both the Kabuki actor and the bride, however, do have clearly defined roles to play. He has his role in the specific play, and she has hers as a 'Japanese bride'. As such, her beauty is judged even more by the way she fulfils this role than by her physical features. In this respect, as well, she is like the Kabuki actor who 'is not in any way dependent upon physical beauty, or even attractiveness . . . His theatrical beauty is provided solely by the materials of the theatre' (Ernst 1974:195). Thus, the bride's 'beauty' depends more on the ability of her dresser to 'make' her similar to a Japanese doll than on her inherent attractiveness.

One of the concerns of this book is the relations between the Japanese and the Western. In this chapter, we were able to discern another aspect of this complex duality. Here these two styles are clearly presented as *consumer products* in the thriving industry of weddings and brides. They sometimes compete, as, for example, when the *furisode* seems to be losing points in favour of a second Western party dress, and are sometimes shown as co-existing side by side. However, as two aspects of a highly commercialized world, their positions in the hierarchy are always open to change. Thus, while the traditional-Japanese now holds a slightly higher status in the context of the beauty shop, it is not clear that this style will retain its position with the 'new generation', for in the world of commercial weddings – and in Japan in general – the Western increasingly symbolizes high status. Even today, prestigious hotels often offer Western weddings which include a chapel ceremony and sometimes omit the Japanese aspect altogether.

In this context, 'the West' is also viewed abstractly. An extreme example of this kind of 'West' is offered by the overseas weddings being promoted in some travel magazines. 'Become the heroine of a story in a Walt Disney Wedding', one such magazine advertisement promises. Another magazine contains an offer for a 'pumpkin horse-carriage tour' from Disney hotel (Rosenberger 1993). Although these 'dreams' are promoted by travel (as well as bridal) magazines, place is really irrelevant in these Western adventures. As Rosenberger puts it: 'The appeal lies in the international, fantasy-inspiring, and opulent qualities of the tours offered.'

The horse-drawn pumpkin carriages advertised as essential parts of overseas weddings are connected with the 'Cinderella Dream' so prevalent in the wedding industry and advertising. For becoming a Cinderella means attaining the status of a princess with the Western ideas of luxury and wealth which this implies. Advertisements that carry this idea – like the one of a costume rental shop that reads: 'We can dare [to fulfil] the bride's Cinderella dream' (*hanayome no shinderera durimu o okashi dekimasu*) – usually use caucasian models (see Plate 13).

The use of Western models in advertising has been on the rise since the late 1960s (Fields 1988:23–31). That these models represent an abstract West disconnected from real people was made clear to me when I was asked to participate in a bridal fair. After I had been fully made-up and dressed in a 'gorgeous' Western dress, the reaction of the people I had been working with for almost two years was 'After all, [you are] a foreigner' (*yappari gaijin*). Of course they knew I was a foreigner all along; but in heavy Western make-up and elaborate Western costume I was the foreigner incarnate, the *gaijin* they knew from television and the movies, from women's magazines and from advertisements.

Although overseas weddings and domestic chapel weddings are not all that popular in Japan, their existence sheds light on the general attitude towards things Western. It seems that the appeal of such weddings is very similar to that of a trip abroad; both endow their partakers with the image of being part of the high-level global culture (Rosenberger 1993).

This high-status cosmopolitanism is also considered a way to acquire *kosei-teki* or individuality. *Kosei-teki* has become a keyword in wedding and travel advertisements (Rosenberger 1993) as well as in young women's fashion magazines (Tanaka 1990). Tanaka, who has conducted a systematic search of magazines aimed at young women, concludes that the word 'individuality' is equivalent to 'fashionable' and 'cosmopolitanism', both of which are related to 'elitism'.[31] It is clear then, that the Japanese have 'neatly adopted and adapted' the word 'individualism' (Moeran 1984b:263). But even more important for us is that this Japanese 'individualism' is equated with the Western as fashionable, modern, international and of high status.

In the process of being packaged in her traditional-Japanese and Western packages, the modern Japanese bride is objectified by the packagers and, moreover, collaborates in this objectification. Aiming to fulfil her 'Cinderella Dream', she collaborates as a customer of both the wedding industry and of the products advertised for brides, and also as a woman who 'puts in evidence her masters' ability to pay' (Veblen 1957).

6

THE PRODUCTION OF TRADITIONS
IN THE CEREMONIAL OCCASIONS
INDUSTRY

novelty is no less novel for being able to dress up easily as antiquity
(Hobsbawm 1983b:5)

Wedding parlours not only created the commercial wedding in Japan but have also been responsible for inventing the new ideas which are now an integral part of the fixed wedding pattern they created. This is what the daughter of the founder of Shōchikuden, the most inventive and 'showy' (*hade*) wedding parlour group, had to say about the Shōchikudeden's development of its wedding reception:

> We decided that people at wedding receptions were bored by all the speeches at a reception, so we added a slide show of the bride and groom. This was back in 1968, when we were still conducting weddings in a shrine. The cake-cutting ceremony was initiated later, in 1973, when we opened our first wedding parlour in Kyoto. When one of our parlours invented the 'gondola' in 1977, it was only adopted by a few other parlours . . . Now, we always have new things, like the laser effects. We encourage every parlour to invent new things and adopt them as long as they fit into the time allotted for a complete wedding at one of our parlours.

The description of a wedding day at the Kobe Princess Palace with its Western and traditional-Japanese ingredients with which this book opens, was presented as a puzzle to the uninformed reader. The chapters that followed helped to fill in some details about the cultural product called the 'commercial Japanese wedding'. Before generalizing about the process involved in the many aspects of this cultural production, it is worthwhile to delve into the ways in which both

135

Japanese and Western 'traditions' are continually being invented and manipulated by wedding parlour operators and suppliers of related goods and services.

As we have seen above, the Japanese wedding industry has since its inception eagerly sought new ideas to add to the fixed pattern, especially those for which the customer can be charged separately. Although costume changes are one of the main areas of invention both because they are financially very beneficial to the parlour and because multiple changes of costumes do not interrupt the course of the wedding – which continues in the absence of the bride – the possibilities for inventions are indeed endless.

The re-invention of Japanese 'traditions'

The Japanese contemporary commercial wedding is replete with 'ancient Japanese traditions' which appear to be crucial in supporting its role as an emblem of Japaneseness. However, an investigation into the sources of these elements indicate that they are not really that old.

One of the most traditional-Japanese elements of the fixed wedding pattern is the popular Shinto ceremony. The image of 'traditional antiquity' portrayed by this (and other similar) ceremonies is enhanced by the elaborate 'ancient' costumes worn by the Shinto priest and his female attendants, as well as by the 'authentic' Shinto sounds of the beat of a large drum and the music of a traditional Japanese flute. However, as we have seen, the Shinto ceremony was not introduced into the wedding until the late Meiji period, after it was used in the imperial wedding of 1900.

It is therefore safe to assume that the 'traditional' Shinto ceremony has been deliberately promoted by interested agencies such as the wedding industry – with the *gojokai* organizations as its core. In this light we can see that, although Shinto ceremonies did begin to be held after the imperial wedding, they did not become popular until after World War II (Hendry 1981:195–196,n.64) with the rise of the nascent wedding industry.

The traditional-Japanese costumes

The bride and groom begin their wedding in Japanese attire. While the bridegroom's traditional clothing consists of the formal but relatively simple *hakama* (pleated skirt), the bride wears an elaborate and heavy costume which is never seen except at weddings. While these

136

'appearances' are considered traditionally Japanese enough to suit the Shinto ceremony which opens the formal part of the wedding, their 'antiquity' is open to question. In what follows I shall endeavour to trace the 'traditional' aspects of what the bride and groom wear on their big day.

The uchikake

The *uchikake* is an elaborate, heavy upper coat which is worn over a white kimono. It is considered today the most traditional bridal attire. It is usually a bride in *uchikake*, wig and head-covering which is said to create the 'bridal appearance' (*hanayome sugata*).

When questioned as to their motivation for wearing *uchikake*, all brides stress both its Japanese (*nihon-teki*) and traditional (*dentō-teki*) aspects as the reason for deciding to include it instead of marrying in a Western dress alone – which would also mean getting married in church, and that is far from common. At the Kobe Princess Palace there has never been a case where a bride has chosen to wear only the Western wedding gown. Choosing traditional-Japanese attire seems to give them a feeling of continuity with their traditional Japanese past despite the fact that their mothers and grandmothers never wore the *uchikake* or anything similar to it.[1] Indeed, the *uchikake* did not become part of the traditional bridal attire worn by most brides until the late 1960s, when the wedding industry began its boom period. Before that it was worn only by brides who could afford to follow what had been known as part of the ceremonial court wear. With the rise of the specialized wedding parlours and its fixed pattern there was no room for other outfits. Moreover, there are researchers who doubt the Japanese origin of the 'pure white' image promoted by the wedding industry as 'traditionally Japanese' in promotional captions like: 'Wear your hair in the traditional Japanese wedding style (*Takashimada*), put on a pure white kimono (*shiro muku*), take the oath of marriage', viewing it instead as a later influence based on the white wedding gown worn in the West.[2]

The tsunokakushi ('horn concealer') and watabōshi

The 'bridal appearance' is not complete without the special *Takashimada* coiffure – a style known to be worn by daughters of the Samurai class – which used to be accomplished by a professional hairdresser using the client's own hair, but which has now been replaced by a wig. Over the *Takashimada* hairdo goes one of two head coverings to complete the traditional and 'pure' bridal image: the *tsunokakushi*, a thin strip of white silk cloth that envelops the wig and some of the forehead; or the *watabōshi*, which veils the whole wig and also some of the face. But, like the *uchikake*, the *tsunokakushi* is a recent trend. According to Ema (1971:225), it too originated in the late Meiji period and is a result of the Western influence of that time. Some brides chose to wear what is claimed to be a former version of the *tsunokakushi*, the *watabōshi*, which used to be worn by noblewomen outside their homes and by women of the Ikko Buddhist sect when they visited the temple.[3] Modern brides consider both head-coverings traditional and decide which one to wear on the basis of aesthetics, or form.

The bridegroom's formal wear

Since the groom's appearance at home weddings never received much attention, it has been almost totally ignored in the literature. With the rise of the commercial wedding, however, he has gradually become a co-star in the production, albeit in a supporting role. Thus, he too now changes outfits during the course of the wedding. Continuing our 'search' for the origins of the 'ancient' bridal costumes, we need not go very far back in the case of his *hakama* (pleated skirt) or his black cloak (*haori*) with the white house crests. These garments were originally designed by the chancellery in 1877, as ceremonial dress for low-ranking nobles and ordinary officials. Later they became common formal dress for all men (Yanagida 1957:12). Grooms did not begin to wear Japanese-style clothing until quite recently. Through the Taishō (1912–1925) and a large part of the Shōwa (1926–1989) periods, grooms usually wore formal Western black morning dress (*mōningu*). It was not until the early 1970s that wedding parlours began to promote formal Japanese wear for the groom to complete the traditional picture. After all, the perfect form of a wedding production would be spoiled if a Western groom stood side by side with his 'pure traditional-Japanese' bride in the wedding portraits.[4]

Before the 'age of the uchikake'

Of the three bridal appearances (*hanayome sugata*) of the late Meiji period which Ema (1971) lists in his extremely detailed history of weddings in Japan, the only one worn by contemporary brides is the *uchikake-tsunokakushi* combination. The other two bridal appearances, which were common in the Taishō and the early Shōwa periods were black *tomesode* and *furisode*.

From a variety of sources[5] we learn that in the early post-world war period, Japanese brides wore a black short-sleeved formal kimono (*tomesode*) similar to the one worn by female wedding guests today, although its pattern was slightly more heightened and elaborately coloured. In the late 1940s and 1950s, with the growing popularity of Shinto ceremonies and restaurant receptions, the black *tomesode* was replaced by a long-sleeved black kimono (the *furisode*). The change from short to long sleeves is related to the wedding being moved from the private to the public domain. When weddings were held at home, the short-sleeved *tomesode* allowed the bride to serve the guests during the wedding reception, which would have been impossible in the long-sleeved *furisode*, as long-sleeved kimono were deemed proper for ceremonies but improper for work. This change presaged another change: that of the role of the bride on her wedding day from someone showing her ability to assume the role of daughter in her new household to a passive 'doll-like' actor in the commercial wedding production.

The flexibility of tradition

While it is true that the 'Japanese appearances' of the contemporary bride and groom are inventions of the wedding producers, such inventions are not created from thin air but are based on the 'store' of ancient materials that has 'accumulated in the past of any society' (Hobsbawm 1983b:6). However, that practices adopted are not necessarily adapted from practices related to weddings becomes clear in, for example, the case of the bride's head-coverings, which were originally worn either in court or in temple and not by brides. Thus, it seems that various 'ancient' practices and forms are taken eclectically from the accumulated past in order to create the perfect form for a bridal couple and a wedding.

The same is true with regard to *ironaoshi* or the practice of changing outfits during the wedding – an excellent example of the flexibility with which past customs are treated. It has been suggested by Ema (1971:154, 208) that changing clothing on this day began during the Tokugawa period, when the bride changed from a more formal kimono to a kimono from her own trousseau between the formal ceremony and the banquet. Some Japanese scholars (e.g., Nakayama 1928:828; Ema

1971:90–91) argue that this was an abbreviation of an even older practice in which the bride would wear white for the first and second days of her wedding and change into a coloured garment for the third.

There are also reports of the custom of changing costumes in rural home weddings, although the time and number of changes reported varies. The only constant in this instance is that a bride at a home wedding changed into one of her trousseau kimono to show members of the community part of the clothing she was bringing to her new home and as a sign of the wealth of her parents' household. Smith (as well as Beardsley *et al.*:1959:325) argues that the only reason this practice was not universally observed was that 'few brides have enough kimono of sufficient quality to carry on the display' (Cornell and Smith 1956:79).

According to informants, the practice of changing outfits hardly existed at all in the pre-war period and even later. A veteran bride dresser and the owner of a beauty shop, said that 'When I started the beauty shop 31 years ago (in 1957). . . there was almost no *ironaoshi* . . . if the bride did change kimono it was for her own kimono.'[6] However, as in their adoption and promotion of the *uchikake*, the wedding parlour entrepreneurs made clever use of 'tradition' in advocating multiple costume changes (*ironaoshi*). They did so by reviving a so-called traditional practice – albeit one that had never really caught on in the past, leaving only its *form* and filling it with different materials. The flexibility of this 'custom' can be seen in the way new fashions replaced some of the 'old-new' traditions, for example, in the gradual replacement of the Japanese *furisode* by a Western party dress. The introduction of *ironaoshi* among grooms is even more interesting, since it is not grounded even theoretically on any past practices, and was introduced only to complement the bride's change from Japanese style to Western style.

Imagining the 'Western'

In her discussion of the elaboration of the fixed wedding package, the daughter of the Shōchikudeden group's founder emphasized the Western ingredients like the cake-cutting and candle-lighting ceremonies. Inventing the Western is much easier than doing the same with the traditional-Japanese since there is no 'real' past to limit the Western customs dreamed up. Thus, there was no necessity to investigate the continuity with the past in this instance. The interesting point concerning mini-dramas like the cake-cutting and candle service is that no attempt is made to imitate any 'real' Western wedding of any sort. The startling fact is that, like the traditional-Japanese inventions of the wedding producers, the imagined Western 'traditions' satisfy their customers as authentic. Thus, when the mother of a future bride, who came to check the Kobe Princess Palace at one of the bridal fairs, asked me if the candle service is part of the wedding reception in my country and I told her that I had never seen it, she was surprised because she was certain it was performed in the West and probably concluded that I was not a reliable source.[7]

The West imitated in the candle service and the cake-cutting ceremony, with its four-foot high inedible wax cake decorated with a miniature bridal couple in Western wedding attire, of course) at its top, is an abstract West imagined by the wedding producers and willingly accepted (and paid for) by the consumer. It is the same Disney World West that is promoted in the Cinderella dream and the pumpkin tours abroad. This imagined West offers the image of cosmopolitanism so eagerly sought by young people in Japan today. The proliferation of Western elements since the mid-late 1980s is part of the wedding industry's attempt to appeal to the young couples directly.

Looking at the Western elements of the commercial wedding one can not ignore the feeling that there is something grotesque about the way the 'West' is treated. This is true not only of the Western clothing worn but also of the inedible wedding cake, as well as of the candle lighting service – the only part of the wedding reception which has a relatively comic aspect in the way the groom's friends tease him by wetting the candle's wick. Whether this comparatively lighter attitude towards 'Western' elements has something to say about the Japanese real attitude towards the West I leave as an open question.

Western wedding attire

One of the Western highlights of the commercial Japanese wedding has long been the opportunity to wear the white bridal gown. However, today most brides do not stop at the traditional Western white dress. They change into at least one other elaborate gown, thereby extending the concept of *ironaoshi* to the Western segment of the wedding. Interestingly enough, just as the Japanese costumes worn were adapted from unrelated practices of the past and then manipulated for use in the commercial wedding, so were the Western costumes.

The wedding dress, like its traditional-Japanese counterpart, the *uchikake*, was introduced by the wedding industry in the 1970s together with other Western elements of the programme. It was not long before it was joined by the coloured party dress in the early 1980s to 'round out' the Western aspect of these weddings.

Wedding parlour owners contend that the growing popularity of the Western dress is related to that of hotel weddings and church ceremonies, to which they are much more suited. But the low percentage of Japanese who marry in church (about 7.3 per cent in 1990) and the fact that the white dress is now worn no matter what the venue of the wedding is suggest that this argument is not valid. Nevertheless, the reasoning itself is interesting in that it reveals the tendency of those concerned to envisage the 'Western' as a whole 'package', one which is conceived quite abstractly. For example, the coloured party dresses bear this out. Their elaborate design, elegant materials and colours – as well as the layers of crinoline to puff out the skirts – ape the gowns of the nineteenth-century European bourgeoisie, as they are conveyed in films and on television. Since the process of invention and elaboration is endless, we may expect to see still more new items added to emphasize the 'Western' picture. Such was a new fashion of tucking a bustle under the skirts to add to the puff of the crinoline.

An anecdote from my fieldwork illustrates the general attitude towards these Western dresses. While working with a middle-aged clothing department employee, I was asked if 'over there' (mukō, a quite typical way of referring to the West) we still wear these bustles when we dress for parties. This woman's image of the West is not very different from that of others with whom I worked at the Kobe Princess Palace.

As for the groom, he started out by wearing a Western-style suit, but his attire too has grown increasingly elaborate. Today, grooms usually open the Western segment of their *ironaoshi* in an elegant tuxedo in a variety of colours, with a flower which matches those in the bride's (fake) bouquet in the lapel. Some grooms change to a second tuxedo with the third *ironaoshi* of their brides.

Even the Western clothing of other wedding participants, who do not change their outfits, evinces some illuminating abstracts of Western fashion. Although the principal female participants wear traditional-Japanese kimono, the main men wear morning suits (usually rented at the parlour), which still symbolizes 'the West' for the Japanese even though they are considered old-fashioned in the countries were they originated.[8] Most other male wedding guests wear black suits and white ties (as contrasted with the black tie worn at funerals). They do not wear suits of elegant material, and their clothing may be quite old.

What is important here is that Western wear is used in a 'Japanese' way, emphasizing formality and form.

Although most of the elderly female guests wear a kimono or a tailored black suit, which they enliven with a colourful flower broach or the like in order to appear different than they would at a funeral where solid black is required, some young women wear elaborate Western cocktail dresses, often rented from the clothing department. When the latter is the case, the dresses look more like old theatre costumes than party wear. These dresses, too, belong among the rest of the elements abstractly interpreted – or imagined – from the West, thereby creating an interesting parallel with their exaggerated version of the Japanese.

The production of new Japanese traditions

The ongoing process of invention involves not only the fabrication of Western (or 'modern') effects and the re-invention of Japanese traditions, but the production of new 'traditions' as well. This involves a diversity of producers of traditional wedding artifacts. These vary from special bridal make-up, to special traditional wigs and other traditional decorations.

The case of a Cosmo-Fani wig company, a sub-company of the large oil company, Cosmo, illustrates this endless process of invention. Cosmo-Fani is a relatively new company in the field of wig production and rental. Although its literature presents Cosmo-Fani as 'aiming at the development of a rational (gōri-teki) lease-system of wigs', the company had a hard time breaking into the wig business at the Cinderella Beauty Shop despite its participation at the parlour's bridal fairs, frequent visits to the beauty shop, as well as training the beauty shop's experts in the use of their wigs.

Cosmo-Funi's main problem was the existence of another style of wigs which, although heavier and not made to order, were included in the bride's package. But the Cosmo-Funi representatives persisted until, after a few years, Cosmo wigs were almost as popular as the 'free' wigs, although they never completely replaced the latter. The beauty shop noting the popularity of the Cosmo wigs,[9] then decided to enter into competition with Cosmo-Funi by contracting the production of its own 'light' wig to a small wig company.

Although the above demonstrates that the traditional artifacts business operates like any other competitive market, a closer look at the way in which Cosmo-Funi promoted its product sheds additional light on the 'production' of traditions. While Cosmo-Funi did indeed present itself as a modern 'rational' (gōri-teki) wig service whose wigs are produced in a modern factory,[10] they by no means neglected the traditional aspect of their product. Thus, the Cosmo-Funi catalogue is titled 'The Time When Tradition (dentō) Shines Beautifully'. It is the association of 'modern' and 'rational' production methods with 'traditional' products which is most striking. Like almost all of those involved in marketing traditional artifacts, Cosmo-fani not only imitates and improves on tradition, it produces new traditions, to order.

Even more striking is the fact that this process seems to be conscious (or 'rational' – in the company's own language). A conversation about 'modern' girls, between Cosmo-Fani workers and beauty shop veterans at a Cosmo-Funi training session at the Cinderella Beauty Shop was interesting in this respect. One of the Cosmo-Funi employees was discussing the fact that fewer girls today wanted to don traditional costumes at their wedding. The shop's head dresser interrupted to say that there were still plenty of girls who yearned (akogare) to wear kimono at their weddings. But the Cosmo promoter continued: 'Our company must think of the future. That is why we have begun to think about new uses for our wigs.' He was referring to Cosmo-Funi's idea of introducing wigs for the 'Coming-of-Age-Ceremony' celebrated on 15 January for young men and women who have reached the age of twenty, as well as for personal twentieth birthday parties. While the coming-of-age day is strongly connected with kimono wearing and other traditional appurtenances – but does not include wigs – twentieth birthday private parties are not usually celebrated in traditional outfits. Thus, if such a practice is introduced it will create yet another new 'tradition'.

The beauty shop's expert dressers were almost as enthusiastic about the idea as the wig promoters themselves. The coming-of-age day is the most profitable day of the year for the beauty shop. During the busy day the large part-time staff prepares more than 100 girls for the ceremony. All girls are dressed in kimono and have their hair done in the 'right' Japanese way. Thus, the way they view it, it would bring more business into the shop and allow the dressers to 'process' customers more quickly, since arranging a wig is a much shorter process than setting a customer's own hair.

Although this conversation was only hypothetical and there are no signs that wigs have become popular in the coming-of-age ceremony, its implication is intriguing. One can only wonder what will happen if Japanese girls begin wearing wigs for the coming-of-age day or for their twentieth birthday. I have no doubt that, after a few years, the practice of 'wigs for twenty year-old girls' will be considered just as traditional as 'wigs for brides' are today.

'Playing' with tradition

While the new, lighter wedding wig represents a case in which the wedding industry 'modernized' an already existing 'traditional' artifact, there is an even more daring kind of invention which I call 'playing with tradition'. These kinds of ventures are usually entered into by the wedding parlours themselves and generally involve a relatively small out-of-pocket investment. They involve the 'invention' of a 'custom' – usually involving clothing – which was originally related to a very specific group or occasion. However, whereas the aristocratic history of the *uchikake* has been disguised, in these cases the origin of the attire is stated openly.

Such a case was the introduction of a special traditional wedding attire called *jūnihitoe* (literally, twelve layers), as a set for bride and groom in imitation of the full court dress (*sokutai*) worn by Prince Akishino and Princess Kiko at the royal wedding in June 1990. Not long after the imperial wedding, advertisements for *jūnihitoe* began to be seen everywhere, and Cobella jumped on the 'twelve-layer' bandwagon by devising a particularly expensive set which they rented out for picture-taking (only) at a price of ¥250,000.[11]

However, although the details of the imperial wedding were the focus of a great deal of attention on the part of the Japanese public, the attire was not as popular as Princess Diana's wedding dresses were in England after the Diana-Charles wedding. For example, in the Kobe Princess Palace only one customer chose this 'package'. The parlour manager attributed this lack of success to the expenses involved and the fact that it was very uncomfortable to wear. He also admitted that they might have been wrong to think that the set would be popular, since apparently young Japanese, who have recently been the main target of new ideas, did not 'long for' (*akogare*) the imperial costumes.

One of the reasons for court dress failing to catch on may be related to the attitude of Japanese young people towards the imperial family. Unlike other countries like England, where young women imitate any new fashion introduced by Princess Diana, in Japan the imperial family is more detached from the people and therefore more likely to be venerated than imitated. This attitude can be understood in the face of the modern myth, designed by bureaucrats in the late Meiji period, who created a state of orthodoxy around the figure of the Japanese emperor and then imposed it on the people (Gluck 1985:5).

What becomes clear here is that the wedding industry is endlessly occupied in producing new ideas. In this process the producers do not hesitate to utilize any kind of playful idea which may have a chance of appealing to their customers. The logic of the market applies here also, considering the fact that Cobella found it necessary to promote the *jūnihitoe* because other wedding facilities were doing so.

Exoticizing the 'Japanese'

'I am only trying to make my customers happy', the manager of the Kobe Princess Palace responded to my question regarding yet another invention which he introduced to potential customers at a bridal fair: an optional bridal change into a young geisha (*maiko*) 'appearance'. This innovation reveals the multitude of still untapped possibilities of manipulating Japaneseness by 'playing' with tradition. For the bride who was to wear the young geisha outfit was certainly not to be identified with an actual geisha.[12] Here, the 'exotic' image of the geisha was being used as a beautiful *form*. In this case, too, the producer of this new tradition was aware of his invention, even using the Japanese word *asobi* ('play') when he described it to me. 'It may seem a little strange from the traditional point of view', he said, 'but today's young people are not interested in difficult things. They prefer light things, light things to look at.'

The parlour manager's observation concerning the young generation are in line with what I have been saying herein about form. If we look beyond the words themselves, we see that what he is really saying is that young Japanese do not care about historical truth but are interested instead in the 'forms' which bolster their own sense of Japaneseness. It is this sense of cultural identity which is of interest to us here. For we have seen how the Western and the traditional-Japanese play dialectically opposing roles in this Japaneseness offered by wedding producers – to the point where they are sometimes interchangeable consumer choices. But here the parlour manager was offering a 'light' approach towards the traditional-Japanese which is generally typical of the Western. It is only when we regard the *Westanese* and the *traditionese* as interchangeable 'goods' that we can understand the manager's attempt to take a 'lighter' attitude to the 'Japanese' aspect of the wedding reception.

Dressing brides in geisha outfits – and also to some extent in the twelve-layer set – has more to it than that. It is a kind of self-exoticism which can be seen as 'reverse Orientalization' (see Miller 1982:209–211).

Conclusion

The wedding industry is involved in the production of traditions as much as it is committed to the introduction of novelties. However, in this chapter I was mainly interested in questions related to the production of traditions. The manifold examples drawn here have emphasized the 'selective' nature of the invention of tradition (Williams 1977, Handler and Linnekin 1984). We have seen how traditions are not only produced, imagined, constructed, played with, but also discarded when necessary.

This perspective pertaining to tradition is one of the main reasons why I view the production of a commercial Japanese wedding as cultural production. When the entrepreneurs and their minions produce a traditional-Japanese bride or manufacture traditional wigs, they are producing cultural as well as material goods and services.

Using somewhat blunt words, a ceremonial occasions entrepreneur described the relation between the industry and its young customers as follows:

> The young people, and the people who do business from their desires, are soon coming together (*atsumaru*), the businessmen (referring to the wedding industry entrepreneurs) think only of the profit (*okane mōke bakari*).

The entrepreneur was referring to the well worked-on *akogare*, or yearning, young girls are supposed to have for being both a Western princess and a symbolic traditional-Japanese woman for a day. This frank remark exemplifies the character of the process with which we are dealing here that can be defined in consumerist terms.

Hobsbawm (1983a:307) argues that the most successful invented traditions are those which meet 'a felt – not necessarily a clearly understood – *need* among particular bodies of people' (my emphasis). The wedding industry has obviously identified such a need, and constantly strives to reproduce it. Moreover, in regard to the commercial Japanese wedding, this 'need' seems no different from any other demand in a consumer market.

Appadurai – who takes his lead in defining 'need' and 'demand' from writers like Veblen (1957), Douglas and Isherwood (1978) and

Baudrillard (1975, 1981) – contends that 'demand is a socially regulated and generated impulse, not an artifact of individual whims or needs' (Appadurai 1986:32). In emphasizing the reciprocal relationship between producers and consumers, Appadurai instructs us to look at 'consumption (and the demand that makes it possible) as a focus not only for *sending* social messages (as Douglas has proposed), but for *receiving* them as well' (Appadurai 1986:31). He then goes on to a point which is relevant to the discussion of manipulation:

> Demand thus conceals two different relationships between consumption and production: 1. On the one hand, demand is determined by social and economic forces; 2. on the other, it can manipulate, within limits, these social and economic forces. The important point is that from a historical point of view, these two aspects of demand can affect each other.
>
> (Appadurai 1986:31)

Thus, the production of traditions elaborated in this chapter should not be viewed as a one-sided activity involving only a 'strong' wedding industry, or in terms of 'total domination', but as a process in which both the 'desires' – which undoubtedly are often created or re-created by producers – and the 'supply' by the wedding industry play important roles.

On the other hand, it is equally misleading to view consumption in a capitalist society without taking account of those who have the power to create new needs and desires, for these creators of tradition are society's 'taste-makers', in Bourdieu's (1984) and Baudrillard's (1981) terms. Thus, in the case of the Japanese wedding industry – or in that of the consumers of this industry's products we should not neglect what Appadurai (1986:32) calls rules of 'appropriateness (fashion)'. In this game of 'appropriateness', trends dominated by the media, advertising, television stars – called *tarento* (talent) – and other 'taste makers' influence the acceptance or rejection of new traditions as well as of novelties thrown onto the market, such as the twelve-layer set.

Finally, it seems that the ongoing co-existence of the Western and traditional-Japanese elements in the commercial Japanese wedding is neither accidental nor surprising. On the contrary, by 'Japanizing' or 'domesticating' (Tobin 1992) the West and at the same time 'traditionalizing' the Japanese, the ceremonial occasions industry – and other similar endeavours – aims straight at the heart of the Japanese cultural identity.

Plate 1 A view of the Kobe Princess Palace wedding parlour

Plate 2 Wedding mini-dramas: the cake cutting ceremony

Plate 3 Wedding mini-dramas: the candle service

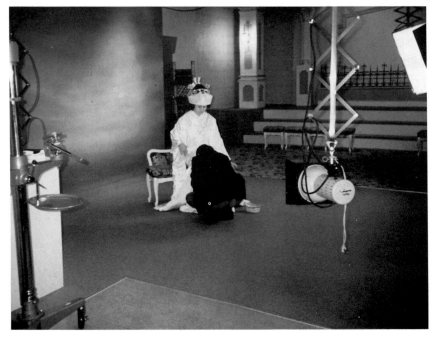

Plate 4 At the photo studio: preparing the 'perfect bridal appearance'

Plate 5 At the photo studio: the bridal appearance (*hanayome sugata*)
(in *uchikake* and wig)

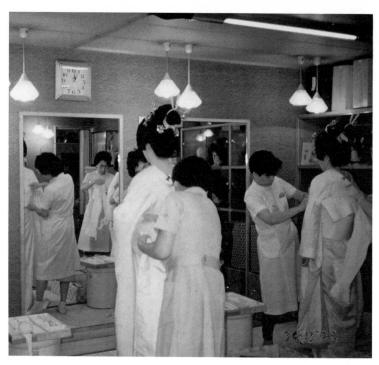

Plate 6 At the beauty shop: dressers preparing brides

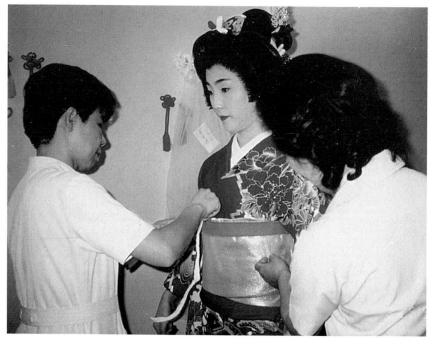

Plate 7 At the *Ironaoshi* room: a change to a second kimono

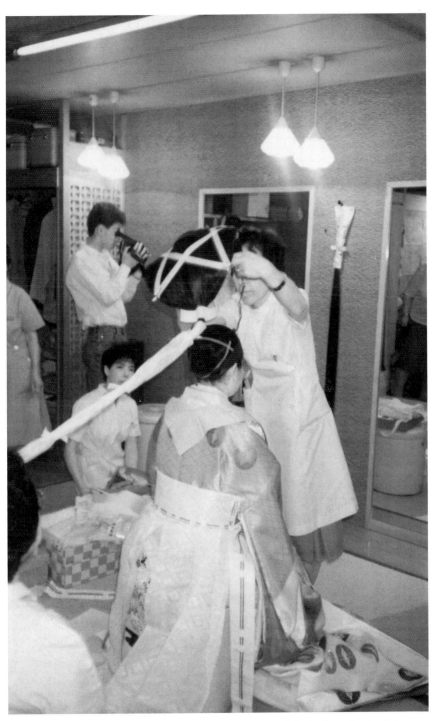

Plate 8 At the beauty shop: the head-dresser dons a special wig for a 'twelve layer set (*12 hitoe*)' costume

Plate 9 At the bridal fair: two models sharing their experiences

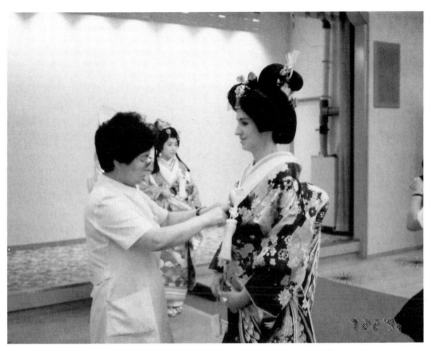

Plate 10 At the bridal fair: the beauty shop's chief corrects the appearance of the anthropologist as a model

Plate 11 Wedding and party dresses display at the bridal fair

Plate 12 Wedding advertisement: 'A flower of Japan, a flower of the West, Ginza-made bride'

日本の花。西欧の花。銀座でつくる花嫁。

花嫁のシンデレラ・ドリームをおかしできます。

Plate 13 Wedding advertisement: 'We can dare [to fulfil] the bride's Cinderella dream'

CONCLUSION: CONSUMING
JAPANESENESS

The complex ceremonial occasions industry in Japan is heavily involved in a continuous process of manipulating, re-inventing, constructing and imagining traditions. While the preoccupation with tradition may seem natural in a primarily anthropological work, it should by now be quite obvious that the 'traditions' referred to herein are not to be found in either the past or the 'nature' of any society, including Japan with its strong sense of preserving what it has come to view as its Japaneseness. As I see it, tradition should be regarded as a kind of mould into which various materials are poured, and which gives these materials a gloss of historicity.

In the context of the commercial Japanese wedding, the traditions adhered to are cultural rather than historical products. They are cultural not only in the sense that they are not transmitted from the 'past' as 'objective deposits' (see Shils 1981:167), but, more importantly, in a sense that they, like culture itself, are seen as dynamic and not as static and homogenous products. From this perspective, the commercial Japanese wedding, (like similar weddings elsewhere) is a symbolic commodity which involves continuous negotiation between its producers and consumers regarding 'the Japanese' and 'the Western'. This is effected in the context of a more general dynamic process in Japanese society, that of the construction of a sense of cultural identity or Japaneseness.

The dialogue between East and West in Japan has been analysed as part of the dynamics of identity and difference (see Creighton 1992; Tobin 1992; Ivy 1995). A related and not less intensive discourse of identity has evolved around the interest in things Japanese and in *dentō* (tradition). This 'renewed, shifting and multifaceted discourse of tradition' (Kelly 1990:69) has taken many forms. Among them were several 'booms', including a '*furusato būmu*' (home-village boom) that

149

sought to locate and preserve 'a world we have lost' both on the local village level (Robertson 1987, 1991), and in domestic tourism (Ivy 1988; Martinez 1990). Another manifestation of this search for the 'real' Japan can be found in another fad, generally termed '*matsuri-būmu*' (festival-boom) (Bestor 1989) which pertains to the revival and re-invention of local ceremonies.

Other examples of this spirit of nostalgia consist of growing interest in Japanese folk-craft (Moeran 1984a), as well as a history boom (*rekishi būmu*) which includes a media celebration of the Japanese past (Kelly 1990:69). Other aspects of the boom, pertaining to women, include the growing popularity of such artistic pursuits as the Japanese tea ceremony, flower arranging and kimono dressing. The promotion of the commercial wedding pattern, and in particular those of its aspects that I have termed 'traditional-Japanese', is part of this nostalgia wave, and like other aspects of nostalgia should be regarded in a critical light as I will show later on.

Another heritage fad related to the search for an 'authentic' Japanese 'self' (*jibun*; Ivy 1988:22) which has been actively encouraged by interested businesses in a context of economic prosperity, has been the flourishing market for literature preoccupied with questions of Japanese national identity and uniqueness, a genre called *nihonjinron* ('discussions of the Japanese'). While the popular success of this literature can be seen as one manifestation of the demand for products which emphasize Japanese uniqueness, the explosion of *nihonjinron* is itself a key factor in what Benedict Anderson (1991) sees as the effect of 'print-as-commodity' on the formation of 'imagined communities' (Yoshino 1992:85–6). In other words, *nihonjinron* is not merely another product in the market of Japaneseness but plays a central role in promoting Japanese distinctiveness and dictating the kind of community to be constructed (or imagined), and therefore in the creation of additional grounds for the continuing invention and production of tradition.

Dale (1986:ii), one of the most outspoken critics of the *nihonjinron*, explains the scope of its influence by directly suggesting that the reader imagine it 'as something which filtered down through newspapers and regional media to everyday life, and you have something of the picture of what has taken place in Japan, where almost any discussion from the formally academic to the colloquial market-place exchange can reflect this ideology of nationhood'. It is, then, against the background of the mass consumption of Japaneseness (Befu 1983:253) that the mass promotion of invented Japanese traditions has succeeded.

Most critics of *nihonjinron* (e.g., Mouer and Sugimoto 1986) have been primarily concerned with the genre as an academic issue, showing its limited academic value. However, Yoshino (1992:164) contends that business elites have played an important role in shifting the notion of Japanese distinctiveness from the economic nationalism characteristic of pre- and early post-World War II Japan to the cultural nationalism that began to develop in the 1970s. Closely related to this shift in emphasis was the belief that Japan's economic success was largely due to 'Japanese style' management and business, which the elites stressed as a product of Japan's cultural tradition. The main themes promoted by spokesmen of this rediscovered national identity, among them academics like Nakane (1984), were 'harmony', 'consensus' and 'group orientedness'.

It is clear that business elites, and business interests in general, benefit from promoting such ideas. Indeed, Kawamura (1980:159), another critic of the *nihonjinron*, claims that such norms 'can be utilized to discipline members of the organizations they lead'. However, I have emphasized elsewhere the importance of another image, that of 'homogeneity' (see Goldstein-Gidoni 1993:331–336). Harootunian (1989:65–66) sees the attempt of the state and intellectuals (including Nakane) to declare '"homogeneity" in a "heterogenous" present' as an attempt to instal a 'master code' that 'would eradicate the scandal of difference'.

The idea of a homogeneous Japanese is easily translatable into that of the 'homogeneous' consumer. This is how the wedding industry succeeded in promoting '*uchikake* for everyone' in the 1970s, when the image that 'all will benefit equally from Japan's new wealth' was being propounded by bureaucrats and politicians (Goodman 1992:11). Interestingly enough, this view of a classless Japanese society was offered to me by a leading Ceremonial Occasions entrepreneur as we sat in her chauffeur-driven luxury automobile. Explaining how the *uchikake*, worn only by the samurai class in the past, has become available to everyone, she said: 'Japan has become much better for the people since the war. Everyone is equal now that we have democracy. Now all the Japanese [including samurai] have become ordinary people (*futsū no hito*). So the people who were discriminated against in the past and longed (*akogare*) for *uchikake* now want their daughters to wear it.'

Now that we have seen how the *akogare*, which all Japanese females allegedly have for wearing traditional-Japanese bridal costumes, and kimono in general, has been promulgated and exploited by the

151

producers of ceremonial occasions, we shall take a look at how such ideas of homogeneity are 'bought' by the customer or, in other words, how the consumer culture in Japan has grown to a point where it shapes the national culture. We find that, in the case of the commercial wedding industry, this includes the acquiescence of the Japanese woman in allowing herself to be made into an object.

The objectification of women has been discussed in feminist writing (e.g., Rubin 1975) as well as in relation to consumerism and clothing (Ewen and Ewen 1982:147–149; Haug 1986:73). In the modern Japanese wedding the objectification of the bride can be seen in her 'packaging' or 'wrapping' in layers of clothing and images. Indeed, in Japan wrapping has become such an important 'ordering principle' (Hendry 1990, 1993) that it (or 'form') is almost more significant than the content itself.

With regard to the *uchikake*, Rudofsky (1974:46) considers the confinement of women in their clothing as a sign of their objectification and subordination. This is particularly true of the *uchikake* and other kimono which Japanese women allow themselves to be wrapped in (Higuchi 1985:115; Beard 1953:98). On the other hand, Elizabeth Wilson (1985:244) has written that 'to understand all "uncomfortable" dress as merely one aspect of oppression of women is fatally to oversimplify'.

Japanese brides actively collaborate in the process of their own packaging, or in buying the packages in which they are wrapped by the producers of their weddings. Whether it is because young Japanese women are constantly bombarded with advertisements offering a multitude of products and services to enhance the female body (Moeran and Skov 1993), or whether today's 'Yenjoy girls' (Moeran 1989a) are major consumers in the market who are actively involved in consumption, they should perhaps be characterized as what Veblen (1957) termed 'vicarious consumers' for men and therefore 'a form of social capital' (Ewen and Ewen 1982:147) in consumerist society.

It should be clear by now that 'what is [being] consumed is not simply a material object that satisfies an all too rational need, but a symbolic meaning' (Baudrillard 1975:8–9). As Baudrillard (1981:5) sees it, 'consumption' has become a kind of labour, 'an active manipulation of signs', a sort of *bricolage* in which individuals desperately attempt to organize their privatized existence and invest it with meaning.

Douglas and Isherwood (1978:57), like Baudrillard, view consumption as 'the very arena in which culture is fought over and licked into shape'. In my terms, what we are talking about here is the consumption of culture and meaning. Although it is true that customers of the wedding industry buy services, they are also buying images and representations, or, in Baudrillard's terms, symbols or 'signs'. What is consumed in this 'system of sign exchange value' (Baudrillard 1981:113) is not the object itself, but the 'system' of objects, or a 'code'.

In this respect, although the cultural production and products used to construct the *traditionese* and *Westanese* elements of the modern Japanese wedding are invented and promoted by the industry's entrepreneurs, there is no doubt that this has been in response to the yearning (Davis 1979) or *akogare* for nostalgia, which is part of the construction of cultural identity or Japaneseness. In Chapter Six I proposed that the production and consumption of traditions are reciprocal, or in other words that Japaneseness is not produced and then imposed on a passive consumer. Instead, it should be regarded as the production *and* consumption of symbols. Again, in Baudrillard's terms, we 'reproduce' the system as we 'consume' the code (1981:5).

This 'creative consumerism' (Miller 1993a:22) of the middle class has also been observed with regard to modern interpretations of Christmas in Japan (Moeran and Skov 1993) and other parts of the Christian and non-Christian world (Miller 1993b). In this respect, the case of Japan seems to give the most evident example of the way in which 'capitalist commodity culture becomes a kind of language through which a national discussion takes place as to the future form of culture' (Miller 1993a:22).

Consuming Japaneseness can therefore be seen as part of the general process of negotiation and construction of the 'future form of [Japanese] culture'. Moeran and Skov (1993) describe the significant role which the media and advertising play in promoting the Japanese Christmas. They play no less important a role in the promotion of commercial weddings. I have suggested that Japanese wedding advertisements, like advertisements in general, are selling people not only services or consumer goods but also the idea of 'themselves' in terms of cultural identity (see Chapter Five). This view is related to that of consumption articulated by scholars like de Certeau (1984:166) who contends that consumption should be treated as an active, committed production of self and society.

One of the most striking characteristics of wedding advertisements in magazines aimed at young women is the over-representation of Western as opposed to traditional-Japanese brides. While this might be facilely explained by the all-too-familiar view concerning the ongoing process of Westernization or Americanization of Japan, a look at train-station advertisements gives us pause for further reflection. For, here, there is a quite fair representation of Japanese brides, including a profusion of advertisements for the imperial twelve-layer set as wedding attire.

One of the main reasons for the difference in advertisements between the magazines and train stations is the intended audience. While the 'cosmopolitan' Western images are aimed at young prospective brides (and possibly their grooms), it is their mothers, fathers and possibly their grandparents who will see the bridal representations in large train stations.

The same distinction applies to shows held at wedding parlours to display the range of possible outfits and accessories available. While the Kobe Princess Palace initiated modern bridal fairs with a central stage for Western attire to appeal to the young, it has not neglected the older-style smaller fairs aimed at *gojokai* members, mainly mothers, at which traditional costumes get the same attention as Western attire.

The diversity of images is also evinced in the specific commercial venue chosen for weddings, that is the wedding parlour versus the more prestigious modern hotel. As with the battle over what properly constitutes the modern Christmas (Miller 1993a:22), the market for the modern Japanese wedding is packed with competing images. While, in the case of the wedding, hotels, with their Western image, have not yet replaced wedding parlours, they have succeeded in capturing a large percentage of the market. And in the struggle over the definition of Japaneseness, the customers-*cum*-objects – the young brides – often come into conflict with beauty shop dressers who criticize them for feeling more comfortable in Western dress instead of understanding 'real' Japanese beauty.

Although the contested definition of Japaneseness may be genera-tional, it does not necessarily imply the Westernization of the young as opposed to the more traditionalist way of thinking held by those who are older. Instead, I propose to view these preferences as consumer choices in an active market which do not have to be made at the expense of either the traditional-Japanese or the Western. While more young couples (though many fewer than implied in the media) may have a 'chapel wedding' in Japan or go abroad for a 'Cinderella' wedding, these couples will often have a Japanese ceremony as well, or at least (if only for their parents' sake) have their picture taken in full traditional-Japanese regalia.

154

For the people involved, such a mixture of styles is not considered strange at all. The same young women (or prospective brides) may also willingly participate in English conversation lessons or French cooking classes in the same department store in which they take courses in calligraphy, flower arranging or tea ceremony (Creighton 1992:54). As Ivy (1988:27) puts it: 'The seemingly indiscriminate cultural mixing and matching that some have taken as a hallmark of contemporary Japan becomes, in the global postmodern situation, the simple prerogative of an affluent nation.'

Indeed, Japan may be the archetypical example of the contemporary consumer society which is more 'saturated with signs and messages' than any society has ever been (Jameson 1979:139). In a social formation in which culture is 'the very element of consumer society itself' (Jameson 1979:139), the *traditionese* and the *Westanese* cultural products may, like culture, merely be 'stylistic reference points' (Ivy 1988:27).

If, as I have suggested, 'traditions' (which are always invented) are, in the case of the modern Japanese wedding, related to form at least as much as to content, we return to Simmel's point about the inseparability of form and content (cited in Tenbruck 1959:72). Or, as Benjamin might have put it, only when we understand that 'the contents are just more images' (Jameson 1991:ix) can we see how the seemingly indigenous Japanese has become one more stylistic consumer choice. I would go even further and venture to suggest that the 'Japanese' and the 'Western' as presented herein – or more accurately, as they appear in the Japanese commercial wedding – should also be viewed as matters of style.

I have related the promotion of Japanese-style in the Japanese commercial wedding to the wave of nostalgia that began to spread in Japan in the 1970s. The study of nostalgia has taught us that in contemporary society – Japan included – waves of nostalgia are not 'innocent' or divorced from the interests of the state or other political and economic powers and the media (cf. Davis 1979:ch.6; Lasch 1984; Dominguez 1986). Indeed, the mechanisms of the 'politics of nostalgia', or those of the 'politics of heritage' (Kelly 1990) are very interesting and deserve much more attention in the Japanese case where 'in the current politics of heritage, traditionalism . . . is both state policy, metropolitan fetish and local identity' (Kelly 1990:80). This intriguing discussion pertains not only to questions of political abuse (Lasch 1984:65), but also to questions of the relationship between past and present.

Although the political implications of the nature of weddings in Japan are not that implicit, in other places in Asia such as the Republic of Korea, the wedding pattern has become part of an overt public and political discourse (Kendall 1994). In the case of Korean weddings where in the late 1960s 'traditional weddings' were reenacted as entertainment in theme parks, the past, evoked through nostalgia (as Anthony Brandt (1978) and Christopher Lasch (1984) understand the term), 'remains frozen in an ahistorical reconstruction' (Kendall 1994:181). It is clear that in such a reconstruction, nostalgia only 'uses the past – falsely, accurately, or in specially reconstructed ways – but it is not the product thereof' (Davis 1979:10–11).

Ivy (1988) presents an extreme example of the kind of nostalgia in which the sense of 'traditional' resides in the present. She describes a whole industry, including cosmetic companies and candy manufacturers, which is involved in producing 'nostalgia products' (*nosutarujii shohin*) and 'nostalgia advertisements' (*nosutarujii kokoku*). In this kind of nostalgia 'there is no appeal to return, no sense of loss, and no reference to actual memory. Instead it is nostalgia in quotation marks, citations of nostalgia' (Ivy 1988:28). In other words, it is a nostalgia that is related more to the production of 'style' than to a reproduction of the past.

These 'nostalgia products' are not only disconnected from any 'real' past but also displaced or 'decontextualized' (Appadurai 1986:28). Appadurai speaks of the 'aesthetics of decontextualization' which is 'at the heart of the display, in highbrow Western homes, of the tools and artifacts of the "other"'. However, whereas Appadurai refers to the presentation of artifacts which belong to the 'exotic' other, the Japanese – by creating such exotic artifacts as a 'geisha' bride – exhibit a similar attitude towards Japaneseness.

This Japanese propensity for 'self-Orientalization' or 'reverse Orientalization' (Miller 1982:209–211) is related to the way in which the Japanese see themselves, or more accurately present themselves to the Other – which has long been the West – and also to themselves. This 'presentation of self' (expanding Goffman's (1959) term from individual to nation or culture) is closely connected with the Japanese cultural identity.

In the same way that the 'West' plays an important role in the construction of the Japanese sense of self, it also plays a part in the peculiar 'Orientalism' (Said 1991) in which the Japanese tend to be involved. This has two channels: while the Japanese are involved in Orientalizing or exoticizing themselves to enhance the 'Japanese' character as unique, this reverse Orientalism also pertains to the 'monolithic' way (Mouer and Sugimoto 1986:32) in which they perceive the West. Moeran (1990a:9) suggests that this mirrors the same 'large collective terms' and 'abstract ideas' with which the West used to view Japan.

Thus, if the 'Japanese' has come to be a matter of style which thus can be decontextualized and displaced, the 'Western' is no less so. It is something that exists 'over there' or on 'the other side' (*mukō*) where neither historic accuracy nor geographical location play any significant role. The Western elements of the commercial wedding – such as the wax wedding cake and the candle service – are symbols of the 'imagined' West. They are taken eclectically from different parts of the Western world with no thought or interest about their origin or whether there is in fact *any* basis for their being considered Western. In this connection, Creighton (1992:55) tells us that 'the symbols and images of the West packaged by depāto [Japanese department stores] do not necessarily reflect the reality of any part of the Western world'.

The question is whether the fact that the traditional-Japanese (or *traditionese*) and the Western (or *Westanese*) are abstract perceptions, disconnected from 'reality', is really relevant. In this sense, the *Westanese* and the *traditionese* may be seen as part and parcel of Appadurai's (1990) 'imagined world', which is an extended version of Benedict Anderson's 'imagined community', in which contemporary Japanese – like other 'complex cultures' (Hannerz 1992) – live today. Whether one labels this world as 'late capitalism', 'postmodern' or 'global' I will leave others to define. What is apparent, however, is that such a 'culture' may be seen as a 'network of perspectives' or as an 'ongoing debate' (Hannerz 1992:266).

The *traditionese* and *Westanese* brides described in Chapter Five reflect this 'ongoing debate' as it applies to the construction of cultural identity. But here we must consider the complex role of Japanese women in this dialogue, since they play an active role as major consumers but are still constrained by the traditional image of women in Japanese society.

Bernstein (1993:13) considers the role and place of women in Japanese society crucial to the discourse on that society's identity. In her Introduction to *Recreating Japanese Women, 1600–1945* she writes: 'Indeed, Japan may be unique in having waged such a conscious discourse on women for such a long period of time, for since the early days of the Tokugawa rulers the "woman question" has engaged political leaders and the intellectual and moral elite alike.' According to Bernstein, this has meant that Japanese women 'have never been without clear role models' (p.14). However, as people relegated to the role of 'repositories of tradition' (see Chapter Four), Japanese women have always been in the midst of the conflict between tradition and modernity in Japan.

This position of Japanese women is evinced, for example, in the public fascination as well as debate over the 'Modern Girl' (*moga*) of the 1920s (Silverberg 1991) which captured all the ambiguity associated with the emergence of autonomous, liberated working women. Silverberg (p.240) sees the 'Modern Girl' as a 'highly commodified cultural construct crafted by journalists who debated her identity'. The interesting question here is how 'a female symbol came to portray all the contradictory values that were pulling Japanese society apart in the interwar period' (Bernstein 1991:11).

The 1920s Modern Girl, who was 'both Japanese and Western – or possibly neither', not only posed a 'threat to tradition' but also 'called into question the essentialism that subordinated the Japanese woman to the Japanese man' (Silverberg 1991:263). On the surface, our wedding-parlour bride seems quite similar to the 'Modern Girl', for she, too, is packaged in both Japanese and Western clothing and images. And she, too, is featured exclusively in the mass media, which celebrate her 'Once in a lifetime' or her 'Cinderella' dreams.

But does the modern bride pose any real threat to tradition? Silverberg (1991:263) argues that the Modern Girl of the 1920s 'played with the principle of cultural or national difference'. But what does she mean by 'play'? If, however, the Western and the Japanese are viewed as matters of style, can the same not be said of the two images and appearances of the modern Japanese bride? Although in terms of Baudrillard's (1981:51) 'game' between the 'old' and the 'new', the Modern Girl's Western appearance would seem to be an 'emblem for the threats to tradition' (Silverberger 1991:266), I view the modern bride's Western and Japanese appearances more as symbols of the 'good wife and wise mother' – the ideal Meiji woman, who continues to enjoy currency in today's Japan as a 'repository of the past' (Sievers 1983:15, 22–23; Goldstein-Gidoni 1993:228–231).

None the less, as Papanek (1977:15) has argued, women have often been assigned the role of repositories of 'traditional' values by active actors – usually men – typically in response to the stress the latter face in a rapidly changing society. In the case of Japan, the male-oriented West has played a role in assigning this 'Oriental' role to Japanese women. Early visitors to Japan such as Lafcadio Hearn (1894) and Townsend Harris began propagating what Robins-Mowry (1983:xviv) calls a 'remote aesthetic viewpoint' of the Japanese woman. Thus, Lafcadio Hearn (1904) enthused that: 'the most wonderful aesthetic *products* of Japan are not its ivories, nor its bronzes, nor its porcelains, nor any of its marvels in metal or lacquer – but its women' (my emphasis).

Robins-Mowry (1983:xviv) describes the objectification of Japanese women as symbols of Japaneseness as follows: 'The world gently placed this living, breathing woman into the glass box used throughout Japan to encase all treasured kimono-clad and artistically hand-wrought dolls. She was entrapped in the legends of her own perfection – a likeness that harmonized with those other perpetuated symbols of Japan: cherry blossoms and Mount Fuji'. However, Robins-Mowry's 'world' is too abstract to describe the reality. The addition of Said's (1991:6) 'male', 'Western' or 'wealthy' (or even 'Japanologist') would be more accurate. None the less, it is clear that the attitude towards women which Robins-Mowry criticizes helped create the image of the Japanese woman as similar to all the other (erotic) 'Oriental' women[1] as depicted by visitors to the 'Orient' (Said 1991:6). If she is presented as 'typically Japanese' in the first instance, she is presented as 'typically Oriental' in the second.

Although Robins-Mowry (1983:xviv) rightly accuses Japanese men of being 'equally guilty of limited visions about the distaff members of their society', one cannot ignore the role that Japanese women play in enhancing their 'mysterious and romantic aura', or, to put it more precisely, in objectifying themselves. Since, as I have pointed out, the Japanese bride collaborates in her own objectification, and Japanese women in general in the reproduction of their own objectified image, it seems clear that they actively collude in their own subordination. Thus, what Kandiyoti (1988:280) would view as 'bargaining with patriarchy' would also include reproduction of the 'Oriental/ Japanese' image of women in Japan, by women as well as men.

The commercial wedding, saturated as it is with a collage of images and representations of the Japanese and the Western, may seem to represent a mass of contradictions. However, one must never forget that, in a world where 'individuals are forced to negotiate life style choices among a diversity of options' (Giddens 1991:5), the choice between *Westanese* and *traditionese* is only one of many. Moreover, it should be reemphasized that this particular ambiguity is offered to wedding customers as a carefully packaged representation of their Japaneseness and sense of cultural identity, which they willingly purchase in their continuous attempt to imagine their world.

NOTES

Introduction

1 The quotation marks around 'traditional-Japanese' and 'Western' are meant to indicate exactly the point about their being 'cultural concepts' or discursive constructs rather than objective referents. I will generally not use quotation marks around these words (and similar words, such as 'Japanese') in the rest of the book, now that this point has been made.

Chapter one

1 Buddhist ceremonies are held mainly for members of the Sōka Gakkai sect. Although the Kobe Palace does not offer Christian weddings, other wedding parlours do have a church or a chapel. In all parlours there is also an option of having a non-religious ceremony, 'in front of people' (*hitomae*), in which case the shrine altar is covered. Unlike religious ceremonies conducted by priests, this type of ceremony is presided over by a front desk employee of the wedding parlour.

2 These gifts are given by the groom-to-be to his prospective bride in the *yuinō* (or betrothal) ceremony which is generally held a few months before the wedding, usually at the bride's house. For a detailed account of the *yuinō* ceremony, see Edwards (1989:78–83). The *yuinō* set consists of symbolic items which are used as a decoration for the main gift of cash (now accompanied by an engagement ring). The cash payment is now typically set as roughly three times the prospective groom's monthly salary (see Hendry 1981:158; Edwards 1989:82; Shiotsuki 1991:62). The symbolic set offered by the parlour includes a decorative set of pine, bamboo and plum (*shōchikubai*) which symbolizes happiness and celebration, in addition to a few other symbolic decorations (see Hendry 1981:159–160).

3 The word *kyaku* refers here both to the guests of the couple's families and to the clients of the parlour; *o* and *san* are added as honorifics.

4 While the wedding parlour attendant serves several weddings at the same time, this is usually not the case in hotel weddings, where a more prestigious ceremony is offered (see Chapter Two). There, a single attendant is nominated for each couple whom she serves and guides throughout the day. In both hotels and wedding parlours the attendants –

160

being the ceremonial guides – are dressed in kimono, unlike other workers, who wear Western style uniforms.

5 The photo studio is rented from the wedding parlour company by a privately owned company. Apart from the owner himself, there are three workers: two men and a young woman in her thirties. While the men are professional photographers, the woman acts as an assistant. (For more on the organizational aspects of the studio, see Chapter Three.)

6 These relatively rare cases are usually of couples who choose to marry abroad in one of the 'chapel weddings' offered by the wedding industry in Hawaii or Australia; this kind of wedding is considered more Western and therefore more modern. Others decline to have a full ceremony for a variety of family reasons, as in the case of a second marriage.

7 The difference between the bride's softer position, with hands held in front, lightly holding a fan, and that of the groom may be regarded as symbolic of gender relations in Japan. It should be noted, however, that while the groom's hand is fisted in his Japanese outfit, when he is photographed later in Western clothing, his pose, too, becomes softer and more open.

8 For the role of women as public announcers, see Moeran (1989a:22). In the Kobe Princess Palace women also act as the ceremonial 'attendants' (*kaizoe*) as well as the assistants in charge of arranging the 'objects' to be photographed. Moeran depicts Japanese society as a film in which it 'is usually women who act as mediators between [the film] frames' (1989a:20). Later on we shall see how even the periods between the 'frames' of the wedding day are used for taking photographs (or for being 'framed').

9 Group pictures are very popular throughout Japan. All famous tourist spots thus provide a set of benches of different heights so that all those in the group will be seen. Professional photographers are ready to snap the pictures of these groups, whether they be school children in their dark uniforms or groups of employees on a company trip (see Graburn 1983:49).

10 This 'division of labour' is characteristic of relations between studio workers and the dressers. While the former take care of the picture as a whole, the dressers' main task is to check the bride.

11 In some cases, as in hotel weddings I have witnessed, two priests conduct the ceremony (see also Edwards 1989:16). In prestigious hotels their costumes are often more elaborate, adding to the 'traditional' flavour of the 'performance'.

12 Although most people think of the *san-san-ku-do* (literally three-three-nine-times) only in connection with marriage, its meaning and use are broader. The sharing of ritual sake creates a deep and solemn bond between two people who are ordinarily considered unrelated. This symbolic tie can also bind the older and younger sisters in the geisha world (see Dalby 1983:41–43). This symbolic sake exchange in the wedding is also not necessarily connected to the Shinto ceremony. According to some accounts, in the past it was conducted in private, in front of the *nakōdo* (see Embree 1939:207–208; Bacon 1902:63). For a more detailed description of the Shinto ceremony, see Hendry (1981:178–180); Edwards (1989:15–19).

13 The Princess Palace endeavours to increase its variety of traditional-Japanese entrances. One such scenario is for three men, usually friends of the groom, dressed in a traditional *happi* coat (with the name of

Shōchikuden emblazoned on its back) to enter after the bride and groom carrying a wooden case and lantern to symbolize the carrying of the bridal trousseau. Like other invented traditions this dramatic scene does have some historical basis; however, it seems that in the process of invention (see mainly Chapter Six), two separate processions (that of the groom's side carrying a barrel of sake, fabric and a lantern, and that of the bride's side carrying an oblong chest [*nagamoci*] containing the bridal clothing (see Lebra 1984a:106–107)) were combined for a greater dramatic effect. None the less, this particular entry is not very popular, most young couples, according to the parlour's manager, preferring the standard entrance.

14 The 'gondola' may be in the shape of an Italian gondola or of a carriage. This device is not used at the Kobe Princess Palace, but is in use at other Shōchikuden parlours.

15 Using an employee as a master of ceremonies is typical of Shōchikuden. At the parlours of other companies, however, the master of ceremonies may be a friend of the groom (see Edwards 1989:20). But the strict pattern set by Shōchikuden is another example of this company's production efficiency.

16 Every wedding produced is programmed in advance, beginning with a detailed form giving the names of every speaker and every scheduled activity, including such particulars as the number and the type of costume changes and the names of guests who will offer songs or dances. There is a time limit for each activity, for example, three minutes for each congratulatory speech.

17 Here Creighton follows Judith Williamson (1978:13) ideas about advertisements. Williamson argues that 'in providing us with a structure in which we, and those goods [promoted by advertisements], are interchangeable, they [the advertisements] are selling us ourselves'.

Chapter two

1 'Ceremonial occasions' is the usual English translation used by those organizations for *kankon sōsai* and refers to initiation rites (*kan*), weddings (*kon*), funerals (*sō*), as well as to other festivals (*sai*).

2 The exchange of sake cups between the bride and groom as a seal of marriage seems to go back to the Heian period (794– 1185) (see Edwards 1989:38).

3 According to Smith (1978), the practice of home weddings continued much later in rural areas. They were one of three forms of weddings in the village he studied as late as 1975. The two other practices he mentions were dividing the wedding between the groom's house and the wedding parlour (most common), and a full wedding-parlour affair.

4 Indeed, even today, this remains the only direct service offered by Shōchikuden, other than the physical space in which the wedding is held. All the other services are offered by companies who rent space at the wedding parlours and share their profits with Shōchikuden.

5 Mr Utsunomiya used the membership fees to purchase the altar and decorations. Today these rites are offered to members in a special hall owned by the *gojokai* while the cremation is conducted at the municipal crematorium.

6 I must admit that it was difficult to get more details concerning the exact relations between the three companies. What came up over and over again in interviews with people at the top of each company, including members of the Utsunomiya family, was the duality of being separate companies as well as one entity. Business confidentiality, I suppose, is only one reason for the difficulty in getting such information; family relations and possibly family intrigues are another.

7 This system is similar to that of other large commercial household confederations in Japanese history. Such confederations are called *noren uchi* (within the shop curtain). They all had a main household (*honke*) to which two types of branches were related; those headed by blood-related kin (*bunke*), and those headed by non-kin (*bekke*). Apparently, merchant households were especially receptive to non-kin members, for merchants were not dependent on land as their chief resource (see Kondo (1990:162–175); see also Nakane (1967) and (1984); Hamabata (1990)).

8 I should note that I was given this version in which parlour owners were always former apprentices by Utsunomiya Chikajidō's daughter. According to her, no one has ever paid for the right to use their name. However, I heard a slightly different version from the manager of the Kobe Princess Palace, who insisted that the right has sometimes been purchased. It is difficult to establish whether this discrepancy is a result of lack of knowledge of a company employee (the manager) or one between ideology and reality. If the latter is the case, it is interesting to see it as an attempt to attach a 'traditional' attribute to the company.

9 There are various theories concerning what constitutes an auspicious day. For example, April is not considered a good month because the cherry blossoms are falling then and because it connotes death; although its name, *shigatsu*, literally means fourth month, *shi* in a different character also denotes death. May with its spring atmosphere is regarded as a very good month. Although seasonal considerations have not been totally abandoned, the wedding industry has succeeded in promoting 'June Weddings'. The sparse summer months are gaining in popularity since the parlours are offering cheap weddings during these months and enticing customers by explaining that, with air-conditioning, their ceremony and reception will be just as comfortable as in the autumn or spring.

10 The most auspicious day for weddings is considered to be *daian* (or *taian*), which is considered lucky for any ceremony. For more about the lunar-month system see Hendry (1981:240–242). On the issue of scheduling weddings from the customers' point of view, see Edwards (1989:83–86).

11 The links between *gojokai* organizations have some formal expression, in collaborative associations such as *Zen Nihon Kankon Sōsai Gojo Kyōkai* (All Japan Ceremonial Occasions Mutual Benefit Association) and *Zen Nihon Kankon Sōsai Gojo Kyōdō Kumiai* (All Japan Ceremonial Occasions Mutual Benefit Cooperative Association). These organizations each have their own publications which they circulate to the wedding parlours. *Zen Nihon Kankon Sōsai Gojo Kyōkai* also occasionally publishes material for the general public, including comic books (*manga*) which explain all that prospective members need to know about the *gojokai* organizations.

163

12 One magazine explicitly for brides-to-be is *Bright Bridal*, which provides up-to-date information about wedding outfits, honeymoons and usually includes a lengthy review of one wedding facility. In March 1987 it featured a forty-page promotion on Shōchikuden paid for by the Shōchikuden Group. Among the general women magazines which have recurrent references to weddings are *25 Ans* and *Classy* – which carry English names as an indication of modernity and style.

13 One of these magazines is *Hanayome* (Bride) which is aimed specifically at professional dressers. This magazine is often used by the wedding parlour as a source for imitating new fashions for their inventory of rental clothing.

14 The same accounts for the rise in popularity of church weddings (3.2 per cent local churches in 1982; 7.3 per cent in 1990). To young Japanese, churches symbolize Western modernity, and having their wedding ceremony in a church has nothing to do with religion.

15 Although I use a pseudonym, I stay loyal to the spirit of the real name as well as to the explanations given by the company.

16 In a television advertisement, the company gave another interpretation of the new name in which 'Bella' represented a bell, which was present in the advertisement. Of course, this bell was supposed to 'ring a bell' to ('Western') wedding bells.

17 The same concept lies behind the name Princess Palace. Indeed, this tendency seems prevalent throughout Japan; in 1991 ten companies listed on the Tokyo Stock Exchange changed their corporate names, 'hoping to create a modern and international image' (*The Daily Yomiyuri*, April 1991). This spate of corporate name changes hit Japan as a result of the 'CI' (or corporate identity) boom in the early 1980s (Fields 1988).

18 The old-style bridal show is a one-day event which includes a free lunch for members and prospective members while the Bridal Fairs extend over two or three days. Some of the participants, all of whom are invited to attend by saleswomen, are long term members who have scheduled a wedding or are planning one for a son or, more probably, a daughter who has reached the right age for marriage. Others are prospective members invited in the hope that the show's displays of costumes, available mini-dramas and special effects will convince them to join the association.

19 The Nishinomiya wedding parlour was torn down in 1990. Although the reason given was that business did not go very well there, that parlour looked old-fashioned compared to Cobella's newer halls, with its facade in a (shrine-like) Japanese style and its interior much less luxurious and spacious. Thus, it appears that the decision to tear it down was based on its being out of date (which was most likely why business was relatively slow there).

20 These figures are from 1989, when Cobella celebrated its 20th anniversary. The number of establishments is probably slightly higher now, since new facilities are added every year. Most of Cobella's parlours have been established by the company, although it has also taken over less successful existing parlours. These mergers have been with competing *gojokai* companies as well as within the Shōchikuden Group itself (*Kankon Sōsai Times*, 1989).

21 At about the same time the total number of *gojokai* members in Japan was said to be seventeen million (Sanda and Tsuda:1988). At the end of March

1991 payments made to *gojokai* businesses by members totalled ¥1.018 trillion (about £4 billion sterling at the 1991 conversion rate; up 7 per cent from the previous year). This is the amount reported by *gojokai* organizations to the Ministry of International Trade and Industry (*The Japan Times*, 18 July 1991).

22 It is important to note that although I refer here mainly to wedding packages, the money accumulated in each grade can be used for the funeral of any family member, if such a need arises.

23 The pamphlets distributed to the members emphasize that 'No matter how much prices rise, the content of the service stipulated in the contract when you subscribed is not going to change.' In addition, according to the contract, Cobella promises 7 per cent interest on the money over five years. There is no mention of a case in which the services will be used after five years.

24 One can also transfer one's rights to a different *gojokai* if one moves to a different area; but this is subject to certain conditions, including the consent of the second *gojokai*. When this is approved, however, the member always sustains a loss.

25 A rather cynical expression of Edwards' (1989:120–123) main argument about the incompleteness of each sex finding its solution in 'harmonious' marriage.

26 This is not related to the covering of wedding costs which are usually shared by the families and the couple themselves, who often contribute a relatively high share of the costs.

27 One bride married in a hotel because her groom felt a wedding parlour to be beneath the honour of his guests. However, they chose a 'traditional' Shinto ceremony because, in the bride's words, 'a modern wedding was out of the question because the groom was from the countryside'.

28 There is a bringing-in fee (*mochikomi-riyō*) which customers must pay when they supply their own clothing. This fee is covered by Cobella. In the rare cases in which brides bring their own clothing to the Princess Palace, they too must pay a fee.

29 The manager of the Kobe Princess Palace boasted of his success in keeping most of the couples in the wedding parlour. But even in his case more than 20 per cent of the brides use their 'packages' at other facilities. And the percentage goes as high as 50 per cent in other Cobella parlours.

30 This does not include the large number of snapshots taken throughout the wedding. Nor does it include optional studio photographs such as that of the *nakōdo* couple or the bridal couple photograph with their parents.

31 Sanwa Ginkō (Sanwa Bank) 1990 *Kyoshiki zengo no suitōbo* (A Ledger of Wedding Expenditures). Tokyo: Sanwa Ginkō Kōhōbu Home Consultant.

32 The total expenditure includes expenses such as the cash payment for the engagement and a cash gift to the *nakōdo* from which the wedding industry does not benefit directly.

Chapter three

1 Using subcontractors is not uncommon in the Japanese economy. It is very common in the automobile industry, where a firm like Nissan sub-contracts

70 per cent of the cost of goods and services used in the production of a small car. The percentage is even higher in other industries (see Clark 1987:68). In these cases, however, the majority of the sub-contracted work is done outside and then brought into the plant.

2 In the two latter instances, they promote the products (furniture and honeymoon plans) of sub-companies of the Shōchikuden Group. The furniture is offered by a company called Shōchikukagu (Shōchiku-Furniture) which produces and sells bridal furniture (*konrei kagu*). The honeymoon plans service is called Shōchikuden-Travel Service.

3 Even though most workers are employed on a part-time basis, some – like the young student shrine maidens – have a lower status, being employed as *arubaito* (as opposed to *pāto*). The word *arubaito*, which originally meant student job, is now used in reference to all jobs which are insecure or casualized (Saso 1990:155).

4 I was not able to extract information on the Princess Palace's percentages in this case. However, from figures that I received for companies which supply their goods through the beauty shop, I estimate that the parlour takes at least 30 per cent, and possibly more.

5 One direction to follow in looking at this relationship is that of 'Japanese company' studies. Such studies (e.g., Abegglen 1958; Rohlen 1974; Vogel 1979; Nakane 1984) tend to emphasize harmony in both Japanese companies and society. In this respect, such interdependence and the resultant internal conflicts raise serious questions regarding such views (see Goldstein-Gidoni 1993:132–138)

6 Their name derives from the combination of business (or trade) (*eigyō*) with the common honorific attached to any name in Japanese (*san*), here translated as 'sales lady'.

7 The *seijin shiki* is a ceremony conducted on 15 January for twenty year-olds all over Japan in which girls are usually dressed in kimono which can be rented at relatively low prices through the *gojokai*. The same goes for the 7-5-3, representing the ages of children who go and visit shrines dressed in kimono.

8 Using middle-aged women as relatively cheap labour can be viewed as another way in which the parlour uses people (and companies) to its own best interest. These sales ladies usually start working after their children are grown. As one of them put it: 'There is no use being at home after the children have grown up, is there? (*kodomo ga okiku natta kara uchi ni iru no wa mottainai, deshō*)'.

9 Although Mrs Suzuki presents herself as a widow, she is actually divorced. She has kept this 'flaw' in her life a secret because she thought it might interfere with her job. As she puts it: 'People who are involved in auspicious work are not supposed to have such an experience.' She disclosed her big secret confidentially to the beauty shop manager and to me in a hotel coffee shop while we were waiting for a chapel ceremony to end on an 'outside job'. After telling us her story, she asked us not to repeat it to anyone.

10 The Japanese mother usually sees it as her responsibility to marry off her children. Her duties include the successful execution of matrimonial ceremonies (Lebra 1984a:260–262).

11 The Japanese are very fond of comic books and use them frequently as guide books on various aspects of life.

12 The Japanese over-inclination to rely on formal sources regarding etiquette and the importance they give to 'form' is presented cynically by one of Japan's leading film directors. In *Sōshiki* (Funeral, or *Death Japanese Style* in the English version) Itami Jūzū, who is known for his satirical films about Japanese society, tells the story of a family's struggle with the difficult formalities surrounding the funeral of an old father. In one of the more sarcastic scenes, the hero, who is very concerned about his ability to perform in the funeral, watches a video about funerals over and over again while trying to memorize the role he will have to play.

13 There are some clear signs that someone belongs to the *yakuza*. Men can be distinguished by tattoos which usually cover their bodies (Lebra 1976:185–186, Raz 1992:219). Although the tattooing may only be discovered by the dresser, other symbols such as a missing finger, permanent-waved hair, a gold bracelet, or sun-glasses suggest the same. It is usually more difficult to detect when a woman is related to a *yakuza* family. Here one must rely on more subtle signs such as her relatively rude behaviour, the way she wears her kimono, or a slightly daring style of Western clothing.

14 It was also interesting to note how the definition of 'relatives', the people who participate in the Shinto ceremony, was elaborated to include the wife of the head of the *yakuza* group in the area (*oyabun*). This is not surprising considering the organization of the yakuza group along lines of fictive kinship (Lebra 1976:172–176).

15 Lebra (1976:170) writes that, despite the fear or disapproval most Japanese feel towards the *yakuza*, some aspects of their behaviour are considered beautiful and morally valid. This is one of the reasons for the glorification of *yakuza* in popular literature and films (Moeran (1989a:161–176)). Raz (1992:211) also mentions this dual image 'of both romance and terror' which conventional society holds of the *yakuza*. In this respect, it is interesting to note the attitude of the parlour workers which was characterized by extreme curiosity. Employees came to 'watch' the couple and their guests as they would popular idols (*tarento*). The participation in this wedding of some actual film stars only added to the admiration.

16 This correlation between company size and productivity, level of wages, and stability of labour force is usually referred to as 'dual economy' (Broadbridge 1966; Yasuba 1976) or 'industrial gradation' (Clark 1987).

Chapter four

1 Because of their role in bridal preparations, hairdressers had business connections with the kimono rental shops which were involved in the establishment of the *gojokai* organizations, the forerunners of the comprehensive wedding parlours.

2 Interestingly enough, towards the end of my fieldwork there was a plan to have a dresser act as the bride's attendant throughout the ceremony. Although I do not know if this plan was ever put into effect, the idea is interesting in itself as another example of the 'invention of tradition' – the

invention in this case taking the form of 'playing with tradition'. This clearly illustrates how the wedding industry manipulates former 'traditions' to attain more efficient – and profitable – weddings.

3 The designation *kitsuke no hito* used in the wedding parlour context is a recent term which developed during the 1970s along with kimono schools that teach kimono 'dressing' (*kitsuke*).

4 Lebra (1984a:60) argues that it was the stigmatization of working women as 'low-class' which until recently blocked them from occupational careers.

5 The phrase used is *hanayome o tsukuru*, literally 'making a bride'. The term refers specifically to the Japanese appearance of a bride in *uchikake* (overgarment) and wig.

6 The story of Sakamoto Sachiko is not the only story of a beautician, or rather of a bridal expert, who knew how to take advantage of the changes in the wedding industry. An even more remarkable story is that of Tamura Keiko, now owner of three wedding parlours and nine funeral parlours in a rival company. Tamura started to work as a beautician at the age of fifteen. Like Sakamoto, she was left without financial support after she divorced her husband at the age of twenty-three. Tamura actually 'sensed' the developments in the wedding business much earlier than Sakamoto when she decided to open a kimono rental shop soon after the war. Then, she joined the *gojokai* with its establishment in 1948. Although she left the beautician's profession long ago, her know-how, together with her contacts in the kimono rental business and, of course, her prominent business skills, have made her an outstanding success.

7 One clear example of the respectful attitude towards Sakamoto Sachiko is that she is referred to as '*sensei*' ('master' of a certain art) even by the owners of Cobella and the Shōchikuden Group.

8 Sakamoto Sachiko's two sons play no part in the business; both are salary-men. When asked why her husband is not involved in the business, her daughter-in-law Sakamoto Keiko first said that it was because men could not do the women's work of dressing (*kitsuke*). Then she added that, on second thought, there were men who 'did beauty (*biyō*)', as in hair styling. Another reason she gave was that her husband saw the profession as a low-level one in which there were no university graduates. Ironically, her husband, an engineer educated in America, has suggested that their son – who has tried unsuccessfully for the last three years to enter university (*rōnin*) – should join the beauty business and take advantage of his grandmother's property. Apparently, however, the young man himself is too proud to agree: 'Only people who cannot enter an ordinary university are becoming beauticians.'

9 Sakamoto's daughter was described by one of her sisters-in-law as a 'weak' (*yowai*) person, whose 'illness' has never been clearly defined: 'She has always had a weak body and she has always caused worries. . . . Also it is in her character to always worry.' The sister-in-law went on to say that the hard work in the shop made her start losing weight. This sort of explanation for a physical condition connected to both personality and social and work pressures is not uncommon in Japan.

10 Using a loan word for the beauty shop's name is not unique. While the first shop opened by Sakamoto had a Japanese name – Shōchiku (literally 'pine

and bamboo') – the newer shops have names like Baron and Cinderella. (See Chapter Two for a similar trend with wedding parlour names.)

11 About five women are employed in the clothing department. The two who work as advisors to customers have been employed for a relatively long time (more than two years). One of these women is fully employed, the other is employed as a part-timer (earning ¥600 per hour) even though she works almost every day. Another more recent part-timer also works as an advisor, but she is only summoned to work on busy days. Apart from these, there are two or three part-timers who work at the back (*ura*) and are in charge of costume maintenance. Their salaries are lower.

12 Only the area of the beauty salon and the brides' room which is attached to it is rented by the beauty shop. The other space it uses in its work belongs to the wedding parlour.

13 This is important because it makes the room a 'restricted' area of the beauty shop into which 'outsiders' such as the sales ladies can not enter freely. When outsiders do enter the room, they feel obliged to apologize for their rudeness (by using the appropriate Japanese phrase *shitsurei shimasu*).

14 It seems that horses are sometimes viewed as bringers of good fortune. Horses were given as offerings to shrines in early Shinto because, being expensive objects, they represented a sincere feeling on the part of the donor. It was also believed by many that horses were a kind of go-between between humans and the gods (*kami*). One can still see sacred horses at some Shinto shrines. At the most famous shrine – Ise – they are white. It is even possible that the white horses for the shop were bought there. (Personal communication from Ian Reader, whom I would like to thank.)

Nevertheless, although the horses were treated like gods, either Keiko nor her mother-in-law could answer the question why these white horses were sacred. I was only told that they were given as a present to Sakamoto when she opened the shop. It seems, however, that the beauty shop employees take the horses less seriously than do the owners. Once, when an expensive melon was put into the glass box as an offering, one of the veterans, a humorous person, said: 'I wish I were god' (*kami-sama ni naritai*). It is, however, also worth noting that the melon was later given to the owner, Sakamoto Sachiko, which may reflect her importance in the eyes of her employees.

15 These envelopes, like those given on happy celebrations, are tied with red and white paper strings (*mizuhiki*); black string is used for funerals. On the ceremonial role of this kind of 'wrapping' see Hendry (1990:21; 1993).

16 Recently, brides have taken to wearing both a white and a coloured *uchikake*; naturally, they are photographed in both. Since the change from one *uchikake* to another is relatively simple (because it is just an overgarment), it is performed in the photo studio itself. Another dressing task which is performed in the studio is re-binding (or packing: *karage*) the bride's *uchikake* after it has been opened for the photograph.

17 Kimono schools are relatively recent institutions that were established in order to teach contemporary Japanese women the forgotten art of how to wear kimono. First established in the 1970s, they have gained enormous success during recent years (see Goldstein-Gidoni 1993, ch. 6).

18 It seems that Sakamoto Sachiko divided her property in this way not only because she wanted to help her children – or because, as she puts it, her

daughters-in-law wanted to help her – but also for tax reasons. (See Chapter Two for a similar process in Shōchikuden itself.)

19 As the one in charge of bride-making she is supposed to be, if not a licensed beautician, at least a graduate of advanced courses in kimono dressing, as she is actually considered by other employees and customers. I was surprised when she told me that she had never taken any advanced classes in kimono dressing, but learned most of what she knows from Sakamoto Sachiko and, as we shall see later on, this may have helped her adjust so well to the beauty shop's particular way of work.

20 In Japan people tend to greet each other more by commenting about the situation than by inquiring about the other's well-being. As such, greetings describing the weather are very common. In the wedding-parlour context, a common greeting is 'It is busy today, isn't it?'.

21 I have chosen to use the Japanese mainly because of the connotation that the word 'mistress' sometimes has in English.

22 While all wedding parlour workers and clients call every dresser *sensei*, novices at the shop are corrected when they call their seniors '*sensei*'.

It is interesting then, that Sakamoto's daughter-in-law, Keiko is called Keiko-*sensei* an unusual combination of first name and the title, with a clear touch of familiarity. In Keiko's case, the title is more a (capitalist) sign of ownership than of (respected) mastery of art. The clear difference in the shop employees' attitude towards the two Sakamotos is another sign of their different status. While Sakamoto Sachiko is indeed treated as a 'mistress' – especially by shop veterans who act as her servants, dressing her, combing her hair, carrying her bag – this treatment is not given to Keiko, who is on more friendly terms with the employees, especially the full-timers.

23 The brides prepared by the *ō-sensei*'s own hands were considered very fortunate. In many cases they were told how lucky they were to have been 'made up' by the mistress of our company (*uchi no sensei desu*). (About the use of *uchi* (literally the inside, the interior) to signify the speaker's company (or household, or school) see Nakane 1984:3–4, Hamabata:1990:46–47.)

24 The *ō-sensei*'s orders were usually given in a very direct, superior way: 'You, do the back . . . You, why don't you do something . . .' The terms *anata* or *anta* ('you') sound almost derogatory in a society like Japan, where direct approach is usually avoided. In any case, they are a clear sign of the speaker's superiority.

25 New part-timers actually earn only ¥500, since the shop deducts ¥50 for training them. By comparison, a high school or college student who works in a fast-food restaurant can earn between ¥700 and ¥800 per hour.

26 Acquiring a dressing licence at one of the Kimono schools is usually expensive. The schools charge not only for the lessons (about ¥3000 per meeting), but also for accessories and textbooks. I was told by one of the part-timers that she had spent one million yen on her licence.

27 When satisfied customers (mostly brides' mothers) give tips (*oshūgi*) to the dressers, they are collected by the *ō-sensei*, who decides how to divide the money. It is then added to the dressers' salaries, in a separate envelope. The veterans view this addition to their pay more as acknowledgement of their work by the beauty shop founder and owner, whom they thank warmly, than

as money they have earned. (It is also a way in which both sides avoid taxes.) Loyal veterans may also receive other extras in the form of trips or invitations to restaurants with the owner. Such treats are an example of the attempt to create a 'company as family' (Rohlen 1974; Kondo 1990).

28 Lebra (1984a:240) argues that one of the most gratifying rewards for professional women is social; social relations between the *sensei* and her previous disciples exemplifies this kind of reward.

29 Kondo (1990:235–236) argues that the most exemplary form of *kurō* (hardship) occurs when one must leave one's natal home, for separation from one's circle of attachments is a form of suffering. The importance of being trained outside the natal home still seems prevalent. The *ō-sensei* told me about the young daughter of one of her apprentices who went back to the countryside and opened a shop and had recently sent the girl to study with the *ō-sensei* at the Himeji shop.

30 Moeran (1984a:201–204) finds that the co-existence of aesthetic and practical in the field of pottery-making has a major bearing on aesthetic appreciation. He also argues that the link between practicality and beauty is related to the subconscious Shinto beliefs with which Japanese aesthetics in general are imbued (1984a:24).

31 These skills are part of a social expertise which, according to Lebra (1984a:239–240), is a necessary supplement to technical expertise. Lebra tells of a beautician who used to give a morning class to her employees every day, on how to improve their attitude towards customers.

32 Although the common translation of *shutchō* is 'business trip', I am not convinced that this serves in the current context; 'outside (out) job' is perhaps more suitable.

There are two kinds of outside jobs: (1) When dressers are sent to the bride's house to prepare her for a wedding taking place at the wedding parlour, which is quite rare today since most brides are prepared in the wedding facility. This is a relatively short job. (2) The most common outside job today is when dressers are sent to another wedding facility where they handle the bride's costume changes during the wedding and dress close family members, as well as take care of the initial preparations. This usually takes a full working day.

33 Reminiscence about the past (*mukashi*) may be connected with building an ideal image of the past. Moeran (1984a:165–166) argues that it is the decline of community solidarity which has led to the construction of an ideal image of the past 'community' among the potters he studied. It seems that the notion of *mukashi* is prevalent in Japan, mainly – but not only – in rural society. Dore (1978:65–66) comments on the frequency with which Shinohata people reminisce about the past, mainly about the hard times before the war as compared to the relative luxury of the present. It seems that, in all these cases, nostalgic tones are used more when speaking to an outsider. (The relationship between *mukashi* and *dentō* (tradition) mentioned by Moeran (1984a:165) will be dealt with below.)

34 The fact that Keiko specializes in Western dressing, which does not have the aura of traditionalism, is also important in this respect.

35 The Himeji shop which the *ō-sensei* manages evinces the influence of the *ō-sensei*. This shop is much better organized and employs much younger

women who are more careful of their appearance (high heels, no short socks) than the Kobe shop. Moreover, they are much more rigorously trained and severely treated.

36 Sakamoto Sachiko's greatest pleasures apart from her work – which she also sees as pleasure – is playing mah-jong (a Chinese game for four resembling rummy) with her friends. However, although she enjoys playing the game in her free time, she is actually worried that it will begin boring her if she were to do only this.

37 Keiko's daughter had just begun to study music at university, as her mother had done earlier.

38 Dalby (1993:65; ch. 4) explains how Japan of the Meiji period that 'became obsessed with its 'national essence'', 'revived', or even better so, invented the kimono primarily for women.

39 Sievers (1983:14–15) argues that the banning of short hair for women is revealing in this respect; while men (particularly samurai) were strongly advised to forgo long hair-styles in favour of the shorter, more 'practical' Western hair-cut, a law banning short hair for women was issued in 1872.

Chapter five

1 According to the Sanwa Bank survey, in 1990 only 2.5 per cent of 600 surveyed brides had no costume changes (Sanwa 1990). Costume changes are also reported by Hendry (1981) and Edwards (1989).

2 In her view, the *uchikake* would lose its importance in a few years. She was the only wedding entrepreneur who held this view, others generally predicting a more optimistic future for the *uchikake*, although they usually said that it was hard to predict.

3 This event consists of speeches by public figures as well as the young people themselves, all on becoming an adult. Recently, however, girls' costumes have come to be the most striking feature of the day (see Hendry 1981:206, Goldstein-Gidoni 1993:194–204).

4 Although the appropriate marriageable age for girls has shifted over the years, it remains in the twenties – preferably no later than twenty-five. According to the 1990 Sanwa Bank survey the average bride's age was twenty-five years and eight months. Lebra (1984a:90) argues that the notion of *tekireiki* limits the woman's bargaining power in marriage negotiations. One of her informants quoted a tea ceremony instructor's counsel that a woman must retract one demand (or requirement in a husband) for each year she added to her age. In such a marital strategy, twenty-five seems to be a turning point. A Japanese woman who does not marry when 'the time is ripe' risks being ridiculed as a 'Christmas cake' (*kurisumasu keeki*): the elaborate Christmas cake is so desirable before December 25 but, like the Japanese woman, totally useless after the twenty-fifth.

5 The fashion of wearing white and coloured *uchikake* is quite recent. Before, it was either of them. It has also become fashionable to add a long plait (*naga*) to the bride's wig for her entrance to the reception hall.

6 A similar attitude towards the wedding dress could be observed in the 1995 Australian film, *Muriel's Wedding*, which tells the story of an unattractive young woman whose greatest dream is to get married. For some time she materializes

her aspiration by visiting all bridal attire shops in Melbourne and gathering her photographs in elaborate wedding dresses in an elegant photo album.

7 The workers of the various companies are not called by their own names but rather by their company name followed by the suffix *san* (Ms, Mrs or Mr).

8 Although the bride might be unaware of this competition, she may well feel the pressure. This may be one of the reasons why the parlour manager decided towards the end of my fieldwork to exclude workers from outside companies from the fair and to hand over all responsibility to the beauty-shop owner and her employees.

9 These advertisements are found mainly in women's magazines. Prices for the treatments vary from ¥9,000 for a body treatment to ¥12,000 for hand treatments and 'from ¥60,000' for a 'comprehensive plan'.

10 Interestingly enough this excessive concern with the female body is also typical of advertisements for 'Christmas Eve', which has become 'a night for two' in Japan (Moeran and Skov:1993). In both cases the language is that of consumerism aimed at the young women.

11 The generation gap between the new generation (*shin jinrui*) and the older generation can be observed here, as the bows of the dressers and the bride's mothers are generally much deeper than those of the bride. Even the younger bride-makers usually bow less deeply than those brought up according to older codes of etiquette.

12 The relatively easy task of painting the bride's arms and hands (in a more pinkish liquid paint) is sometimes performed by an assistant (*joshu*) to save time.

13 The notion of the beauty of fair skin goes much beyond the wedding and the bride. Even today, Japanese women make every effort to avoid the sun, using a parasol and avoiding beaches, although this attitude applies less to younger women. The preference of white skin for women is probably related to the notion that upper-class women never had to expose themselves to the sun. Therefore white skin has always been prized as evidence of social superiority. (White face colour is also used by geisha and Kabuki actors.)

14 On the similar geisha make-up, see Dalby (1983:1321–1333).

15 The wig is fashioned in the *Takashimada* coiffure, a style of hair dressing known to be worn by daughters of the Samurai class in the past. On the wig and wig decorations as another 'playground' for market competition, see Chapters Three and Six.

16 The verb 'to make' (*tsukuru*) is used only for bridal make-up and dressing. For other kimono dressing, the special term *kitsuke* (literally, dressing) is always used. The verb *tsukuru* has a very broad meaning in Japanese; according to the Kenkyusha New Japanese Dictionary, it also means 'to create' and 'to manufacture'.

17 While other 'correction' sets are made in the beauty shop, the bride's set is purchased from a professional *hosei* maker at a very high price. In 1990 the beauty shop had to pay as much as ¥3,000 for a set of this kind, even though the fee the shop received from the wedding parlour for dressing the bride was only ¥10,000.

18 According to Jeremy and Robinson (1989:116–117), the bride used to carry seven objects on her journey by foot to the ceremony. These, called

hakoseko, comprised needle and thread, fan, purse, mirror, comb, and a pair of scissors. Embree (1939:206) described a similar practice in which 'a traditional purse containing a mirror, pin, and crystal ball, and a fan were tucked in a very wide and very tight belt'.

19 The original function is interpreted as being to hide the face and avoid the evil eye (*jashi*), and to stop the horns of jealousy (Hendry 1981:195, n.54).

20 Today these garments are seen only in wood-block prints, and, to some degree, in the world of the geisha. Such feminine figures are known in the West as belonging to the 'floating world' (*ukyiyo-e*: pictures – *e*, of the *ukiyo* – floating world) of the Edo period, i.e., the world of theatre and the pleasure quarters.

21 Townsend Harris, one of the first Western visitors to Japan, wrote that the Japanese lady 'minces her steps as tho' her legs were tied together at her knees' (Rudofsky 1985:46).

22 Ben-Ari (1991) mentions the teaching of a stylized way of walking to young archers in a village 'rite of passage' which initiates male youth aged twenty into the adult community. This stylized way of walking, he argues, resembles that used in Japanese theatre performances.

23 While we find continuity in the passivity of the bride, it seems that the groom has come to have a much more passive role than he used to in home weddings. This point may be considered in the light of the commercialization and formalization of the wedding ceremony in which both bride and groom are objects.

24 Japanese girls and women use relatively more make-up than in the West. From adolescence onwards, foundation cream and lipstick are indispensable to their appearance.

25 This beauty shop advertisement was published in a women's magazine. It showed a bride in a white *uchikake* and *watabōshi* (head covering) with a stripe of red collar and a red belt. Although a touch of colour to the collar is a common practice, a belt is never used when wearing *uchikake*. Thus the red belt which obviously catches the eye is meant to emphasize the red over white with all its social-cultural connotations, especially that of beauty.

26 The phrase is often used during the training of bridal dressers when the *ō-sensei* creates a 'perfect' bride. When I acted as a model at one of the bridal fairs and was 'made' by the head of the brides' room, I (or was it the dresser?) was also paid this compliment.

27 A perfect example of a protected 'girl in a box' is Yukiko, the youngest of the Makioka sisters in the novel of the same name (Tanizaki 1958). Although already over thirty, Yukiko was raised in such a protected environment that she is too shy to speak on the telephone or to meet serious prospective husbands on her own.

28 These are usually Western dolls. In the early 1990s, the Seven Dwarves from Walt Disney's 'Snow-White' were very popular as car decorations.

29 An example of the ultimate 'cutie' was Seiko Matsuda, Japan's most popular female singer of the early and mid 1980s, who conveyed a childish image in both her voice and her body.

30 It is interesting that the Japanese bride is not in *uchikake* but in a black *furisode*, which was worn by brides before the wedding industry promoted the *uchikake*. The beauty shop may be trying to present a more traditional

image or to promote the black *tomesode*. A similar attempt has been made by the wedding industry before. A special issue of 'The Bride' (*Hanayome*) (October 1987), the magazine for professional dressers, devoted to the 'Old Days' Boom' (*orudo daizu bumu*), had as its central figure the 'classical' (*koten*) bride in a black kimono.

31 See Winship (1983:50) on the interesting relations between consumption, individuality and fashion in Western women's magazines.

Chapter six

1 The tendency or preference of young Japanese brides and their mothers to ignore historical facts is somewhat similar to that of visitors to the Mikimoto Pearl Island Museum, who seem not to notice the written information that the white clothing of the *ama* (diving women) was designed by Mikimoto himself, preferring to believe that it is 'traditional'. Martinez (1990:102) regards this as a kind of symbolic invention of tradition.

2 See Ema (1971) and *Kindai Nihon Fukusō-shi* (History of Dress in Modern Japan) (1971) for the variety of wedding fashions and how they have changed since the Meiji period, and for the origins of the white colour of the *uchikake*.

3 Hendry (1981:170, 195, n.54) says that the *tsunokakushi* – which is generally interpreted as covering the 'horns of jealousy' or the bad traits of the woman's character which must be hidden to signify the future obedience of the wife – is a more recent and simplified version of the *watabōshi*.

4 The 'balance' (*barancu*) between bride and groom is strictly kept in the wedding parlour. For example, grooms choose the colour of their tuxedos in accordance with the bride's dress. Moreover, the black *haori* has recently begun to be offered in colours as well, which only emphasizes the point that the 'traditional' is open to innovation, adjustments and fashions.

5 These include: Norbeck (1954:179–180); Cornell and Smith (1956:80 photo), and Beardsley *et al*. (1959:102), as well as information gathered from informants, and a perusal of Japanese literature, including professional 'dressing' magazines.

6 Quoted in *Hanayome* ('The Bride'), a professional magazine for 'dressing' (*kitsuke*). '*Kitsuke Zuisō*' ("Dressing" – Occasional Thoughts'), in *Hanayome* 1988, Vol. 4:108.

7 It is interesting to note that Kendall (1994:171) observed exactly the same attitude of Koreans towards what they defined as the 'new style' wedding. As Kendall puts it, many of her interviewees assumed that the new wedding was identical to the American custom.

8 On November 1872, the Chancellery proclaimed the morning suit a substitute for the Japanese formal attire worn by noblemen at court (Yanagida 1967:11) and it has since remained Western formal wear for Japanese men. According to Ben-Ami Shiloni (personal communication), this can be termed 'freezing tradition'.

9 The incentive for the beauty shop to promote Cosmo wigs was a commission of 30 per cent of the rental price of each wig.

10 This 'modern' image is important *vis-á-vis* the more 'traditional' image of small workshops which produce old-style wigs.

11 Another possibility was to have this attire (which was circulated among the parlours according to orders) as part of a '¥1,000,000 package', which included a designer wedding dress.

12 It is important to note, however, that the geisha's place in Japanese society and the relations between wives and geisha are more complex than they might seem. One aspect of the special attitude towards geisha is that they are regarded as symbols of Japanese femininity. For more about the complex relations between geisha and wives, see Dalby (1983:167–175).

Conclusion

1 Although an erotic image of Japanese women or particular groups of women in Japanese society does exist (Martinez 1990; Moeran 1990a:9), the 'aesthetic' image prevails in early writings. The erotic image can, however, be found in a more modern and vulgar image, presented, for example, in a guide book for the Western man titled *Women of the Orient: Intimate Profiles of the World's most Feminine Women* (De Mente: 1985), in which Japanese women are accorded the compliment: 'Good Things Come in Small Packages'. Vulgar as it may sound, both in the 'aesthetic' image of Lafcadio Hearn and in the modern version, women are reduced to 'things'.

REFERENCES

Abegglen, James C. 1958 *The Japanese Factory: aspects of its social organization*, Glenco: The Free Press.

Anderson, Benedict 1991 (1983) *Imagined Communities*, London:Verso

Appadurai, Arjun 1986 'Introduction: commodities and the politics of value', pp.3–63 in A. Appadurai (ed.) *The Social Life of Things: commodities in cultural perspective*, Cambridge: Cambridge University Press.

—— 1990 'Disjuncture and difference in the global cultural Economy', pp.1–24, *Public Culture*, 2 (2).

Bacon, Alice M. 1975 (1902) *Japanese Girls and Women*, New York: Gordon Press.

Barthes, Roland 1982 *Empire of Signs*, translated by Richard Howard, New Work: Hill and Wang.

Baudrillard, Jean 1975 *The Mirror of Production*, translated by Mark Poster, St. Louis: Telos Press.

—— 1981 *For a Critique of the Political Economy of the Sign*, translated by C. Levin, St. Louis Press: Telos Press.

Beard, Mary R. 1953 *The Force of Women in Japanese History*, Washington, DC: Public Affairs Press.

Beardsley, K. Richard *et al.* 1959 *Village Japan*, Chicago: The University of Chicago Press.

Befu, Harumi 1980a 'The group model of Japanese society and an alternative', pp.169–187, in *Rice University Studies*, 66 (1).

—— 1980b 'A critique of the group model of Japanese society', pp.29–43, in R. Mouer and Y. Sugimoto (eds.) *Japanese Society: reappraisals and new directions* a special issue of *Social Analysis* nos. 5/6.

—— 1983 'Internationalization of Japan and Nihon Bunkaron', in H. Mannari and Befu H. (eds.) *The Challenge of Japan's Internationalization: organization and culture*, Tokyo: Kodansha International.

—— 1984 'Civilization and culture: Japan in search of identity', in pp.59–75, in T. Umesao *et al.* (eds.) *Japan Civilization in the Modern World*, Osaka, National Museum of Ethnography (Senri Ethnological Studies 16).

—— 1989 'The emic-etic distinction and its significance for Japanese studies', in Y. Sugimoto and R. Mouer (eds.) *Constructs For Understanding Japan*, London and New York: Kegan Paul.

177

—— 1990 'Four models of Japanese society and their relevance to conflict', in S. N. Eisenstadt and E. Ben-Ari (eds.) *Japanese Models of Conflict Resolution*. London and New York: Kegan Paul.

—— 1992 'Symbols of nationalism and *nihonjinron*', in R. Goodman and K. Refsing (eds.) *Ideology and Practice in Modern Japan*, London and New York: Routledge.

Ben-Ari, Eyal 1991 'Posing, posturing and photographic presences: a rite of passage in a Japanese commuter village', pp.87–104 in *Man* (N.S), 26 (1).

Ben-Ari Eyal *et al.* (eds.) 1990 *Unwrapping Japan: society and culture in anthropological perspective*, Manchester: Manchester University Press.

Benjamin, Walter 1973 *Charles Baudelaire: a lyric poet in the era of high capitalism*, translated by H. Zohn, London: New Left Books.

Berger, John 1984 *About Looking*, London: Writers and Readers Publishing Cooperative.

Bernstein, Gail Lee 1983 *Haruko's World: a Japanese farm woman and her community*, Stanford: Stanford University Press.

—— 1991 'Introduction', pp.1–14, in G. L. Bernstein (ed.) *Recreating Japanese Women, 1600–1945*. Berkeley: University of California Press.

Bestor, Theodore C. 1989 *Neighborhood Tokyo*, Stanford: Stanford University Press.

Bird, Isabela L. 1984 (1880) *Unbeaten Tracks in Japan*, with a new introduction by Pat Barr, London: Virago Press.

Bishop, I. L. 1900 *Unbeaten Tracks in Japan*, London: John Murray.

Bourdieu, Pierre 1977 *Outline of a Theory of Practice*, Cambridge: Cambridge University Press.

—— 1984 *Distinction: a social critique of the judgement of taste*, translated by R. Nice, London: Routledge and Kegan Paul.

Broadbridge, Seymore 1966 *Industrial Dualism in Japan: a problem of economic growth and structural change*, London: Frank Cass.

Chamberlain, Basil Hall 1902 *Things Japanese*, London: John Murray (4th edition, revised).

Charsley, Simon R. 1991 *Rites of Marrying: the wedding industry in Scotland*, Manchester and New York: Manchester University Press.

—— 1992 *Wedding Cakes and Cultural History*, London and New York: Routledge.

Cherry, Kittredge 1987 *Womansword: what Japanese words say about women*, Tokyo and New York: Kodansha International.

Chodorow, Nancy 1974 'Family structure and feminine personality', in M. Z. Rosaldo and L. Lamphere (eds.) *Woman, Culture, and Society*, Stanford: Stanford University Press.

Clark, Rodney C. 1987 (1979) *The Japanese Company*, Tokyo: Charles E. Tuttle.

Cornell John B. and R. J. Smith 1956 *Two Japanese Villages*, New York: Greenwood Press Publishers.

Cort, Louise A. 1992 'Whose sleeves . . .? Gender, class, and meaning in Japanese dress of the seventeenth century', pp.183–197 in R. Barnes, and J. B. Eicher (eds.) *Dress and Gender: making and meaning in cultural contexts*, New York and Oxford: Berg.

Creighton, Millie R. 1992 'The Depāto: merchandising the West while selling

Japanesness', pp.42–57 in J. J. Tobin (ed.) *Re-Made in Japan: everyday life and consumer taste in a changing society*, New Haven and London: Yale University Press.

The Daily Yomiyuri, '10 companies change names', April 2, 1991.

Dalby, Liza 1983 *Geisha*, Berkeley: University of California Press.

—— 1988 'The cultured nature of Heian colours,' pp.1–19, in *Transactions of the Asiatic Society of Japan* 3.

—— 1993 *Kimono: Fashioning Culture*, New Haven: Yale University Press.

Dale, Peter 1986 *The Myth of Japanese Uniqueness*, London: Croom Helm.

Davis, Fred 1979 *Yearning For Yesterday: a sociology of nostalgia*, New York: The Free Press.

de Certeu, M. 1984 *The Practice of Everyday Life*, Berkeley: University of California Press.

De Mente, Boye 1985 *Women of The Orient: intimate profiles of the world's most feminine women*. Arizona: Phoenix Books Publishers.

Dominguez, Virginia R. 1986 'The marketing of heritage', pp.546–555, in *American Ethnologist* 13 (3).

Dore, Ronald P. 1958 *City Life in Japan: a study of a Tokyo ward*, Berkeley: University of California Press.

—— 1973 *British Factory-Japanese Factory: the origins of national diversity in industrial relations*, Berkeley: University of California Press.

—— 1978 *Shinohata: a portrait of a Japanese village*, New York: Pantheon Books.

Douglas, Mary and B. Isherwood 1978 *The World of Goods: toward an anthropology of consumption*, Great Britain: Penguin Books.

Edwards, Walter 1982 'Something borrowed: wedding cakes as symbols in modern Japan', pp.699–711 in *American Ethnologist* 9.

—— 1984 'Ritual in the Commercial World: Japanese society through its weddings', PhD Dissertation, Cornell University.

—— 1987 'The commercialized wedding as ritual: a window on social values', pp.51–78, in *Journal of Japanese Studies* 13(1).

—— 1989 *Modern Japan Through Its Weddings: gender, person, and society in ritual portrayal*. Stanford: Stanford University Press.

Eisenstadt, S. N. and Eyal Ben-Ari (eds.) 1990 *Japanese Models of Conflict Resolution*. London and New York: Kegan Paul.

Ema, Tsutomu 1971 *Kekkon no Rekishi* (History of Marriage), Tokyo: Yuzankaku.

Embree, John F. 1939 *Suye Mura: a Japanese village*. Chicago: University of Chicago Press.

Emori, Itsuo 1986 *Nihon no kon'in: sono rekishi to minzoku* (The History and Folklore of Japanese Marriage), Tokyo: Kōbundō.

Ernst, Earle 1974 *The Kabuki Theatre*, Honolulu: University of Hawaii Press.

Erskine, William 1925 *Japanese Customs: their origin and value*, Tokyo: Kyo Bun Kwan.

Ewen, Stuart and Elizabeth Ewen 1982 *Channels of Desire: mass images and the shaping of American consciousness*, New York: McGraw-Hill.

Fields, George 1988 *The Japanese Market Culture*, Tokyo: The Japan Times.

Foucault, Michel 1972 *The Archeology of Knowledge*, translated by A. Sharidan, London: Tavistok and New York: Pantheon.

—— 1979 *Discipline and Punish*, New York: Pantheon.

—— 1980 *Power/Knowledge*, New York: Pantheon.

Frager, Robert and T. Rohlen 1976 'The future of tradition: Japanese spirit in the 1980s', pp.255–278 in L. Austin (ed.) *Japan: the paradox of progress.* New Haven and London: Yale University Press.

Fujisaki, Hiroshi 1957 *Kankonsōsai Jiten* (Dictionary of Ceremonial Occasions), Tokyo: Tsuru Shobō.

Gellner, Ernest 1964 *Thought and Change*, London: Weidenfeld and Nicholson.

Giddens, Anthony 1991 *Modernity and Self-Identity: self and society in the late modern age*, Stanford: Stanford University Press.

—— 1994 'Living in a post-traditional society', pp.56–109 in U. Back *et al.* (eds.) *Reflexive Modernization*, Stanford: Stanford University Press.

Gluck, Carol 1985 *Japan's Modern Myths: ideology in the late Meiji period*, New Jersey: Princeton University Press.

Goffman, Erving 1959 *The Presentation of Self in Everyday Life*, New York: Doubleday.

Goldstein-Gidoni, Ofra 1993 'Packaged Weddings, Packaged Brides: The Japanese Ceremonial Occasions Industry', PhD dissertation, University of London.

Goodman, Roger 1992 'Ideology and practice in Japan: toward a theoretical approach', pp.1–25 in R. Goodman and K. P. Refsing (eds.) *Ideology and Practice in Modern Japan*, London and New York: Routledge.

Graburn, Nelson 1983 'To pray, pay and play: the cultural structure of Japanese domestic tourism', pp.1–89, in *Centre Des Hautes Etudes Touristique* (Series B) 26.

Haga, Kōshirō 1989 'The wabi aesthetic through the ages', translated by M. Collcutt, pp.195–230, in P. Varley and I. Kamakura (eds.) *Tea in Japan: essays in the history of Chanoyu*, Honolulu: University of Hawaii Press.

Hamabata, Matthews M. 1990 *Crested Kimono: power and love in the Japanese business family*, Ithaca and London: Cornell University Press.

Hanayome (The Bride) 1987 Vol.10, Tokyo: Hyakunichisō.

Hanayome (The Bride) 1988 Vol.4, Tokyo: Hyakunichisō.

Handelman, Don 1990 *Models and Mirrors: towards an anthroplogy of public events*, Cambridge: Cambridge University Press.

Handler, R. and J. Linnekin 1984. 'Tradition, Genuine or spurious', pp.273–290, in *Journal of American Folklore*, Vol. 97. No. 385.

Hannerz, Ulf 1992 *Cultural Complexity: studies in the social organization of meaning*, New York: Columbia University Press.

Harney, Nicholas 1992 'Buste, bomboniere and banquet halls: the economy of Italian Canadian weddings', pp.263–275, in *Studi Emigrazione – Etudes Migrations* 29 (106).

Harootunian, H. D. 1989 'Visible discourses/invisible ideologies', pp.63–92, in Masao Miyoshi and H. D. Harootunian (eds.) *Postmodernism and Japan*, Durham and London: Duke University Press.

Haug, Wolfang F. 1986 *Critique of Commodity Aesthetics: appearance, sexuality and advertising in capitalist society*, translated by R. Bock, Cambridge: Polity Press.

Havens, Thomas R.H. 1982 *Artists and Patrons in Postwar Japan*, New Jersey: Princeton University Press.

REFERENCES

Hearn, Lafcadio 1894 *Glimpses of Unfamiliar Japan* (Vol. I and II), London: Kegan Paul, Trench Trubner & Company.

—— 1904 *Japan: an attempt at interpretation*, New York: The Macmillan Company.

Hendry, Joy 1981 *Marriage in Changing Japan*, Rutland and Tokyo: Charles E. Tuttle.

—— 1990 'Humidity, hygiene, or ritual care: some thoughts on wrapping as a social phenomenon', pp.18–35, in Eyal Ben-Ari *et al.* (eds.) *Unwrapping Japan: society and culture in anthropological perspective*, Manchester: Manchester University Press.

—— 1993 *Wrapping Culture: politeness, presentation and power in Japan and other cultures*. Oxford: Oxford University Press.

Higuchi, Keiko 1985 *Bringing up Girls*, translated by Tomii Akiko, Kyoto: Shōkadoh Book Sellers.

Hobsbawm, Eric 1983a 'Mass-producing traditions: Europe, 1870–1914,' in pp.263–307, in E. Hobsbawm, and T. Ranger (eds.) *The Invention of Tradition*, Cambridge: Cambridge University Press.

—— 1983b 'Introduction: inventing traditions', pp.1–14, in E. Hobsbawm, and T. Ranger (eds.) *The Invention of Tradition*, Cambridge: Cambridge University Press.

Hobsbawm, E. and T. Ranger (eds.) *1983 The Invention of Tradition*, Cambridge: Cambridge University Press.

Hutchinson, John 1987 *The Dynamics of Cultural Nationalism: the Gaelic revival and the creation of the Irish nation state*, London: Allen and Unwin.

Ishihara, Shintaro 1991 *The Japan That Can Say No* (translated by F. Baldwin), London: Simon and Schuster.

Ivy, Marilyn 1988 'Tradition and difference in the Japanese mass media', pp.21–29, in *Public Culture Bulletin* 1 (1).

—— 1995 *Discourses of the Vanishing: modernity, phantasm, Japan*, Chicago and London: University of Chicago Press.

The Japan Times 1991 'Growth seen in wedding, funeral-related services', July 18.

Jackson, Jean E. 1995 'Culture, genuine or spurious: the politics of indianess in the Vaupes, Colombia', pp.3–27, in *American Ethnologist* 22 (1).

Jameson, Fredric 1979 'Reification and utopia in mass culture', pp.130–148, in *Social Text* 1.

—— 1991 *Postmodernism: or, the cultural logic of late capitalism*, Durham: Duke University Press.

Jeremy, Michael and M. E. Robinson 1989 *Ceremony and Symbolism in the Japanese Home*, Manchester: Manchester University Press.

Johnson, Chalmers 1983 'The internationalization of the Japanese economy', in H. Mannari and H. Befu (eds.) *The Challenge of Japan's Internationalization: organization and culture*, Tokyo: Kodansha International.

Kamata, Satoshi 1982 *Japan in The Passing Lane: an insider's account of life in a Japanese auto factory*, translated by T. Akimoto, London: Counterpoint, Unwin Paperbacks.

Kamishima, Jirō 1969 *Nihinjin no kekkonkan* (The Japanese View of Marriage), Tokyo: Chikuma Sōsho.

Kandiyoti, Deniz 1988 'Bargaining with patriarchy', pp.274–290, in *Gender and Society* 2 (3)

181

Kankon Sōsai Times 1989 published by Zennihon Kankon Sōsai Gojo Kyōdō Kumiai, Tokyo: All Japan Ceremonial Occasions Mutual Benefit cooperative association.

Kawakatsu, Kenichi 1936 *Kimono*, Tokyo: Maruzen Company.

Kawamura, Nozumu 1980 'The historical background of arguments emphasizing the uniqueness of Japanese society', pp.44–62, in R. Mouer and Y. Sugimoto (eds.) *Japanese Society: reappraisals and new directions*, a special issue of *Social Analysis* 5/6.

Kawashima, Takeyoshi 1954 *Kekkon* (Marriage), Tokyo: Iwanami Shoten.

Kelly, William. 1986 'Rationalization and Nostalgia: cultural dynamics of new middle class Japan', pp.603–618, in *American Ethnologist* 13(4).

Kelly, William 1990 'Japanese No-Noh: the crosstalk of public culture in a rural festivity', pp.65–81, in *Public Culture* 2(2).

Kendall, Laurel 1994 'A Rite of Modernization and its Postmodern Discontents: of weddings, bureaucrats, and morality in the Republic of Korea', pp.165–192, in C. Keyer *et al.* (eds.). *Asian Visions of Authority: religion and the modern states of East and Southeast Asia*. Honolulu: University of Hawaii Press.

Kindai Nihon Fukusoō-shi (History of Dress in Modern Japan), 1971 Showa Joshi Daigaku, Hifukugaku Kenkyushitsu.

Kinzley, W. Dean 1991 *Industrial Harmony in Modern Japan: the invention of tradition*, London and New York: Routledge.

Koike, Kazuo 1988 *Understanding Industrial Relations in Modern Japan*, translated by M. Saso, London: Macmillan Press.

Kondo, Dorrine K. 1985 'The way of tea: a symbolic analysis', pp.287–306, in *Man (N.S)* 20.

—— 1990 *Crafting Selves: power, gender, and discourses of identity in a Japanese workplace*, Chicago: Chicago University Press.

Krauss, E. S. *et al.* (eds.) 1984 *Conflict in Japan*, Hawaii: University of Hawaii Press.

Krauss, E. S. *et al.* 1984a 'Conflict: An Approach to the Study of Japan', pp.3–15, in Krauss E. S. *et al.* (eds.) *Conflict in Japan*, Hawaii: University of Hawaii Press.

Krauss Ellis S. *et al.* 1984b 'Conflict and its resolution in postwar Japan', pp.377–397, in E. S. Krauss *et al.* (eds.) *Conflict in Japan*, Hawaii: University of Hawaii Press.

Kuhn, Annette 1985 *The Power of the Image: essays in representation and sexuality*, London: Routledge and Kegan Paul.

Kurita, Isamu 1983 'Revival of the Japanese tradition', pp.130–134, in *Journal of Popular Culture* 17 (1).

Lasch, Christopher 1984 'The politics of nostalgia: losing history in the mists of ideology', pp.65–70, in *Harper's* (November).

Lebra, Takie, Sugiyama 1976 *Japanese Patterns of Behaviour*, Honolulu: University of Hawaii Press.

—— 1984a *Japanese Women: constraint and fulfilment*, Honolulu: University of Hawaii Press.

—— 1984b 'Nonconfrontational strategies for management of interpersonal conflicts', pp.41–60, in E. S. Krauss *et al.* (eds.) *Conflict in Japan*, Hawaii: University of Hawaii Press.

MacCannell, Dean 1973 'Staged authenticity: arrangements of social space in a tourist setting', pp.589–603, in *American Journal of Sociology* 79 (3).

—— 1976 *The Tourist: a new theory of the leisure class*, New York: Schocken Books.

Martinez Dolores, P. 1990 'Tourism and the *ama*: the search for a real Japan', pp.97–116, in E. Ben-Ari *et al.* (eds.). *Unwrapping Japan: society and culture in anthropological perspective*. Manchester: Manchester University Press.

Matsushima, Hiroko 1990 *Matsushima Hiroko no Kimono Saijiki* (Matsushima Hiroko's Kimono Almanac) Osaka: JDC.

Miller, Daniel 1993a 'A theory of Christmas', pp.3–37, in D. Miller (ed.) *Unwrapping Christmas*, Oxford: Oxford University Press.

Miller, Daniel (ed.) 1993b *Unwrapping Christmas*, Oxford: Oxford University Press.

Miller, Roy Andrew 1977 *The Japanese Language in Contemporary Japan: some sociolinguistic observations*, Washington, DC: American Institute for Public Policy Research.

—— 1982 *Japan's Modern Myth: the language and beyond*, New York and Tokyo: Weatherhill.

Minami, Ryōhei 1953. *Konrei-Shiki to Kekkon no Kokoroe* (On Marriage and the Marriage Ceremony), Tokyo: Taibunkan.

Moeran, Brian 1984a *Lost Innocence: folk craft potters of Onta, Japan*, Berkeley and Los Angeles: University of California Press.

—— 1984b 'Individual, group and seishin: Japan internal cultural debate', pp.252–266, in *Man (N.S)* 19.

—— 1986 'One over the seven: sake drinking in a Japanese pottery community', pp.226–242, in J. Hendry and J. Weber (eds.) *Interpreting Japanese Society*, Oxford: JASO Occasional Papers No. 5.

—— 1989a 'Homo harmonicus and the Yenjoy Girls: the production and consumption of Japanese myths', pp.19–24, in *Encounter*, LXXII (5).

—— 1989b *Language and Popular Culture in Japan*, Manchester: Manchester University press.

—— 1990a 'Introduction: rapt discourses: anthropology, Japanism and Japan', pp.1–17, in E. Ben Ari *et al.* (eds.) *Unwrapping Japan: sociey and culture in anthropological perspective*. Manchester: Manchester University Press.

—— 1990b 'Making an exhibition of oneself: the anthropologist as a potter in Japan', pp.117–139, in E. Ben Ari *et al.* (eds.) *Unwrapping Japan: sociey and culture in anthropological perspective*, Manchester: Manchester University Press.

Moeran B. and L. Skov 1993 'Cinderella Christmas: kitsch, consumerism, and youth in Japan', pp.105–133, in D. Miller (ed.) *Unwrapping Christmas*, Oxford: Oxford University Press.

Moore, Henrietta L. 1988 *Feminism and Anthropology*, Cambridge: Polity Press.

Moore, S. F. and B. G. Myerhoff 1977 'Secular ritual: forms and meanings', pp.3–24, in S. F. Moore and B. G. Myerhoff (eds.) *Secular Ritual*, Amsterdam: Van Gorcum.

Morita, Akio 1986 *Made in Japan: Akio Morita and Sony*, New York: Signet.

Morris, Ivan 1964 *The World of The Shining Prince*, Harmondworth: Penguin.

Mouer, Ross and Yoshio Sugimoto 1983 'Internationalization as an ideology in Japanese society', in H. Mannari and H. Befu (eds.) *The Challenge of Japan's Internationalization: organization and culture*, Tokyo: Kodansha International.

—— 1986 *Images of Japanese Society: a study in the social construction of reality*, London: Kegan Paul International.

Nakane, Chie 1967 *Kinship and Economic Organization in Rural Japan*, New York: Humanities Press.

—— 1984 *Japanese Society*, Tokyo: Charles E. Tuttle.

Nakayama, Tarō 1928 *Nihon Kon'in Shi* (A History of Marriage in Japan), Tokyo: Shunyoō-dō.

Namihara, E. 1984 *Kegare no Kōzō* (The Structure of Ritual Pollution), Tokyo: Aonisha.

Niwa, Motoji 1990 *Japanese Traditional Patterns*, translated by J. W. Thomas, Tokyo: Graphic-sha.

Niyekawa, Agnes M. 1984 'Analysis of conflict in a television home drama', pp.61–84, in E. S. Krauss *et al.* (eds.) *Conflict in Japan*, Hawaii: University of Hawaii Press.

Norbeck, Edward 1954 *Takashima: a Japanese fishing community*, Salt Lake City: University of Utah Press.

Norman, Henry 1892 *The Real Japan*, London: T. Fisher Unwin.

Omachi, Tokuzō 1962 *'Kon'in'* (Marriage) pp.175–202, in T. Omachi *et al.* (eds.) *Nihon Minzoku Gaku Taikei* (An Outline of Japanese Folklore) (Vol. 3) Tokyo: Heibonsha.

O'Neill, P.G. 1984 'Organization and authority in the traditional arts', pp.631–645, in *Modern Asian Studies* 18 (4).

Ortner, Sherry B. 1974 'Is female to male as nature is to culture?', pp.67–87, in M. Z. Rosaldo and L. Lamphere (eds.) *Woman, Culture, and Society*, Stanford: Stanford University Press.

Ortner, Sherry B. and H. Whitehead 1981. 'Introduction: accounting for sexual meanings', pp.1–27, in S. Ortner and H. Whitehead (eds.) *Sexual Meanings*, Cambridge: Cambridge University Press.

Papanek, Hanna 1977 'Development planning for women', in *Wellesley Editorial Committee. Women and National Development: the complexities of change*, Chicago.

Parkin, David 1978 *The Cultural Definition of Political Response: lineal density among the Luo*, London: Academic Press.

Pascale R. and Athos A. 1981 *The Art of Japanese Management*, New York: Warner Books.

Pharr, Susan J. 1976 'The Japanese woman: evolving views of life and role', pp.301–327, in L. Austin (ed.) *Japan: the paradox of progress*, New Haven and London: Yale University Press.

Raz, Jacob 1992 'Self-presentation and performance in the Yakuza way of life: fieldwork with a Japanese underworld group', pp.210–234, in R. Goodman and K. Refsing (eds.) *Ideology and Practice in Modern Japan*, London and New York: Routledge.

Richie, Donald 1987 *A Lateral View: essays on contemporary Japan*, Tokyo: The Japan Times Ltd.

Robertson, Jennifer 1987 'A Dialectic of native and newcomer: the Kodaira citizen's festival in suburban Tokyo', pp.124–136, in *Anthroplogical Quarterly* 60 (3).

—— 1991 *Native and Newcomer: making and remaking of a Japanese city*, Berkeley: University of California Press.

Robins-Mowry, Dorothy 1983 *The Hidden Sun: women of modern Japan*, Boulder: Westview Press.

Roden, Donald T. 1991 'Book review: modern Japan through its weddings: gender, person and society in ritual portrayal by W. Edwards', pp.236–240, in *Journal of Japanese Studies* 17 (1).

Rodesdale, Lord 1908 *Tales of Old Japan* (including translation of Sho-rei Hikki, a 'Record of ceremonies' published in 1706 by Hayashi Rissai), London: Macmillan.

Rohlen, Thomas P. 1970 'Sponsorship and cultural continuity in Japan: a company training program', pp.184–192, in *Journal of Asian and African Studies* 5 (3).

—— 1974 *For Harmony and Strength: Japanese white-collar organization in anthropological perspective*, Berkeley: University of California Press.

Rosaldo, Michelle Z. 1974 'Woman, culture, and society: a theoretical overview', pp.17–42, in M. Z. Rosaldo and L. Lamphere (eds.) *Woman, Culture, and Society*, Stanford: Stanford University Press.

Rosenberger, Nancy R. 1993 'Media construction of elite cosmopolitanism among Japanese women: contradictions and domination', unpublished paper presented at the American Anthropological Association, Washington, DC, November.

Rubin, Gayle 1975 'The traffic in women: notes on the 'political economy' of sex', pp.157–210, in R. Reiter, (ed.) *Toward an Anthropology of Women*, New York and London: Monthly Review Press.

Rudofsky, Bernard 1974 *The Unfashionable Human Body*, New York: Garden City.

—— 1985 *The Kimono Mind*, Tokyo: Charles E. Tuttle.

Said, Edward W. 1991 (1978) *Orientalism*, London: Penguin Books.

Sanda, E. and Tsuda 1988 *Kurashi ni Ikasō: kankon sōsai gojokai* (Making the Best of Living: ceremonial occasions gojokai), Zennihon Kankon Sōsai Gojokyōkai (All Japan Ceremonial Occasions Mutual Benefit Association).

Sanwa Ginkō (Sanwa Bank) 1976 *Kyoshiki Zengo no Suitōbo* (A Ledger of Wedding Expenditures), Tokyo: Sanwa ginkō okyakusama centa josei chōsa group.

—— 1982 *Kyoshiki Zengo no Suitōbo* (A Ledger of Wedding Expenditures), Tokyo: Sanwa ginkō gyōmu kaihatsubu, Home Consultant.

—— 1986 *Kyoshiki Zengo no Suitōbo* (A Ledger of Wedding Expenditures), Tokyo: Sanwa ginkō gyōmu kaihatsubu, Home Consultant.

—— 1990 *Kyoshiki Zengo no Suitōbo* (A Ledger of Wedding Expenditures), Tokyo: Sanwa ginkō kōhōbu Home Consultant.

—— 1991 *Kinsen kara Mita Tsukiai Chōsa* (A Survey of Association from a Monetary Perspective), Tokyo: Sanwa ginkō kōhōbu Home Consultant.

Saso, Mary 1990 *Women in the Japanese Workplace*, London: Hilary Shipman.

Sen, Sōshitsu XV 1989 'Reflections on chanoyu and its history' (translated by P. Varley), pp.233–242, in P. Varley and I. Kamakura (eds.) *Tea in Japan: Essays in the History of Chanoyu*. Honolulu: University of Hawaii Press.

Shibusawa, Keizō 1958 *Japanese Life and Culture in the Meiji Era*, translated and adapted by Charles S. Terry, Tokyo: Obunsha.

Shils, Edward 1981 *Tradition*, London: Faber.

Shiotsuki, Yaeko 1991 *Shin Kankon Sōsai Nyōmon* (A New Introduction to Ceremonial Occasions), Tokyo: Kōbunsha.

Sievers, Sharon L. 1983 *Flowers In Salt: the beginning of feminist consciousness in modern Japan*, Stanford: Stanford University Press.

Silverberg, Miriam 1991 'The modern girl as militant', pp.239–267, in G. L. Bernstein (ed) *Recreating Japanese Women, 1600–1945*, Berkeley: University of California Press.

Smith, Anthony D. 1991. 'The nation: invented, imagined, reconstructed?', pp.353–368, in *Millennium: Journal of International Studies* 20 (3).

Smith, Robert J. 1978 *Kurusu: the price of progress in a Japanese village 1951–1975*, Stanford: Stanford university Press.

——. 1994 'Wedding and funeral ritual: analyzing a moving target', pp.25–37, in J. Van Bremen and D. P. Martinez (eds.) *Ceremony and Ritual in Japan: religious practices in an industrialized society*, London and New York: Routledge.

Smith, Robert J. and E. L. Wiswell 1982 *The Women of Suye Mura*, Chicago and London: Chicago University Press.

Sontag, Suzan 1973 *On Photography*, New York: Farrar.

Tagg, John 1988 *The Burden of Representation: essays in photographies and histories*, Houndmills: Macmillan Education.

Takamure, Itsue 1963 *Nihon Kon'in Shi* (A History of Marriage in Japan), Tokyo: Nihon Rekishi Shinsho.

Tamura, Naomi 1904 *The Japanese Bride*, New York and London: Harper and Brothers Publishing.

Tanaka, Keiko 1990 '"Intelligent elegance": women in Japanese advertising', pp.78–96, in E. Ben Ari *et al.* (eds.) *Unwrapping Japan: sociey and culture in anthropological perspective*, Manchester: Manchester University Press.

Tanaka, Stefan 1993 *Japan's Orient: rendering pasts into history*, Berkely: University of California Press.

Tanizaki, Junichirō 1958 *The Makioka Sisters* (translated by E.G. Seidensticker), London: Secker & Warburg.

Tenbruck, F.H. 1959 'Formal sociology', in K. H. Wolff (ed.) *George Simmel, 1858–1918*, Columbus: Ohio State University Press.

Threadgold, Terry 1990 'Introduction' in T. Threadgold and A. Cranny-Francis (eds.) *Feminine, Masculine and Representation*, Sydney: Allen and Unwin.

Tobin, Joseph J. 1992 'Introduction: domesticating the West', pp.1–41, in J. J. Tobin (ed.) *Re-Made in Japan: everyday life and consumer taste in a changing society.* New Haven and London: Yale University Press.

Van Wolferen, Karel 1989 *The Enigma of Japanese Power: people and politics in a stateless nation*, London: Macmillan.

Varley, H. Paul 1986 *Japanese Culture*, Tokyo: Charles E. Tuttle.

Veblen, Thorstein 1957 (1925) *The Theory of The Leisure Class*, London: George Allen & Unwin.

Vogel, Ezra F. 1967 *Japan's New Middle Class: the salary man and his family in a Tokyo suburb*, Berkeley: University of California Press.

—— (ed.) 1975 *Modern Japanese Organization and Decision-Making*, Berkeley: University of California Press.

REFERENCES

—— 1979 *Japan as Number One*, Cambridge: Harvard University Press.

Williams, Raymond 1977 *Marxism and Literature*, Oxford: Oxford University Press.

Williams, Rosalind H. 1982 *Dream Worlds: mass consumption in late ninteenth-century France*, Berkeley: University of California Press.

Williamson, Judith 1978 *Decoding Advertisements: ideology and meaning in advertising*, London: Boyars.

Wilson, Elizabeth 1987 *Adorned in Dreams: fashion and modernity*, London: Virago Press.

Winship, Janice 1983. 'Options – for the way you want to live now', or a magazine for Superwoman', pp.44–65, in *Theory, Culture and Society* 1 (3).

Yanagawa, Keiichi 1972 'The family, the town and festivals', pp.125–131, in *East Asian Cultural Studies* 11 (1–4).

Yanagi, Sōetsu 1972 *The Unknown Craftsman: a Japanese insight into beauty*, adapted by B. Leach, Tokyo: Kodansha International.

Yanagida, Kunio 1957 *Japanese Manners and Customs in the Meiji Era*, translated and adapted by Charles S. Terry, Tokyo: Obunsha.

—— 1967 (1931) *Meiji Taisho Shi: seso hen* (A History of the Meiji and Taisho periods: social conditions), Tokyo: Heibonsha.

Yanagisako, Sylvia J. 1985 *Transforming the Past: tradition and kinship among Japanese Americans*, Stanford: Stanford University Press.

Yasuba, Yasukichi 1976 'The evolution of dualistic wage structure', pp.249–298, in P. Huge (ed.) *Japanese Industrialization and its Social Consequences*, Berkeley: University of California Press.

Yoshino, M. Y. 1968 *Japan's Managerial System: tradition and innovation*. Massachusetts: The Mit Press.

Yoshino, Kosaku 1992 *Cultural Nationalism in Contemporary Japan*, London and New York: Routledge.

INDEX